ANNA'S GOLD

ANNA'S GOLD

Julie Harris

ARROW BOOKS

Arrow Books
an imprint of Random Century Australia Pty Ltd
20 Alfred Street, Milsons Point NSW 2061

Sydney Melbourne London
Auckland Johannesburg
and agencies throughout the world

First published in 1992

National Library of Australia
Cataloguing-in-Publication Data

Harris, Julie.
Anna's gold.
ISBN 0 09 182662 4.
I. Title.

A823.3

Designed & typeset by Midland Typesetters, Victoria
Printed by Australian Print Group, Victoria
Production by Vantage Graphics, Sydney

For my parents and Penny

One

Thirteen months of following Michael's dream two hundred miles across the Great Divide had at last come to an end. The baby in Anna's arms cried, and the cries became impatient, angry wails. Anna was oblivious. Oh my God, she thought. Is this all there is?

Scattered over a vast section of cleared hillside below were thirty or more calico tents, the occasional tin shack, lean-to and humpy.

Bitter Creek. Where the making of a fortune, or the shattering of a dream, waited patiently amid dust, mud and sweat.

Tears welled in Anna's eyes.

At the start Michael's excited anticipation had been contagious. She looked at him now and wiped her dirty face on her even dirtier sleeve. If he noticed her desolation he said nothing. His bright eyes were alive with silent joy. Anna's stung from bitter disappointment.

'Sh, baby,' she whispered, knowing any attempt to placate Susan was futile.

'Come on, Anna.'

The final few hundred yards were taken on foot.

It was too much to hope for, of course, that the rough, ravaged miners wouldn't notice their arrival. All around, perfunctory curses and the noise of machinery began to dwindle, and eventually it faded. The Halls were welcomed with hushed stares, silent perusal and stony wonder at the sight of a woman. A young, pretty one at that.

Again if Michael noticed, there was no reaction. He'd found his paradise, and from it he'd pull a fortune. Nothing else mattered.

Anna could sense the camp's reaction. Her exhaustion was too intense, there was no room for fear. She ached, totally. Make the best of it. Her thoughts whirled. Someone whistled. Instinct traced its source—a wild, unshaven face, curiosity behind the eyes. Anna clasped her angry baby tighter, and watched as her feet trod their uncertain way down the rocky, dusty incline.

We are finally here. Tonight I cannot find words to describe the nothing I feel.

Anna tickled her chin with the quill feather and sighed. The lamplight cast eerie shadows and demonic silhouettes against the tent side. She tried not to see, and to focus her tired thoughts on the events of the day, and of the two before. But travelling so far with an unhappy baby and a silent husband was conducive to despair. If she lay down to sleep now, Susan would wake crying. Michael was restless enough. Anna dipped her pen into her ink bottle.

The baby will wake if I settle to sleep. She seems to read my mind, and she knows how to frustrate me. She refused the breast twice today and screamed when I offered her water. Michael says she will feed when she is hungry and the more I worry, the worse she will get. Fine for him, I have never felt . . .

'Anna, I canna sleep with that bloody scratching!'
'I'm almost finished.'
He'd heard that before, too. Michael reached over, grabbed his wife's diary and flung it across the tent. 'And you'll turn the lamp off this time.'

'But I was waiting for Susan to wake.'

'And I need to sleep!'

'I need to do this, it's the only time I can!'

She was about to say more until she heard an angry intake of breath, and sealed both her lips and her ink bottle. Best not to cause trouble when he was tired. His hand was always heavy and stinging.

Anna retrieved her book, read what she'd written and found she'd have to add a 'ness' to the 'nothing'. Not now, though. She dared not. She extinguished the lamp and settled down beside Michael.

Shadows from a nearby campfire danced against the calico. Anna drew the covers high. Michael kicked them off. 'It's too hot, damn you,' he grumbled while she watched the shapes within shadows and listened to a stranger's high-pitched cackle of laughter. Anna cuddled closer to her husband and felt him flinch and move away.

All was silent again, except for the night sounds of the bush and the light wind whistling through distant treetops.

Her eyes closed involuntarily. Monsters lurked behind the darkness of her eyelids, more fearsome in fact than those she could see in the distorted silhouettes. Slowly, with a will of its own, her arm sought refuge against Michael's strong, muscular side. The rest of her body followed until she was curled safely against him. Here was comfort; nothing could claim her. Nothing.

'Anna. No. I said I was tired.'

He flung her arm off and moved so far against the edge of the cot he almost fell out.

She was used to it, even if it stung her pride. This had been happening almost every night since Susan had been born. Five months was a long, long time.

Another laugh echoed around the Bitter Creek diggings. Anna strained to hear the distant conversations. Young voices, old voices. Men's voices.

''Tis Rose herself for me.'

'Rose is too bloody old, man. Ginger-Lee . . .'

Women?

Where?

The wind changed direction and she heard no more than garbled voices and the beginnings of Michael's snores. Anna nudged him fiercely—it was usually enough to quiet the rumblings which gradually became thunderous.

An obscene peel of laughter split the night.

'Do ye not know there's a lady among us now?'

Anna waited for the reply.

'If she chooses to live here, Billy Squire, she'll have to be getting used to it.'

A lot of voices seemed to agree.

On cue, the baby began to squeak. Squeaks preceded angry cries. Anna scrambled to the baby, and a familiar pungent odour wafted to meet her. Michael stirred. If he woke now, hell would only be a joyful promise. Anna whispered to the baby. A mistake. The voice was recognised and immediate attention demanded. On hands and knees, Anna threw the soiled nappy outside. She'd see to it in the morning. All she could hope for was that someone's foot would not find it first. If she ventured out into the night, she'd probably fall down a mine shaft and never be forgiven.

Forgotten, perhaps. Missed, doubtful. But forgiven? Never.

'Jee-ee-ziz!' someone cried and the echo rebounded around the entire camp. 'We're trying to sleep here!'

Anxiety hit.

Everyone was joining in now, the baby becoming fiercer while Michael snored on. Anna fumbled for the ties on her nightdress and made herself as comfortable as possible, as far as possible from

Michael. He hated the sounds the baby made.

Strangers' voices were unappreciative of a small baby's midnight screams; the baby rejected her mother's nipple. Anna knew if Susan didn't feed soon, her breasts would explode. Anxiety gave way to tears. A soft curse escaped her lips as she fought a losing battle with the baby. 'Please, baby, stop this crying, please . . .'

Then a roar brought silence.

'Let the girl be!'

The hush that fell was extremely loud. Michael stirred, mumbled and rolled over. Susan condescended to feed. Anna's panic ebbed.

I have an ally, she thought and wondered who the voice belonged to. A tiny smile touched her face. In this wilderness, there was someone who cared. For a moment, she felt calm.

Michael was right. He was always proving her wrong. The baby was hungry, almost choking in her starving attempts to fill an empty belly.

Anna touched the soft wisps of fine hair on her child's head. She knew two huge, dark eyes were staring up at her face in the gloom, and after a little while the strong sucking stopped. She felt the child's smile and, for a moment lost in time, all feelings of futility somehow vanished.

Perhaps it wouldn't be as horrendous as she'd first thought. Perhaps there were miracles after all.

The Halls' claim on the southern end of the stagnant, leech-infested waterhole yielded nothing but anger and impatience for the first few days.

Anna's aversion to the place quickly turned to indifference. The days were long and joyless; although she was surrounded by people, she was alone. Hadn't it always been that way? The novelty of having a woman among them was short-lived with the diggers.

They soon accepted her presence and acknowledged it with a short smile. There was rarely any conversation. Her shyness was mistaken for aloofness. One or two would ask after the baby, but that was all. They tried and mostly failed to hold tongues when The Lady was about. She was not Anna, nor was she Mrs Hall. She was The Lady. Day by day, she sat on the creek bank and silently watched her husband at work. Displaced, bored and frustrated, Michael's old hat shielded more than a saddened expression. She longed to hear the call: 'Anna! Quick!', which never seemed to come.

He was just like the rest of them working for hours at a time under the scorching sun, cursing at splinters from new pick handles, cursing misfortune, cursing the Lord for His indifference to their dreams.

Michael cursed at her when he'd exhausted his targets for profanity. But the afternoon he swore at the baby for being such a screaming, complaining little bastard, no wonder it was a female, Anna attacked. The argument aroused idle curiosity amongst the men—boredom was a terrible thing to endure, and a fight between man and wife was a refreshing change. Michael's hand quickly silenced her outburst, and with her pride stinging Anna retreated.

Never let them win. Never.

Michael was rewarded, his acceptance amongst the men on the camp site complete. Each night after supper he'd join the male ritual of socialising: drink, talk of gold, talk of women. The gold and the women were scarce commodities.

Anna stayed away and used the time alone to sketch the images she often saw in her mind's eye—huge, elegant hats that only ladies of society would dare wear. Mostly, the hats were amusing designs and belonged where they stayed—in dreams. After a few hours, Michael would stumble home drunk and tired.

This suited Anna, because when he was drunk he slept heavily, and the scratching of the quill went unheeded deep into the early hours.

To keep him pacified, she cooked his meals, watched him work, fetched this and that, and tried not to antagonise him by breathing too loudly. When he began to find gold, all would change for the better.

It had to.

Her genuine offers to assist were laughed away and the days stretched out to infinity and back again. Uselessness became boredom.

Anna began to watch for the old man to stroll by in the mornings and evenings. He'd never say much except 'Howdy' in his rough American voice. Sometimes he'd nod and half smile. He was always too quick for someone his age, and by the time she'd found the courage to ask if he'd stay and have some tea with her, he was too far away and too deaf to hear.

Or perhaps Tom Manning was just like any man, only willing to hear relevant things, not wanting to listen to a lonely woman who lived in dreams, drowning in the mire of a man's dirty world?

On the eleventh morning, two things occurred: Tom became a friend and Michael found gold.

Anna didn't know which was more valuable.

Tom ambled by the tent with more than a 'Howdy' on his lips. 'How's your eyes, girl?' he barked.

'My eyes?'

He thrust his wrinkled, spotted hand very close to Anna's face. Her eyesight was fine. She dug the huge splinter from the base of his thumb using the small pocket-knife he offered. 'There you are, as good as new,' she said with a smile.

'Don't I wish,' he mumbled and sauntered away.

Anna called out did he want a mug of tea but

her invitation fell on deaf ears.

Later that morning she was painstakingly drawing an apple dangling from the brim of a hat when Michael's bellowing yell thundered up from the creek. The baby woke screaming, and for a moment Anna didn't know what to do. Ignore both? Keep sketching before the vision faded? Feed the baby? Feign deafness or let them both scream as both were prone to do anyway?

Michael came running to her, gold pan in hand. Anna rose and took the baby from the cradle. Susan stopped crying when Anna gave her a finger to suck on. All problems solved. 'Look!' The gold pan was duly thrust under her nose. Did he think she was blind? In the bottom groove of the tin dish sat five flakes of gold, neither small nor large, barely a quarter-inch wide and coarse to touch. Anna looked up into Michael's eyes and the brilliance of the gold was of no comparison. Her heart lifted—a lifelong dream achieved. Even if it was *his* dream.

'Say something!'

'Is it a fortune?'

'No, of course not. It's the beginning, Anna.' She had never seen elation of this magnitude.

Michael kissed her forehead and headed back to the creek. Anna watched him walk away and one thought echoed around her mind: Find a lot of gold, Michael.

Tom Manning spat a lump of chewed tobacco at the piece of tin which substituted for a door. It kept some of the cold out in winter. He looked down at the stiff, decaying photograph, so old now he only touched it once a week, fearing more regular perusal would fade the image completely.

Catherine.

His Katie.

The only surviving memory he could still trust these days lay in that one photograph. Twenty-two when she died, thirty-two years ago. She never got over the birth of the boy. Took her a year to die. 24 April 1835. A cold spring that took his heart.

Katie. Large, dark eyes that touched the core of his soul. Everyone was surprised when the boy's eyes were his father's summer blue.

'He's you, Tom,' she used to say and try to smile.

Just like the girl across the creek there—trying her best to smile when the eyes said something else. Women were good at that. So much like Katie, she was. Hands too. Not the touch though—no, that was nothing but an old man's hope of sliding back into a dead yesterday.

Tom was never comfortable playing anyone but himself. The role came more easily with age and wisdom. 'How's your eyes, girl?' he'd asked while his heart ached to hear Katie's voice again. She wasn't Katie of course, but the mirror image deluded his tired old mind into believing she was. It wouldn't have been hard to get the girl talking. He'd recognised loneliness, tasted it for most of his life.

God knew what she was doing at Bitter Creek in the first place. Young women and babies didn't belong here. This wasn't Ballarat. There were no other women to gossip with, no children. There was nothing.

Just Bitter Creek.

He'd heard her all right. 'Would you like a cup of tea?' she'd called, nice and loud. Dreams had been a lie. He'd used the excuse of old age not to hear, not to respond. She'd only go breaking his heart again. But now, as he sat staring at the image of a wife he still loved more than life itself, he felt lost. He'd missed the damned chance.

Tom slipped the photograph into the tattered Bible.

Hers, not his. He'd not needed God. God never helped the pain when Katie was dying, so Tom never bothered to pray after that.

The old man emerged into the midday sun, glad of the escape from his sweltering tin shelter. His back was aching again, his limp more pronounced. He told everyone it was from a fight at Sutter's Mill, although it was only lumbago, an affliction which had plagued him for the last twenty years. Twenty years that felt like fifty.

Anna was drawing more of her pretties until the husband appeared. Always the way. Tom watched them have their lunch, watched Mick return to his claim, and waited for the girl to take out her pretties again. She took up the axe instead. And as he watched, he wished he was young and good looking again. That was forty years ago when thoughts co-operated with the body, when memories were too shiny to rust.

Tom watched and winced. She'd never split that lump of ironbark. Never. She didn't have the strength or the knowing. It wasn't called ironbark for nothing. Her damned lazy good-for-nothing old man needed a kick in the butt for letting her do this.

Fortified with another wad of tobacco and knowing that soon he'd have to ask Sam to get more, the old man approached, cautiously. Anna didn't see him coming and he heard her soft curses and pretended he was deaf again. Amusement touched his eyes.

'Howdy,' he said.

She jumped in fright and any exasperated anger faded into her smile. Tom's heart kicked against his ribs.

'Hello. How's your hand?'

The crisp English made her sound like a schoolteacher. Well-educated, this one. If she was educated, what the hell was she doing out here?

'Hand's fine,' he lied. It was swollen, and he could

barely move his thumb. She wouldn't know because he kept his hand buried in his pocket. The girl had the light in her eye—she was wondering what he wanted. Tom spat the tobacco and it curved in a glorious arc before splattering on the ground. 'Do that all day, girlie, won't make no difference. You'll just wear yourself out.'

'We'll see. I'm not going to let a block of wood defeat me.'

She had Katie's ways, all right. The same defiance in the voice, the eyes. Only this one caught the back of a husband's hand for her troubles. Tom had seen it too often. But a man could do what he liked with his woman, and although Tom didn't necessarily approve of hitting them—he knew there were other ways to quell spirit without breaking it—he couldn't do much at all. It was none of his business. Could be she enjoyed it. Could be the only way to get noticed. If she didn't like it, she'd soon learn how to avoid it unless she was stupid.

The more he watched, the more he realised she wasn't stupid. Just stubborn. She raised the axe high and brought it down heavily. Tom didn't move away—he knew the axe would bounce again. Bounce right out of her hands soon. She didn't curse this time. She tried to be ladylike about it all and she mumbled.

'Tom's the name,' he said.

'Yes, I know.'

Anna rested the axe on her weary shoulder and wiped sweat from her forehead. She looked at Tom, and almost absently remarked, 'Billy Squire lives there, Joshua McPherson there, Dinny Masterson over there . . . I know of everyone and everyone knows of me, but you happen to be the only man courageous enough to talk to me. I must be an ogre.'

Nope, Tom thought. No one wants to get beat

up by Mick Hall. Tom sent her a short, curdled grin and wished his heart would behave itself because she smiled back.

'Would you care for a mug of tea, Mr Manning?'

'Tom's the name,' was all he said.

'Tom, would you like a —'

'Yep. Don't mind if I do.'

The grins were contagious now. Tom settled on a log near the campfire and held the pint mug between his hands. He sipped the bitter, strong brew. Only one thing he knew of could add some taste. The small flask was drawn from his tattered coat and he glanced up at Anna. 'Whisky. No offence, girl, but any tea needs some help.'

Anna threw a cursory glance to the creek. Michael wasn't looking so she accepted the dash of whisky from the old man. After a few more sips, her smile was very large.

'How long have you been here?' Anna asked.

'Sometimes too long. Nowhere else to go, nothing else to do.'

To Anna, the words seemed to echo how she felt most of the time. Duty to her husband had brought her here. Michael was all the family she had left. Michael and Susan.

The old man heard the whimpers of the wakening baby. For weeks now he'd been wanting to have a good look at the little one, and here was his opportunity. She lay in her cradle, with something like muslin covering her to keep the flies off. Plenty of flies here, mosquitoes too. Damn things. Bloodsuckers everywhere. Leeches on your ankles and hands when you panned, and mosquitoes trying to carry you off alive while you tried to sleep off a hard day's work.

Big dark eyes studied him intently. Apart from the eyes she looked just like an ordinary baby to him,

12

nothing special. 'Girl ain't it?'

'Yes.'

'Looks like you. He's doin' it wrong.'

'Excuse me?'

'He's doin' it wrong,' Tom said, a little louder this time.

'Doing what wrong, Tom?'

'He's tippin' it out his dish, girl. He's got ten ounces of flake sittin' in his tailings. I see it happening.'

Anna chewed on her thumbnail and her dark eyes flickered at him. Tom had seen that look before, many times. In Katie's eyes it meant she was considering a truth. Just took him to find it for her. His heart pounded again. It hurt.

'Are you sure?' she asked. He knew she would.

'I been prospecting for fifty years, and he's doin' it wrong. Could be I might teach you the proper way, seeing that Mick of yours got no ears to listen and no eyes to see and no brain wanting to learn.' Strong words, he knew. But this one could tolerate honesty without having to hide. He could see that in her eyes. He continued. 'He's stubborn. Sometimes being stubborn's good, but with him, not so good. You know that anyways. He don't have the touch, but you, maybe you might.'

'The touch?'

'I been watching you. You wanna learn. You been itchin' to try.'

'I don't follow you, Mr Manning.'

'You want me to teach you how to pan or not?'

'Of course I do!'

As swiftly as it came, her eagerness departed. Her eyes clouded and she looked down into her whisky-flavoured tea. It was as dark as the abyss she'd fallen into. 'Michael won't approve.'

'Mick won't know till you show him how good you are, and then he won't care. All that matters to him's findin' gold, and no amount'll ever be enough. Well?'

'Well what?'

'When do you wanna start?'

'Now?' Anna asked, afraid he'd change his mind.

'Yeah, why not? Yesterday's no damned good to me no more and tomorrow might not get here.'

'But Susan —'

'I don't think she'd mind comin' along,' Tom said and a gnarled finger tickled the baby's foot. The old man was rewarded by a mountainous grin.

And if anyone from Bitter Creek noticed the regular absences and the smiling faces on the crazy old American and the pretty Englishwoman, no one spoke aloud.

I began on the tailings heap whilst Susan slept. At first, Michael was too busy to notice what I was about. I found nothing in the first half hour and began to wonder if what Tom had said that day had been true. Perhaps Michael did know what he was about after all. He surprised me as he usually does when I'm concentrating. 'What's all this, then?' he asked.

'I'm going to pan.'

Michael found it amusing. 'That's the tailings, Anna. Do you know what the tailings are?'

'What you've thrown away, of course.'

'Anna, if there was any gold to be found would it be there?'

'I want to practise. Perhaps you missed some.'

'You're wasting your time.'

Wasting my time, she thought and anger rose. I'm always wasting my time. Whenever I'm doing something you feel is odd, you explain it as a waste of time. Her spark of anger threatened to strike into the flame.

14

'Isn't there something else you could be doing?'

'Such as?'

'Don't speak to me in that tone.'

'There's nothing for me to do, Michael. The baby is alseep, I've hardly any ink left and it's too hot to take walks. I'm doing no harm, I'm not nagging you. Please let me do this.'

Michael rolled his eyes and walked off. 'It's your back. Don't come to me complaining.'

Anna pulled a face at his retreating figure.

'You can sit there all day as far as I care. It'll do you no good. But you never listen to a man, you never have and you never will . . .'

Anna returned to her panning and mimicked his grumbles as he took his woeful complaints to the shaker. She took her sieve, put it on top of her gold pan, scooped a hefty amount of Tom's decreed gold-bearing wash from the tailings heap on the sieve. Even if she did have a sore back she'd keep it a secret. Michael's incessant 'I told you so' was far worse than her grandmother's ever had been. With a sigh, Anna immersed pan and all in the creek and began the underwater shake.

Tom had taught her 'The Art' by salting coarse sand with shotgun pellets. In theory, the pellets, being heavy like gold, would drop through the sieve into the pan. Then came the ritual of washing the lighter sand and dirt away by gently swirling and tipping the dish. Tom made it look easy. Her arms ached, her back ached, her hands and fingers grew stiff and sore. Dish after dish, after dish, and Tom wasn't satisfied until nothing remained except the pellets. All of them. He'd tap her head and huff if she shook too savagely. He sighed if she got the angle wrong and the water lapped too hard against the dish. He only yelled at her occasionally. Now she was on her own without so much as a shotgun pellet to find.

The dish was put aside, the sieve studied. There were no nuggets caught in the mesh but a leech was attached to her wrist. Anna pulled it off, ignored the blood and began to pan. In the bottom of her third dish lay a sliver of gold a quarter inch wide, and when she picked it out it was as long as her little fingernail. She forgot her aches and grumbles. Anna began to smile again.

I panned for three hours until Susan woke. The flakes I found in Michael's tailings now cover the bottom of my bottle. When dried and separated from the black sand as Tom showed me how, I suppose the flakes would fit neatly into my palm. Dare I say it, but I have recovered more gold than Michael has in eight long weeks of work. It is a satisfying feeling. I do not care that it is not a fortune. I have promised myself not to show Michael until he asks to see my bottle. Then, he may realise how useful I can be other than for cooking his meals and catching mosquitoes at night.

Michael shook the bottle and the gold flakes cascaded and settled. It was heavy, the collected gold reaching up to a quarter inch from the bottom. 'Who showed you how to pan?'

'Tom Manning.'

'The American?'

'Yes.'

'When?'

'Oh, recently,' Anna replied and studied her hands.

'All this came from my tailings heap?' Michael asked, shaking the bottle again, watching the flakes cascade to the bottom. The water made them seem a lot larger than they really were. 'All this from my tailings?' he asked again, and Anna thought silence her best reply in this situation. 'Why didn't you tell me you knew how to pan?'

'I didn't know what you'd do. You said it was to be our fortune and I do need to help. There's little else for me to do here.'

Michael was quiet for a little while. He let the bottle drop into Anna's lap. 'Remember what you are. Wife. Mother.'

A conciliatory remark with a bottomless warning. Anna saw it in his eyes when he looked down at her. 'And what's all this? My clothes?'

'I can't do a man's work in women's clothes.'

Michael was about to protest when a scream of agony hushed the entire diggings. Anna scrambled to her feet.

Dinny Masterson's partner, Bert, was dragging his screaming offsider from their shaft, and even from a distance Anna could see the pick embedded in Dinny's boot.

She was running before she realised it and pushed her way through the curious, shocked crowd.

'Someone hold him down!'

'No, Bert! You mustn't panic.' Heart in mouth, Anna couldn't believe her own words. She sank to her knees and her touch to Dinny's face helped to ease his yells and curses. 'Ease the pick out gently, Bert. Someone get clean cloth, quickly! Don't stand here staring, help us!'

Dinny didn't scream when the pick was removed. He lay on the ground, his face covered by his arm.

'Ease his boot off very slowly, Bert.'

Bert's face was as white as a wedding gown. He couldn't move. All he could do was stare, helpless.

Tom pushed him out of the way and knelt beside Anna.

When Dinny's boot was pulled off, the big toe and two others spewed to the ground in a wash of blood. His screams could be heard for miles.

For days he knew he was dying and refused the many offers of transport to town, and to the doctor there. A drunk, they say; not many people in their right minds would let that doctor attend a sick dog. There was nothing I could do to help Dinny. I have seen lockjaw take its slow hold too many times in my life. We all waited quietly for the release of death.

Today, it came.

I shall remember Dinny's smile. His friends will remember him as a glutton for food, drink and women. With me though, Dinny was no more than a quiet child who knew death was near.

He wanted to see his children again. Most of all, he wanted to be held by his wife—a woman, who, as far as I knew, was still in Ireland.

We buried him this day, 4 August 1867. Jokingly, with unhidden tears, Bert said, 'Here the place be, boys. 'Tis too far to ride to have him stuffed and mounted above the bar at Rosie's.' They all laughed because jest can hide the ache in the heart. There were tears for Dinny, and life, such as it is, goes on.

The troopers are expected soon. I suppose they will be notified of Dinny's passing when they check the licenses.

The wake continued late into the night and died in the early hours. As the bottles emptied in honour of Dinny's passing, Joshua's fiddle became louder, and so did the stories.

Anna stayed in the tent and listened. She dared not venture out into the man's night, not even to look at the night rider whose horse cantered by. She listened though to the voice. It spoke to Tom and held the same accent and pitch; a hint of gravel, deep yet melodic. Light-hearted until he heard the news.

'What, Dinny? You're kidding.'

'Just gimme the tobacco, son.'

Son? Tom had a son? Why hadn't he told her?

Sam Manning took his hat off and drew it across his sweating face. He squinted into the blinding sun that seemed to envelop the tiny town in a blanket of gold haze.

The police station was unattended as he knew it would be. A smile creased his face and he fixed his attention to the pub opposite, where loud roars and screams of laughter echoed up to meet him. For a little while, Sam wondered what was the celebration. Sitting up here all day, he'd never find out. He walked his grey mare down to the park, where two boys were playing cricket with a lump of wood and a green lemon.

'Hello, Sam.'

'Boys,' he replied as he went by.

'Traps ain't here, they gone to Bitter Creek. Left last night they did, the Sergeant and Daniel and Billy.'

'Yes, I know,' Sam said with a smile. The boys' grins were conspiratorial. Sam's presence soon forgotten, they returned to their game. Sam tied his horse behind the stables of Rose Keller's establishment.

Ginger-Lee, the plump blonde who today wore red, abandoned her hopeful customer the instant Sam walked in. Curiosity forgotten, Sam let his body decide his immediate course of action. A couple of whiskys could wait. He swept Ginger-Lee into his arms. He knew the way to her boudoir blindfolded and, like always, he was blinded by Ginger-Lee.

'I was worried the traps had you,' she said as he put her down and locked the door.

'I think you'd hear if they had,' Sam said quietly, mouth watering for a taste. It was dark in there, sparsely furnished apart from a washstand and a squeaky iron bed. A faint, musky odour of sex lingered in the stuffy air. Soon, that odour would become powerful. 'It's so good to see you,' Sam whispered and nibbled on her ear while deft fingers parted the ties on her red dress. The full warmth of her breasts fell into his hands. And she sighed. Not for the first time. Sam wondered if she sighed like this for every man, or if she rested her head back against any man's shoulder and played at relishing the touch. With Ginger-Lee it was hard to tell.

'I worry about you, Sam. At times you're all I think of. Lucas won't rest until he has a rope around your neck.'

Sam turned her and lifted her face. 'He's not quick enough,' Sam whispered.

'And don't you be so quick, either.'

The bed protested, the two bodies did not. Before long, she'd forgotten her fears and despair. Sam Manning could make her forget everything. When he'd finally done, there was none of this dressing and leaving. He stayed, holding her in the crook of his arm. Ginger-Lee listened to the strong beat of his heart, the tired sigh and wished he would never go, ever. Wishes were delusions and always would be where Sam was concerned.

'Was it you who knocked off the payroll?'

'Would I do that?'

'You're costing me hard-earned money,' she whined, rising on an elbow, sweeping a stray wisp of brown hair from his bright blue eyes, eyes that were watching her now with a mixture of caution and lingering lust. His fingertips drew invisible spirals on her skin and he touched her face with the same intricate gentleness.

'I don't like the thought of you sleepin' with Luke Hannaford.'

'You'd rather I starved? I've no choice, Sam.'

Marry me, her eyes pleaded. You said you would.
You said you loved me . . .

Sam drew her down once more and his sigh this
time was huge and almost sad. Or was it resigned?
'Tell me where the sub-inspector's gone, Ginger-
Lee.'

She groaned. Each time it was the same! He'd have
his fill, he never paid and he wanted information.
Each time and it wasn't right. Ginger-Lee tried to
move. Sam held her fast. 'Come on, girl, it's
important.'

'And I'm not? What's my life worth if Lucas finds
out I'm telling you things I hear? Things I know.'

'Please?'

His eyes were as hungry as a starving child's.

'Inspector Ritchie's gone to Brisbane. He'll be away
six weeks or more, or so is the whisper. Daniel told
Nelly as much.'

'Luke's in charge, right?'

'God help us all, yes.'

A tiny smile crossed Sam's face and lingered in
his eyes as he stared at the ceiling. It was a smile
she recognised as trouble. 'What are you planning
this time, Sam Manning?'

'I might take myself a bath,' he replied.

She tugged at the few hairs growing on his chest.
'The day you take a bath is the day a toff gentleman
walks me down the aisle.'

The talk of wedded bliss sent Sam bouncing off
the bed to dress in his usual hurry.

Ginger-Lee realised he was serious about taking
the bath when an hour later, Nelly happened to notice
the grey-coated bushranger dragging a tub down the
main street of the small town. 'Oh, Sam, the devil's
in you,' Ginger-Lee whispered to the pane of glass
at her lips.

And as if he'd heard, he turned in his saddle and

looked up to her window. Sam grinned and lifted his tattered hat in farewell.

'He never asks for me,' Nelly said with a pout on her face. Ginger-Lee walked away, happy.

And as always when the traps were away, no one would see a thing.

Anna rarely liked to judge people on first impressions. Not only was it unfair but sometimes impressions could be wrong. So when the two troopers rode in to the Bitter Creek diggings early that morning and her skin began to crawl, it was an impression she couldn't ignore.

Accompanying them was a black man—they called them Native Mounted Police. Anna took little notice of the young white constable, barely nineteen. It was the sergeant who held her attention far too long.

She did not join the queues for the licences to be perused—she kept panning, mindful of the talk she overheard from a distance. The sergeant asked Michael where he was from. 'Brisbane', came the reply. The conversation seemed quite ordinary, and she didn't look up when her name was mentioned in passing. Some time later, the hair on the nape of her neck prickled as it tended to do whenever there were spiders nearby. With approaching footsteps came familiar smells: leather, horse, unwashed male body. She looked up from where she sat on the creek bank with her legs immersed to the knees in the dirty water. She caught the sergeant's cool gaze and her skin crawled yet again. She shivered despite the heat.

'Mrs Hall, is it not?'

The voice was grating, authoritarian, demanding attention and receiving it.

'Sergeant?' she asked, recognising the rank from the uniform coat hanging over his wide shoulders.

He would have been handsome were it not for his eyes. Behind him, the young constable kicked at the dusty ground. He seemed bored, hot and tired. His eyes were dark and kind. He looked directly at Anna and smiled, shyly.

'Constable,' she greeted, quietly.

The lad whispered, 'Ma'am' and filled his lungs with air.

Anna clasped Michael's shirt tightly at her neck. The sergeant's gaze was unnerving.

'I'm told you were with Dennis Masterson when he died, is that not so?'

'I was there, yes.'

'And how did he die?'

'Slowly and painfully, Sergeant. It was lockjaw.'

While Anna recounted the tale in as few words as possible, the sergeant squatted and picked up her bottle of gold. He swirled it about, mesmerised by its glitter. 'And how do you know it was lockjaw, Mrs Hall? Or may I call you Anna?'

Opposing thoughts reflected in both's eyes. The boy seemed surprised at the sergeant's boldness. He smiled to himself when he heard: 'To you and everyone here I am Mrs Hall, thank you, Sergeant. And I know it was lockjaw for I used to work in a hospital before we emigrated.' She emphasised the final word.

He took no notice. 'Ah, hospital. You'd be a handy one to have about then, Mrs Hall?'

Anna said nothing. He hadn't specified what she'd be handy for. He didn't have to. The silence was uncomfortable, perhaps more unsettling than the way the man's gaze crusted her skin. 'His death was accidental and unfortunate.'

'Frankly, Mrs Hall, I don't care. It only means one less to me. You have a baby, is that correct?'

'Yes.'

'How old?'

'Seven months.'

'And has the birth been registered?'

'Registered? No, I haven't had the opportunity —'

'Ignorance is no excuse, Madam.'

'I said nothing of ignorance. If you'd let me finish what I was about to say, you would have known that in any of the towns we passed through the local constabulary was never available. Now if you'll excuse me, I'm rather busy.'

Anna noticed the lad's quick smile before he turned away. Although the sergeant smiled, no humour touched his pale eyes. Despite the innocuous sunshine filtering through the eucalypts, Anna grew suddenly cold.

'I suggest when you're in town next, you call in to see me and register your daughter's birth. Good day.'

The man loped off with the constable following him, and then came to a sudden standstill. The boy crashed into his back and was clipped on the ear for his trouble. 'Your husband's licence doesn't include you. I suggest you refrain from prospecting until you acquire your own permit.'

'Shouldn't we attend to it now while you're here?'

'I don't have the relevant papers with me.'

Liar, she thought. The boy was about to speak on the contrary and even reached into his coat. But something was whispered and the boy was led away. She couldn't hear the argument. The three finally rode away, the brooding, silent black the last to mount his horse.

'Bastards,' and Michael spat into the dirt.

Sooner rather than later, the diggings fell into its normal, punishing routine. Illegal or not, Anna went back to her panning.

Michael had said there was no need to waste days

travelling to town when Harry Ryan's wagon made three-monthly trips to Bitter Creek. How was she to register the birth and obtain her permit if her husband wouldn't take her to town?

Sergeant Lucas Hannaford was lost amid his own thoughts as he crossed Mitchell's Hill. He'd heard about the woman at Bitter Creek and had finally seen her for himself. A beauty sure enough, with one flaw. The delicate face hid a will of iron. She was well-spoken. A nurse? A healer of the ill and dying, indeed.

Police never about when needed? What in hell's name did these people expect of him? Miracles? Three hundred square miles of mountainous territory to police and one snotty-nosed constable too honest for his own good.

Never available when needed indeed. His pride stung.

The finds at Bitter Creek only added to his workload. God knew what trouble would be afoot when the Chinese from Thane or Liston caught a whiff of the gold and converged. The yellow bastards could smell it.

The only trouble Lucas wanted was the kind he could anticipate, incite and prosper from.

'Sarge?' Billy Moonshine asked cautiously, aware of the reverie he was interrupting. 'Down there, looks like a bloke dragging a bathtub to me.'

Daniel Brannigan saw it too. 'It's Manning, sir!'

Hannaford couldn't see a bloody thing. His eyesight at a distance was fading, but the twist of his gut affirmed Daniel's statement. It was Manning.

Daniel's echo reverberated down through the thick bush, giving Manning plenty of time to cut the rope on the tub and canter off up the creek. A three hundred-yard lead might as well have been three hundred miles. The sergeant wished it was.

While Moonshine and Brannigan were in futile pursuit, Lucas guided his mount down the precarious, boulder-ridden slope.

The tub was damming up the creek.

Too tired to curse, Luke rubbed his face, sighed and reached for his tobacco. All he could do now was wait to hear the troopers' return and their inevitable: *Lost him, sir, sorry.*

He'd heard it a hundred times too often. Sometimes he thought they did this on purpose.

Sam watched sadly from the relative safety of his hiding place, high above. Luke was down there, bored, smoking. Idle. The other two finally managed to secure the bath and drag it away.

Damn, they're stealing my tub.

Gone now, the visual impact of imagining Inspector Ritchie's wife heading for her bath and finding it gone. At the first yelp, Harry would think she was stuck. *I say Harry, someone has stolen our bath!* Now all the magic was gone, dammit.

From far away, Daniel was being cursed at. Sam enjoyed listening to Luke's echoing shouts of 'stupidity', 'what is the world coming to?', 'surrounded by fools' . . . It reminded Sam of the sergeant they'd both been unfortunate enough to serve under. Back then, it had always been Luke in trouble. How the past always repeated, and lived to haunt the present, the future. Once the best of friends, now . . .

Sam dozed in the afternoon sunshine. It had been a long, tiring day. The grey picked at grass, tail swishing at flies.

He'd get his tub back, though. He wouldn't let them win, not now, not ever.

Two

Anna emerged from the tent eager to see what was causing all the din. Once in the fresh air, she was enveloped in a dark cloud of hatred which was directed at a rattling wagon making its slow way past the camp. She didn't understand the fuss until she saw a Chinese girl walking steadily behind the wagon.

Chinese. In the battle for gold they were nothing but the enemy.

All Anna could see was the young woman leading a tired pack horse. Her head was lowered throughout the tirade of abuse.

Anna ran farther up the slope to get as close as she dared. She discarded her hat. The mane of long dark hair suddenly free captured the Chinese girl's attention, and for a brief moment gazes locked.

Anna smiled, inspired by hope. The gesture wasn't returned.

Michael was calling her back. She turned. Why was he so upset? When she looked to the wagon again, the Chinese girl was studying her feet as she walked. She couldn't regain her attention now.

'What in God's name do you think you're doing?'

Anna winced from the sudden, tight grip on her arm. 'I was trying to attract her attention.'

'What the hell for?' Michael yelled, eyes wide, disbelieving.

'What for?' Anna couldn't believe he was so stupid. 'She's the first woman I've seen in months! And months seem like years out here!'

'She's Chinese!' he yelled back, disgust in his voice.

He pushed Anna away with the warning, 'Don't even think it. You hear me?'

'Think about what?' Anna snapped at his retreating figure. Michael marched off, muttering things that sounded awfully like 'Why me?'

Rage welled. Why you indeed! Anna kicked the ground, and now her foot hurt as much as her arm did. Damn him, the bruises were already showing. Anna snatched at the hat that lay in the dirt and pulled it on her head. 'They're only people!' she cried, not expecting her voice to carry quite as far as it did. Every face turned to her and she realised her mistake. She shouldn't take sides with the enemy— it would be a quick, certain way to be tarred and feathered. But she refused to let these men win. 'If you hate, it comes back to you! Don't you know that yet?' she called. Disgusted faces turned away, dismissing her stupidity. Her insane logic.

And Tom simply watched. He could feel the beginning of the end. It was as close as a thunderstorm in December. Tom understood her anger and confusion—he'd been the only one who hadn't left his claim to hurl abuse, and he was all too understanding of the thoughts whirling through the girl's head. But it all culminated in a weary sigh. He picked the small, round nugget from the top of the gravel in his pan and rolled it between his fingers.

Females, damn them all, longed for each other's company and it didn't matter what colour they were, female was female. But this union meant trouble. Tom began the routine shake and swirl in the patch of muddy water he called his own. Another mistake, because nothing really belonged to him. He was just borrowing it for a little while. Too bad the others didn't realise it, too.

'Nothin' but trouble,' he mumbled.

Supper cooks. I hope it burns. Michael is away drinking rum.

'I hope he drowns in it,' Anna whispered but didn't write that down. Her anger had intensified during the long day. There was so much anger all she wanted to do was take a long walk and scream to the surrounding mountains. But leaving so suddenly would have made Michael angry and suspicious.

She stared at the words she'd written and tried not to listen to the talk of the murdering, robbing yellow-skins. The pivot of conversation lately was, 'Slanty-eyed bastards, hanging's too good.'

'Aye and too quick.'

How dare they?

And a plan to make contact slowly formed in her mind. Didn't she have to fetch drinking water each day? Didn't she have to wash the baby's clothes, and didn't she have to walk a full mile to the waterhole? Perhaps she would find the Chinese camp site by mistake?

Yes, perhaps, if she searched long enough.

And what Michael never knew could never hurt her.

How dare they? . . .

Sam dismounted, dropped the reins and kept his hand on his hat. The horse followed him as he searched the diggings for his father. It was late afternoon and there he was, sipping tea like he was at the governor's garden party. Sam whistled, and when the old man turned he saw who Tom was sitting with. Too pretty to be a man but from a distance it was hard to tell. The horse rubbed her itchy face up and down Sam's back and put him off balance.

'Here comes trouble,' Tom mumbled as Sam took

his hat off and chased the horse with it. She kept following.

Anna watched the stranger approach. He was perhaps the most handsome being she'd ever seen, and she thought her heart would explode when he smiled at her, impishly, unsurely. Somewhat confused. Had she been wearing a dress there'd be no confusion at all, but she was dressed in Michael's huge pants and shirt, and her hair was tucked up under the old hat.

'Did you bring my tobacco?' Tom demanded.

'Course I did.'

It was the same voice she'd heard the night Dinny had died, a few weeks ago. Tom's son. Yes, it had to be. He had the old man's eyes, and was making a show of searching his many pockets for the precious tobacco. The tins were duly found and slapped into Tom's outstretched hand. Tom pocketed the gifts with a grunt.

She couldn't just sit there and say nothing. 'Would you like to join us?' she asked politely.

'No. He don't want no tea. He's leaving, right now, he's leaving. Git. Go on, git.'

Ignored, of course and Anna was glad. 'I'd love a cup of tea, ma'am. It's been a long ride.'

Sam was happy now. Yes, this was female and very pretty too. 'Call me Sam, ma'am,' he added politely.

'Sam,' Anna whispered. Her hands shook and her face deepened in hue when she caught his smile again. It was the way he watched her—curious, interested.

'Thank you, ma'am.' His words were soft, his actions almost shy as he took the offered mug, but Anna saw no such shyness in his eyes. He was melting her and he knew it.

'My name is Anna.'

'No, it ain't. Her name's Mrs Hall. Hear that? She's married.'

Sam smiled again, and Anna wondered if Michael was watching. As she turned to look, a gust of wind blew her hat off. She was on her feet swiftly, no match for Sam. He killed the flight. He noted the flash of dark eyes, the mane of hair and the white swell of breast peeking at him as he stooped to retrieve the hat. Anna grabbed for the hat as well and heads collided. She took two stumbling steps backwards and fell flat on her behind. 'You right there, ma'am?' he asked, rubbing his forehead. Then with the hat in one hand, her hand in the other, his powerful grip eased her back to her feet. Anna swayed. Vision blurred. 'You have a very hard head, Mr Manning.'

'Here, let me see.' Rough fingers touched her forehead and swept hair from her eyes. Anna looked up into his face. He was too close, just too close. He stepped away as if realising it too, and stared down at the hat. Muddied, squashed. 'Sorry, Anna–ma'am. I'll get you a new one.'

'No! I mean, no, it's not necesary. Accidents happen.'

'I must be a walking accident, ma'am.'

She couldn't tear away from his teasing gaze. She felt her face heat again, and her head was pounding almost as hard as her heart.

Tom closed his eyes. If Hannaford don't hang you, son, Mick Hall will. If I don't get you first.

Tom could see it happening for the hundredth time. The boy had some magnetism that attracted ladies like bugs to light. Tom didn't know where it came from, and even at his age he'd have joined a queue of a thousand men just to get a little thrown his way.

Anna had been hit by a gallon of it.

Trouble, nothing but trouble. She'd be full of questions now, dammit.

Jealousy prompted Tom to sweep the mug of tea from his son's hand, grab him by the collar and drag him off for a little chat that essentially was a waste of time and energy. Too late, the interest was rising. Tom saw its full bloom as Sam rearranged his pants before getting on his horse and riding away.

And he looked back at Anna and nodded. Smiled. I'll be seeing you again soon, that grin seemed to say. Tom groaned and looked at Anna. She had her thumb in her mouth. Chewing her nail, thinking things she shouldn't have been thinking.

Tom read the eyes.

'He's not what you think, girlie.'

Anna turned to him absently. She hadn't heard. No use repeating himself, she still wouldn't hear.

'Are you upset, Tom? You called me girlie.'

'Mick won't like it, Anna.'

'Don't be silly, Tom. I'm married.'

'Yeah? You coulda fooled me.'

You coulda fooled me.

Tom's words haunted her that night as she curled into Michael and tried not to hear his snores. She ran her hand over his chest, his stomach and hips, hoping the feel of her breasts squashing into his back might prompt a little attention. Even being held close for a little while would do. Michael woke and mumbled, he was abusive, telling her to put some clothes on. He was tired.

Anna rolled away, fumbled for her nightgown and felt tears stinging her eyes. Tears of shame.

It wasn't Michael she wanted.

The mail coach drew to a rattling, grinding stop in the middle of Mitchell's Crossing. For a change, it wasn't muddy. There'd been no rain here for weeks and the danger of bogging to the axle was slim.

The bushranger stood with arms casually folded

and his Adams .45 pistol tapping the shoulder of his coat. Five more pistols were tucked into his belt. It was a fearsome sight to anyone who was unsuspecting or unknowing. Sam Manning was easily recognised by the sparkling blue of his eyes even though he wore the appropriate black scarf across his nose and mouth. 'Just the mail today, Sam. Nothing here of importance.'

The eyes narrowed from the hidden grin. 'Depends what you think's important, Lionel. Where's Bill?'

'Broke a leg last Friday, Sam,' Lionel replied as he heaved the mail bag from the rack behind him. It landed with a thud near Manning's grey mare. She sniffed it, like she always did.

Sam thanked him with the normal nod of head and walked to the window of the coach. The canvas was down. Sam peered in anyway. Bert Whipps, the town's postmaster, sat quietly shaking while his new wife cringed in his arms. Sam knew of the union—he'd read most of their love letters. 'Morning, Bert. Ma'am,' Sam greeted, and he noticed Bert's hands tightening around his wife. It was futile defence and a moment Sam had been waiting a long time to experience. 'Out you get, Bert.'

'My wife's ill.'

'My wife's ill,' Sam imitated in matching falsetto. He wasn't entirely stupid. If she was sick, he was the Queen of France. 'Out.' Sam opened the door and stood aside as Bert emerged. The old fart had put on at least twenty pounds during his honeymoon—he probably couldn't do much else but eat, anyway. 'No, I'll help her out.' Adding insult, Sam slapped Bert's hand from his wife's arm and gallantly assisted the lovely Mrs Whipps to the rocky ground.

Two beautiful women within twenty-four hours. Sam felt elated just to touch her hand. Nice legs.

He noticed them when she hoisted skirts to disembark. Nice everything. Lionel was looking and he had a better view from where he sat.

Bert watched, humiliated to the core. Sam had a pistol in one hand and Rebecca in the other. She wasn't trying to get away and now Bert regretted asking her to wear the collarless dress he'd bought in Sydney. Too much bosom showed, not to mention the gold-plated locket half hiding within.

'What's your name?' Sam asked, eyes sparkling.

'Rebecca,' she squeaked.

'Rebecca. Nice name. May I?'

Rebecca turned to her husband the moment Sam let go of her hand, and reached to grope for the locket. Bert was so angry he was studying the ground. Rebecca felt the warm fingers glide over her shoulder, her breasts. Goosebumps followed. Then came the tug as the delicate chain snapped.

'Don't take my locket, please!'

Sam slipped it into his pocket and took her left hand. A beautiful hand. He told her so and smiled at her. Her face turned crimson. On her third finger was a wide gold band and, next to it, a huge array of . . . Sam looked closer. Rebecca tried to pull her hand away. It was more a gesture of propriety than anything meaningful. Sam clung tighter. 'Nice ring, Bert. What's it worth?'

'To you, nothing.'

'Nothing to anyone I think. What'd it cost you, Bert?'

'Leave them be, Sam. You have the mail.'

'Quiet, Lionel. I asked Bert here a question. Didn't I, Bert?'

'Twenty shillings,' came the hoarse whisper.

'Come again?'

'I said, twenty shillings!'

Rebecca was aghast. She pulled her hand from

Sam's and turned to her husband. 'You said they were real diamonds and they cost you a bloody fortune!'

Sam winced at the sudden Cockney outburst. All her beauty faded with the screech.

'Now, Bert,' Sam gently chided. 'You been married enough times to know you can't start off by lying. Don't you know that yet?'

'What's he saying, Bertie?'

'Rebecca please, now is not the time.'

'Now's as good as any,' Sam said, scratching his chin.

Even Lionel was interested in Bert's excuses but nothing more would come from the silent man—his mouth was snapped tight as a rabbit trap. Sam slipped the worthless locket back into its soft, warm nest. His fingers stayed a moment too long for Bert's liking.

'Touch my wife again, Manning and I swear, I . . . I . . .'

'Why don't you shut up and take your boots off, Bert?'

'What?'

'You heard me. Your ears are pretty good hearing gossip, and spreading it around, especially about me. You know the stories. What I do to folks who don't co-operate. Take your boots off, now.'

'I will not!' The little enraged man stamped his foot like an angry ram.

'I could make Rebecca take her clothes off if that's what you'd like. I know *I* wouldn't mind if she did.'

'For God's sake, Bertie, do as he says!'

Bert took his boots off.

'Socks, too.'

Humiliated to the core, Bert discarded his socks and stood barefooted on rocky, hard ground.

'Pants now.'

'I object!'

'Take his pants off, Rebecca.'

She did.

Lionel looked away although he didn't want to. It served Whipps right. The uppity little wombat had it coming. He'd often said nuisances like Manning should be hung from the nearest tree and not necessarily by the neck, either. Somehow, like always, Sam had heard.

Finally, the lovely new wife dropped her husband's boots, socks and pants into the creek. Four pairs of eyes watched expressionlessly as the items floated in a tumble for a little way. The boots sank with a gulping, final pop of despair.

And Sam cantered off into his hills with the Royal Mail bag dragging along behind the horse.

As Rebecca searched the luggage for trousers, Bert screamed, 'I'll see you hang for this, Manning!'

Lionel thought, not bloody likely, but he kept his opinions to himself. It was still a long haul into town.

Lucas Hannaford watched as the coach rattled in and stopped outside Ryan's General Merchandise Store across the street. Lionel Jeffries, the regular driver, jumped down. Children appeared from nowhere, all eager to know if Sam had held up the coach again.

The sergeant saw the nodding head and sighed.

More bloody paperwork. No doubt it was the mail.

A barefooted Bert Whipps emerged from the coach. One hand was holding up beltless trousers, the other was gesturing wildly. The sergeant opened the nearest book and appeared to be busy, looking up only when Whipps, followed by a beautiful young woman, burst in.

With great difficulty, the sergeant kept his smile hidden. He had prayed for this moment a long, long time. After two years of 'Something must be done!', Bert had finally been confronted with the elusive enemy of the postal system, Sam Manning.

The woman looked bored by it all. They usually did.

'I demand immediate action!'

'Sit down, Bert.'

The little man wilted. He sat, and the woman, who Lucas discovered was the new wife, remained standing, gazing about the charmless, somewhat distasteful room. No doubt she would find the town charmless and distasteful, too. Most women did.

'What happened?' It was always the question he need not bother to ask.

'I've been robbed of my dignity and physically assaulted by that . . . that . . .'

'By what, Bert?'

'You know who I'm talking about!'

'I'm not a mind reader.'

'His name is Sam Manning,' Rebecca Whipps said, and picked at her fingernails. They were long. Women with long nails rarely did any work. Lucas knew as much because his wife had talons, and she showed them daily. If it weren't for Maddy nothing would ever be done. He averted his gaze back to Bert.

'We were assaulted by that creature and I demand satisfaction. Hang him!'

'For robbing you of your dignity?'

'Well, he stole my locket but he gave it back,' Rebecca said.

From the depths of the lock-up Daniel Brannigan chuckled.

'You have something else to do, Brannigan?' After a moment, the back door closed.

'You're saying he stole your locket and he gave it back?'

'Here, I'll show you.' The girl's right hand disappeared into the depths of her green dress. Her face was alight with intense concentration for a moment before the locket was found and withdrawn. When the sergeant touched it, it was still hot.

He sighed. 'Perhaps if we start from the beginning?'

The tale was recounted and whenever Bert began to exaggerate on fact, the new wife countered with basic truth. In fact, she ruined Bert's story completely.

'Bert, I can't hang a man for wounding your pride. It wasn't Manning who tossed your clothing into the creek, and as the locket wasn't stolen there's little I can do.'

'He stole the bloody mail!'

'I realise that, Bert. Lionel will give me his usual statement in due course. And as always, the mail will show up on your doorstep in two days' time.'

'What's he going to do?' Rebecca asked.

'Nothing. Bloody nothing!'

'Take me home, Bertie. I'm tired.' She led him away, full of promises of how she'd make him feel better, very quickly.

She left her locket. It wasn't heavy enough to be pure gold so Lucas slipped it into the desk drawer and hoped she'd be back to reclaim it. Alone, of course.

Manning. Why did he persist? Wasn't he tired yet? Stealing mail for God's sake. The only things he ever opened were objects bearing governmental seals and, Lucas had to admit, anything which looked interesting. Keeping his hand in, Lucas supposed. Quietly persistent, extremely annoying.

On a number of occasions, Lucas had ordered a police escort for the mail coach. On those occasions, there was never any sign of Manning. An attempt or two to place troopers in civilian clothing on board the coach had been futile, too. It seemed as though Manning were a fly on the wall, and Lucas needed the annoying antics as much as he needed a broken leg. He'd discovered it was almost impossible to bushwhack a bushwhacker. Especially Manning.

Take, for instance, the bathtub that sat outside the stables. No one had reported a tub missing. Surely to God people knew whether their tubs were there or not? There was only one answer to the problem. Manning was going slowly insane. Unfortunately, he was endeavouring to take Lucas on the journey as well.

Damn him. There was more pressing business to attend to. The Chinese arrival at Bitter Creek was more than rumour now. Give them a month at the most. Or less. The sergeant scratched a message on a slip of paper and called for Moonshine. There was no reply. 'Where the hell are you, Billy?' he roared and a dark face cautiously peered around a corner. 'I want you to take this to the McIntyres.'

Billy hesitated. 'What's going on this time?' he asked quietly.

'Take this to the McIntyre brothers, Now.'

'It's forty miles, sarge . . .'

'It'll be worth it. Believe me.'

'That's what you said last time. They'll want more money. Lots more.'

Money? Lucas almost laughed. A keg of rum and a few pounds and the four brothers could be persuaded to do anything. 'They'll have gold this time, Billy. You tell them they'll have gold.'

Indecision crossed the dark face. 'From Bitter Creek, sarge?'

'Perhaps. Tell them it's the Chinese causing a problem. They'll know what I'll be wanting.'

Billy took the note and tucked it away. An order was an order and who was he to question? But still he lingered.

Lucas took out a bottle of rum from the old boot under his desk, uncorked it and took a huge mouthful.

39

It burnt, and his upper lip broke into a cold sweat. Billy was still there, watching, thinking. 'I gave you a bloody order!'

'You sure you want to do this, sarge?'

'I'm preventing a riot, Moonshine. Go.'

'Riot? Like Lambing Flat, sarge?' Billy caught the look in the sergeant's eyes and fled before his question was answered.

The Chinese. Easy enough targets providing they didn't set up camp too close to the whites at Bitter Creek. Give the Chinas a couple of weeks and they'd be doubling any European finds—they could smell gold a hundred yards underground. Wherever there were Chinese there was wealth for the taking.

Yellow blood meant nothing. It hadn't at Lambing Flat when he'd had the lawful excuse to shoot twelve of them in as many minutes. It certainly didn't matter now.

Anna dipped the bucket into the creek and withdrew the day's quota of clean drinking water. She was close to the Chinese camp site, because over the next hill she could hear the rattles and bangs of the shakers and blowers; now and then a foreigner's impatient call. How she wished she had the courage to find that Chinese girl. Talk to her. It was ludicrous, of course. Michael just wouldn't approve. He'd beat her for certain. Hadn't she already been warned?

Damn Michael. He'd never know.

Anna put the bucket down in a patch of shade and, heaving the baby to her hip, she began the trek up the wearying incline.

The baby gabbled to herself and slobbered on Anna's neck. She was ignored. Anna looked down on tents, wagons, men and machinery. The Chinese camp was little different to Bitter Creek.

Bent over a huge iron crock like a grey-clothed

witch from a fairytale was the object of Anna's latest obsession. The Chinese girl. Her hair was so black, it was almost blue in the sunlight. She was small, thin. She looked so fragile and tired.

Anna's courage rose and faltered with each alternate heartbeat. But she'd come this far, it would only take a few steps more. 'Should I, Baby?' she whispered but there was no answer. Anna took a few tentative steps down the hillside.

All work suddenly ceased, all heads turned after one jabbering shout. It sounded alarmed.

Anna froze. Michael's terrible stories of the Chinese and what they did to white women leapt at her in a thousand tangled forms. Anna tried to smile and held Susan tighter, hoping the baby's warmth and innocence would calm her frantic heart. The Chinese girl turned to her, studied her for a moment and continued with her cooking.

So this is all she will do? I should have expected as much, Anna thought. One glance weeks ago and I expect a cure for my loneliness. Michael was right, and I have no right being here. No right at all. I may need a friend but she doesn't. That was obvious.

Dejected, Anna turned and looked into an aged, oriental face framed by white hair. She stepped back, he stepped forward. He said something, not to her but at her and she glanced down at what he held in his hand.

Her water bucket.

Oh, no, she thought. They've laid claim to the only drinking water for miles. I've stolen his water. I'm dead. Dear God, he's going to murder me because I stole his water.

The old man gabbled at her again. He sounded annoyed, impatient. Demanding. She started to shake and tears filled her eyes. Anna tried to explain. Her words were lost because he couldn't understand her any more than she could understand him. But tears were universal language and fright heralded their fall. Anna screamed when he touched her shoulder. She took a frightened step backwards and the old man saved both her and the baby from tumbling down the hill.

His voice was angrier than ever now.

Anna burbled on and on and on:

'I didn't know it was your water, I don't know why I'm here, I'm so sorry.' The old man stared at her as if she were some kind of life he'd never seen before. He was also amused.

'My father say you leave this.'

Anna spun. The Chinese girl was coming up the steep incline towards her. My saviour, she thought. 'But I can't leave it. It's the only bucket we have.'

'No, no, he say you leave, you forget.'

That would be a good idea, Anna thought. But she couldn't go without her bucket. How would she explain it to Michael? I'm sorry, but I had no choice? An old Chinese man stole it? She didn't know which fate was worse. 'Leave? Forget I came?'

'No, no!' The girl was more impatient than the old man. 'This yours. Do not forget. Father say water precious!'

'Oh, is that what he was saying?' A smile lit her eyes before it touched her face. She'd never felt relief quite as intense, and only now was she aware of her stinging eyes and blurred vision.

'Why you cry? Father see you coming and he follow. He just curious. We see many . . . many . . .' The girl gestured with her hands. Anna was never very good at charades.

'Snakes?' she offered.

'Yes, exact. Snake. Ignore him and come. Please. I expect you long ago.' The Chinese girl took the bucket from the old man and beckoned Anna to follow her down to the camp.

Anna couldn't refuse. Although her knees still shook, there was no turning back. Not now. She was glad, too. Nothing was quite as bad as her imagination led her to believe. These people would not cut her throat and drink her blood. They took no notice of her.

'I am Lu Sun.'

'Anna Hall.'

By the facial contortions, Lu Sun thought the name was very odd. Anna was allowed to sit in the shade and she watched while the men, all of whom looked the same to her, were fed rice and a thick broth. Lu Sun attended to all of them. She didn't speak to Anna until the food had been eaten and the men had dispersed. No one took much notice except for the old man, who watched the baby with the intensity of an eagle after prey. He was disturbing.

'A girl?' Lu Sun asked. Anna nodded and Lu Sun said something in Chinese to the old man. He grunted in much the same way Tom grunted and said something to his daughter. 'Father say it look like boy to him. I once had boy. Dead before born. In here.' She patted her belly.

'I'm so sorry.'

Lu Sun walked off and scraped the bowls out to the waiting magpies. She came back, smiled at Anna and patted her stomach again. 'This one live. I know.'

She didn't look pregnant to Anna. 'Congratulations.'

Lu Sun didn't know what the word meant.

'I'm happy for you, Lu Sun.'

'So is Lu Sun's husband.' She pointed him out amid the tangle of lookalikes at the other end of the dry gully. He was digging around the base of a huge gum tree. Anna couldn't even guess his age. 'Eat?' Lu Sun offered. There was a lot of rice left, so Anna had lunch with her new friend, and all the while the girl's eyes feasted on Susan. 'You can hold her if you wish.'

The offer was declined. 'I must work now.'

Anna could tell by the sun's position in the sky, and the short shadows, that time was passing too quickly. Already it was nearing midday. 'I'd better be going, too. Thank you for the rice and the tea.'

'You come every day here?' Lu Sun asked.

Anna didn't want to lie. She picked up her bucket and steeled herself for the long, hot walk back to Bitter Creek. ' Yes. I do this every day.'

'Good. You see me when you come for water, yes?'

'I'd love to, Lu Sun. Goodbye.'

Michael was very curious. I can't hide happiness very well and nor can I lie effectively, so I told him I'd been walking and had forgotten the time. It is not quite a lie, nor is it quite the truth. I do need to tell someone about Lu Sun.

'Hello, Anna–ma'am.'

The nib Anna was dipping into the ink pot slipped, and ink spread like a black bloodstain across the diary page before the entire bottle tipped down her shirt. Her sins were thereby obliterated forever. She almost swore and looked up into Sam's eyes. He was full of clumsy apologies. 'Sorry, ma'am. I didn't mean to scare you, I thought you saw me coming.'

'That was all the ink I had left,' she moaned.

'Oh. I can get you some more if you want.'

Anna closed her eyes in despair. 'No, it's not necessary.' What had Michael said? When it was all gone, there would be no more? All this writing and drawing hats was a waste of time and money. He was forever buying ink. No more, not now.

'But I caused you to knock it over.'

44

Her gaze wandered to his face again as he crouched down beside her.

'I ruined your shirt, too.'

She looked down at the stained shirt. What would she say to Michael? I fell over? What does it matter what I say, he'll be happy there's no more ink. Anna looked across the diggings and saw Michael working at the creek.

'I'm real sorry. Anna-ma'am.'

Anna said nothing. She closed the diary and slid it into the tent, out of sight, out of mind, until she had another vision and what good would that do now?

Sam scratched his nose. 'I really did it this time.'

'May I ask what you're here for?'

'I came to apologise for squashing your hat the other day, ma'am. Brought you these as my way of saying sorry. Looks like I shoulda brought the whole tree instead.' As he spoke he withdrew a multitude of oranges from the depths of his coat and he thrust them at her, one by one until her arms were crowded and she was juggling fruit.

'But Sam, there's no need for this.'

'Maybe. But I've got a tree full of them. Nothing grows out here except wild limes. Hell, a lady like you might appreciate some oranges. You know, with the baby and all, and I guess I should shut up before there's another accident.'

Anna couldn't stop her emerging smile. He was really very shy and he knew he'd been babbling. Or perhaps that was the impression he wanted to give? 'Are you sure you don't want them?'

Pleasure lit his eyes. 'I'm sure, ma'am.' With the ma'am came a smile. Innocence belied the intelligent knowing in his eyes. A stranger was stealing her heart and the stranger was all too aware of it.

'Thank you, Mr Manning.'

'Mister?' He laughed. 'That sure sounds different.'

Anna purposely let her gaze wander to the creek. Thank God Michael wasn't watching.

Sam looked too. He'd heard about her bearded giant of a husband. 'Sure I can't get you some ink? Pop says you draw a lot.'

'Perhaps your Pop says too much. No thank you, my husband won't allow me to have any more ink.'

'Why?'

'Please, Mr Manning, it's best if you leave, now.'

'Oh. Just being friendly, that's all,' he said quietly, and for a moment he looked like a hurt child. Anna felt awful for turning him away like that but all she could really do was watch him leave. One of the oranges fell from her arms. How on earth would she explain these?

Hide them. Yes. Hide them.

'Got a cuppa for an old man?'

Anna threw the oranges into the tent and innocently turned to Tom.

'Stealin' oranges now is he?'

'Pardon?'

Tom sniffed. Anna knew he'd seen.

'Stealing. That's what he is. A thief.'

'Sam? I mean, your son?'

'Yep. I told you he was trouble. What's all that?' Tom pointed at her clothing.

'I spilled the ink. Michael won't be pleased.'

'It's not right for women to wear a man's clothes anyway.'

'It's comfortable for when I'm panning.'

'And how much did you recover today?'

'I . . . I didn't. I went for a walk instead.'

'You went to meet with that Chinawoman.'

'You know?'

Tom laughed away the shock in her eyes. 'Now, if you'd gone and said what woman? Girlie, girlie, you can make trouble for yourself without even trying.

46

Ah, it's all right. I won't tell nobody but what you tell Michael is this. You say it was him what kicked the bottle of ink over when he was drunk.'

'But that's a lie.'

Tom grinned. 'What he don't know can't hurt. And you be careful with them Chinas, girl. You be careful for me. They're not like us. They're different.'

'They seem very nice people.'

'Anna-girl, everyone seems very nice to you. Just be careful is all I say.'

'Yes, Tom.'

And as he walked away, he knew his warning had fallen on deaf ears.

'I thought you wanted some tea!' she called.

Tom Manning's deafness had set in again. It was sweet revenge.

All he had to do was drag the tub just another hundred yards up the treacherous slope, and hope the hell either it or he didn't slip. Sam stopped for a rest. If he left it here he'd have something to keep his wood dry. Besides, leaving the tub here would save him a busted back, too. Or maybe he was just getting lazier each day.

The mare lovingly rubbed her face up and down Sam's back, and made a quick lunge for his hat. It was a success and Sam caught her after first performing a belligerent little dance full of curses. Sam ripped the hat out of her mouth before she ate this one too. She snorted full in his face. A sign of love. Sam wiped it all off. 'Leave my hat alone. I won't tell you again.'

She probably understood the words, too. She rubbed her itchy face against his back once more. With hat firmly in hand, Sam surveyed the decaying miner's hut otherwise known as home. It was bare of anything decorative, littered with bits and pieces he'd collected over the past couple of years of living alone. He'd lied about the oranges, there was no tree but she'd never know that. No one would except for a couple of trusted friends who knew where he lived. It was safer that way, safer for others. Sam had told Tom a hundred times to move on—for his own safety, get away.

Tom had told Sam to move on. He had his claim at Bitter Creek and the only way he'd leave was to be carted out, dead.

Neither moved. Tom had his home at Bitter Creek and Sam's home was wherever Luke Hannaford was posted. From Lambing Flat where it had all begun, to Muswellbrook, to Brisbane. Now here. Girraween. Ah, yes, the haunting was planned to continue until one of them died.

Sam wanted to live forever, and exact his revenge one lazy, idle day at a time. Sam would never forget, and while Sam lived Luke would not be allowed to forget either. Sam could forgive almost anything except the betrayal, its causes, its effects.

'Damn,' he said and yawned. He left the tub where it lay between the hut and the outhouse. Too tired to care now. He unsaddled the grey and set her free. The horse tried to follow him inside the hut, but with her in there it was too crowded. 'Get out, there ain't no room.' The horse backed out and a squawking, speckled hen followed after a roar of, 'You too! Find somewhere else to lay your damn eggs!'

Sam apeared with his new Spencer repeater and a pocket full of fifty calibre bullets. The hen bided her time before slipping back to her full nest under his bed.

Singing a parodied sea shanty about drunk sailors, Sam loped off towards the creek and the flats beyond. It was his own private peace here, a little hut nestled in, and protected by, the mountains. A good supply of water, rabbits, and the occasional scrub turkey. He even tried to grow his own vegetables after he put up a fence to keep the horse out. He had all a man could need, except a woman. But he couldn't share his life with one, not now. Not again.

When he brought down the rabbit, he wished he had a dog because he had to walk fifty yards to find his kill. As he skinned and gutted the rabbit, he remembered the ink. And Anna.

Mostly Anna. It was impossible to forget her.

He had a box of paper and stationery things from one of the robberies. Where it was in his cave stash remained a mystery he'd solve later, after he ate. First he had to cook. Sam hated cooking. Women's work this.

Anna. Thoughts always returned to her. He wasn't used to ladies being scared of him. Shy maybe but scared? Maybe she had her reasons, maybe not. But eyes never lied. Best to forget about her. Women were nothing but trouble. But he did have ink, and he also had some paper. It was all going to waste where it was and she'd be able to use it.

Sam looked at the rabbit dangling from his hand. The thought of eating stew again turned his stomach. Next time he was in town, he'd go to Harry's and get some tinned bully beef. 'Yeah, something decent to eat,' he whispered to himself.

And as he sat, listening to his supper boiling, he fondled the bottle of ink he'd found quicker than he'd expected. He fantasised about the ink being Anna Hall's face. Smooth, pretty, soft. Then he threw the fantasy aside and put the ink bottle down on the table.

Fantasies, too, caused trouble.

There was a sheaf of old paper he'd found for her drawings. A great heap of it, yellow with age. Dusty. Brittle. He wanted to see her again even if it would be from a distance, even if it meant giving the ink and paper to Tom to pass on to her.

Sam wanted her to have it. He didn't know why but he guessed he liked her. She reminded him of someone, but he didn't know who. That was the worst of it. He liked her, she was married. Funny how it had never mattered before.

When he finally slept around midnight, his last thought was to avoid the lady completely after this one last time, of course.

Three

Sam was set to fill his small waterbag and rest the horse when he heard the sounds which took him by surprise. They were sounds unsuited to the bush stillness and unheard once away from Rosie's establishment.

It was the laughter of girls.

For a moment he wondered if he was awake but the horse heard it, too. The light breeze was an ally for a change because the laughter was coming from the waterhole.

Sam got off his horse, tied it and slunk through the undergrowth, stealing carefully and quietly up the granite outcrop that enfolded the creek.

He'd dreamed of seeing things like this—spying on a bevy of naked females, stripping to nothing and diving in.

So he lay on his gut and watched.

One was Chinese. The other, Anna. The baby was there, too, in the shallows with its mother, happily obstructing Sam's view of nakedness. If they knew or sensed the voyeur, there would be no show. So far, so good. He tried to hear what they were saying but the voices faded to the breeze.

He had all the time he wanted.

The Chinese took hold of the baby and Anna stood. From a distance there wasn't much to see. He blinked at the wrong time and next she was swimming. Graceful, quiet. Hardly a splash. He wanted to reach out and touch until sense returned. Sense, though, didn't make any difference to his suddenly tight pants.

She was another man's wife. Someone else had her first. Shouldn't be here watching. Not her, not like this.

Sam slid down the rockface as quietly as he'd climbed it. Heart pounding, body aching, he retraced his path to the horse and went in search of another waterhole to fill his bag and wash her out of his system.

Water wasn't that strong.

'What's wrong?' Anna asked. Lu Sun had a strange, lost expression in her dark eyes, as if she wasn't really there. Something was wrong. Anna could feel it. She swam back to where Lu Sun sat in the shallows, her long-fingered hands wrapped around the baby. 'Are you feeling unwell?' Anna asked.

Lu Sun couldn't voice her feelings in any language that either of them could understand. Whatever had prompted the sudden oddness was gone. She no longer felt vulnerable, simply lost for an explanation. 'Sun hot. You burn.' And with those curt words, she rose and stepped out of the water. Although Anna didn't want to leave so soon, she followed and reached for her rag of a towel. What was happening? Had she said something amiss? Or was it her lack of conversation again? Somehow, there was no need to talk in Lu Sun's presence. One day they'd be full of frustrated chatter and laughter, the next both would be thoughtful and silent. The silences were mostly enjoyable. Not now. Anna had the feeling something was being hidden. How she hated secrets.

'Lu Sun? Please tell me what's on your mind?'

There was confusion and indecision for a moment. 'Feels how you say, bad?'

'What feels bad?'

'Feels this be last time.'

'Last time for what?'

'Last time we meet. Talk. Laugh. Be fun.' Tears welled in her eyes.

'Don't be so silly. What could stop us from having fun?' Anna didn't wait for Lu Sun to answer. She pulled her dress over her head and fastened it together. But something forced her to look at her friend.

'Lu Sun not be silly. Anna feels it, too. Anna does not lie good.'

Even if it was the truth, Anna couldn't admit it, not even in her thoughts. Perhaps she's been drinking too much of that strange tea. 'I'd better be going. I'll see you tomorrow.'

Half a mile to go to Bitter Creek. Sam was in no hurry, walking the grey along the goat track of a weaving trail. He heard singing. It wasn't very good singing. It made him wince. 'Molly Malone'. He'd never liked that song.

The voice faded as he drew nearer and for that he was pleased.

It was Anna again. She put the bucket of water down, shifted the baby to the other hip and continued her song. She didn't know he was there. Other things on her mind, Sam guessed.

'Morning, ma'am. Nice day.'

Anna squealed in fright and almost dropped the bucket. She spun and there he was, studying her from his seat on his grey horse. He was smiling.

'Sam Manning, are you trying to scare me to death?'

'Who, me?' Sam knew he really should ride on but he sat there for a while, looking at her, smiling at her. Her hair was dry now and pulled back and she wore a dress, too. A colourless grey thing that must have been hot as hell. There were sweat marks down her back, under her arms. And the baby was squinting up at him and jabbering something until it stuck its fist in its mouth and grinned at him. The grin made him uncomfortable—it was as if the baby knew something he didn't. Not only that, she'd called him by his name instead of 'Mr Manning'. He was pleased, and his heart lifted because she made his name sound good. 'Would you like a ride to Bitter Creek, ma'am?' he asked.

'No, thank you. I'm fine.'

It was his cue to ride on of course but his feet wouldn't tap the horse and his brain had gone numb. For the first time in years, Sam Manning was lost for words.

'I hope you have a pleasant day, Mr Manning,' Anna said in her little girl voice. She tried to smile as she picked up the bucket. Sam watched her walk off. He was dejected. First Sam, then Mr Manning. He didn't have a chance. Or did he? If anything he was known for persistence even if the odds were against it.

'I'll take that if you like.'

'No, I do this every day. Really.'

Sam moved the horse on, pacing it with the woman. 'Looks heavy.'

She glanced up at him, shook her head and kept walking.

'I found some ink for you, ma'am. Some paper too.'

Anna stopped walking again and when she looked up this time, he saw an immeasurable amount of sadness in her eyes. 'I thought I told you my husband wouldn't allow it.'

'Why not?'

'He just won't. But thank you for thinking of me.'

Thinking of you? He wanted to laugh. Sam dismounted. 'Here, I'll swap you. Which is heavier?' he asked, glancing from the bucket to the baby.

54

Without giving her time to decide or object, Sam took the bucket and started walking. The protests soon came. He ignored them all. The horse followed lazily. 'What's his name?' Sam asked, quieting Anna's thunder.

'I beg your pardon?'

'The kid. What's his name?'

'Susan Louise.'

'Oh. Nice name. Watch the horse or she'll eat your hat, there.'

Anna promptly moved away from the horse. The horse followed. It was interested in the baby and the baby was interested in the horse.

'I suppose Tom's told you all about me?' Sam asked. He was walking too fast. He slowed.

'He did mention something about you being a thief.'

'Is that all?'

'That's enough, isn't it?'

Sam changed hands. The bucket was heavy all right. 'You really lug this two miles a day, ma'am?'

'How do you know I carry it two miles a day?'

'Pop told me,' he lied. She seemed to accept it. The last thing he needed her to know was how he'd been watching her and her Chinese friend. How he knew almost every move she made. The walk continued in silence for a little way until Anna had to rest. Sam sat too, but not too close in case she got the wrong idea. Getting the wrong idea was probably a good idea, though. Another fantasy was ruined when the baby grabbed a fistful of Anna's nose. Sam winced in sympathy. She didn't seem to mind. She didn't seem to feel it. 'Ma'am?' he asked.

She turned to him but couldn't meet his gaze for long. A lot of women couldn't. He often wondered why. 'Are you happy out here?'

'I don't think that's any of your business, Mr —'

'Would you call me Sam? I like it when you call me Sam.'

'I shouldn't call you anything.'

''Cos I'm a thief?'

'Amongst other things, yes.'

'Other things? What else you heard about me?'

'Please, Sam. Just give me my bucket. If anyone should see us —'

'There's one!' he suddenly cried, changing the subject and surprising her again. Sam put the bucket down, grabbed her hand, heaved her to her feet and darted off into the bush beside the track. Numerous nightmares leapt into her mind until she saw what he was reaching for—a small green fruit. 'Here, I told you.' He was smiling at her. 'Look. Wild limes. See?'

Anna dared not read the signals behind his eyes. 'Please let go of my hand.'

Sam looked down to see and feel his tight grip on her small fingers and he let go quickly. And over her shoulders he saw the horse with its head buried in her water bucket. He cursed and darted off.

Anna closed her eyes and tried not to listen to his apologies. 'It's all right, I'll get more!' Before she could protest, he was on his horse, bucket in hand, and cantering back towards the waterhole.

Michael saw his wife return to the diggings. Sam Manning was walking with her. She was exceptionally quiet at lunch, too quiet. With Anna, quiet was synonymous with guilt.

'Enjoy your walk?' Michael asked. She looked up but said nothing. Her attention went back to the dancing flames of the open fire. Her mind wasn't on meat and damper, that much he knew. 'I think I'll be fetching our water from now on, Anna.' She sent him an alarmed look. Michael sipped at his tea.

She'd sweetened it too much and for a moment he was tempted to throw it into her face, and ask if Manning liked tea this bloody sweet. The urge soon passed. 'I thought you said you'd spilled the last of your ink.'

'Yes.'

'Where'd that bottle come from?'

Silence. She was trying to think of a reasonable lie and wasn't quick enough.

'Anna!'

She jumped and tensed, and when she tensed he was tempted to hit.

'I asked you a question. The least you can do is answer me!'

'Tom's son gave me a bottle. Some paper, too. I said I didn't want it—'

'Tom's son? So you're friendly with a bushranger?'

'A bushranger?' she asked, all eyes now.

He hated her dull innocence.

'I see he carries our water these days!'

'Michael, you don't understand. His horse drank it and he fetched more to save me the long walk. That's all.'

'When was this? Where?'

'I was coming back from the waterhole. He rode by and he stopped and . . .' She faltered. Michael suspected it was to fabricate a little more. He'd heard of Manning and how irresistible he was. But he remained calm. A disquieting harbinger of the inevitable.

'And? Go on, lass. Dare not stop now.'

'He talked.'

'He talked? You didn't?'

'Michael, I've done nothing wrong!'

Tears in her eyes now. Face trembling.

'He seems to visit the diggings a lot of late. Everyone's commenting.'

'I've heard nothing.'

'You're never here!'

'That's not true!'

'You're meeting him, aren't you? Every bloody morning you saunter off with the baby. Fetchin' water's just a bloody excuse! You're meeting him.'

'No!'

'You're supposed to be my wife, can you not act like one!'

'I do! It's you who's not a proper husband!'

The back of his hand struck her mouth, splitting her lip. The force sent her to the ground. On his feet and towering over her, Michael felt like kicking. He resisted. 'No more, you hear me! No more! A man can only take so much!'

Anna covered her face with her ams as he stepped over her, throwing his pannikin mug to the ground. He cursed his way back to his claim.

Anna lay there quite still but shaking inside from fear. And she cried because it wasn't over. It had barely begun. He'd get drunk and he'd never let her forget, never.

Blood was warm and salty and filling her mouth. This time he'd loosened a tooth. Anna struggled to sit up. Her back hurt from the rock she'd fallen against. Her head swam from pain, and sobs came from the depths to scour her lungs. She touched the back of her head and had to wipe her eyes to see her fingertips.

Blood.

Hatred welled. It was pure and deep.

She quinted at the diggings, at the men who had seen and pretended otherwise and her blurred gaze fell on Tom. He made no move toward her yet the message that passed was silent. After a moment, Tom wiped his nose on his shirt sleeve and returned to his work.

Then she heard the baby crying—angry demands she hadn't noticed before. She crawled into the tent and drew the flaps to a close. While Susan fed and quiet tears continued, Anna could barely discern the colour of the one orange that remained. She wouldn't be able to eat it now. It would go rotten.

Like this place. Rotten.

And she'd never see Lu Sun again. That hurt most of all. Lu Sun had been right. She'd said it was to be the last time.

When Michael came home it was very late and he was very drunk. He hadn't returned for any tea, and the food had been wasted. He'd been drinking rum for hours with the mad Yugoslav, and all her fears were realised when Michael stumbled in. Apprehension tickled her spine.

It was hard if not impossible to judge his moods when he'd been drinking. She pretended she was sleeping. If she was lucky, he'd simply fall over and lie there until morning. And in the morning he'd be unaware of anything that had happened.

'Where is it?'

The words were slurred, incomprehensible. Angry.

'What?' she asked, sleepy, innocent. Anna did the best she could under the circumstances.

'Where's it gone? Where is it?'

He began demolishing everything he could find in Anna's trunk.

'Michael!'

'Find it, I want to see it!'

'What?'

'That diary thing of yours! I wanna know what you been writing about him!'

'About who for God's sake?'

Too late, he found her diary and started to tear at its pages, throwing them about, trying to read, swaying on his feet.

'Michael, that's mine, don't!'

But it was more than hers, it was her life's dreams, everything she was or had ever aspired to be, recorded in her infinitely neat handwriting, forever. And he was destroying it. He was destroying her very soul. Despite the paining back and blistering headache, she attacked.

He pushed her away as if she were made of paper. By the time she scrambled to her feet once more, Michael had flung the book outside and into the fire. She tried to go after it, to save it, but he held her fast. She punched at him, screaming out her hate, trying to hurt him. It was futile until she bit. She drew blood on his forearm. His elbow caught her in the chest and she fell, winded. Michael stared down at her and touched his arm. He looked at the blood. Amazement was in his eyes. Shock had sobered him, and Anna's sudden, overwhelming anger was replaced with terror.

'Not a proper husband?'

She couldn't breathe let alone speak to defend herself. But words never helped.

'Not a proper husband? You're nothing but a whore! It's not me you want, it's him! You think I don't know!'

Hate was in his eyes. He reached down and fisting his hand in the front of her nightgown, he heaved her to her feet. 'Did he bed you? Or was it you beddin' him?' Anna closed her eyes. His breath was fouled by rum. She wanted to vomit but all she could do was shake her head. 'And you're a lyin' whore, too!'

Anna tried to get away, as far from his rage as she could.

Futile.

'I'll show you what proper husbands do!'

Tom said nothing. Nor did any of the others who

had heard the commotion and the screams of the night before. From the moment she appeared in the blinding sunlight, faces turned to her, and away just as quickly. Anna pretended she hadn't seen the looks. It was the best way.

Michael was nowhere in sight. His rifle and the tin bucket were gone. There was no kindling for the fire, and all that remained of her diary was the brass clip amid the smoulder. He'd have forgotten. In a few days, he would probably ask why she hadn't touched her piddling book.

Anna sat down slowly, wincing. It hurt to walk. She ached all over and was covered in bruises. Inside, there was nothing left to feel. She was simply numb.

She knew where he'd gone and why he'd taken the rifle. She'd be in for another hiding if by chance Lu Sun was waiting at the waterhole but no, it was far too early. Even Lu Sun had work to do and by now she'd know to hide from Michael Hall. Lu Sun had inquired about a bruise or two, and ordinarily Anna would have lied quite convincingly. Lying became easier with practice, especially where her marriage was concerned, but there'd been no reason to lie to Lu Sun. If she'd tried she'd have been transparent. 'He hits you? What you do?' she'd asked. Anna found it difficult to explain impossibilities.

Michael duly returned with rifle over shoulder and water bucket in hand. There was barely a flicker of emotion. She winced when he walked by. He rarely hit when her face was this swollen and tortured. Anna stabbed at the fire with a long stick and pretended the coals were Michael's soft, hairy belly. She could still feel it sloshing against her body. And he never bathed, ever. It wasn't fair that her Chinese friend had a husband who loved her and cared for her as best he could. Why, the woman who'd lived in the house next door in Brisbane had determinedly refused to let her husband touch her unless he bathed first. Worse, her husband was a meek little creature, always saying, 'Yes, Millie, yes, whatever you say,' and venturing off to wash. Once, Millie had laughed about her new dress and had given Anna all the details of how she'd acquired it.

Michael would have killed her before relenting to a woman's attempts at blackmail.

He mumbled something. Anna was deaf. He went away and returned with an armload of kindling. The fire was soon ablaze.

'Make some tea for me.'

Anna made some tea. When he'd finally gone off to work, she dipped her handkerchief into the water pail and held it to her closed eye, then to her split lip. The coolness seemed to help.

Tom almost stopped on his way past. He would have if she'd looked up. Shame or anger, she didn't know which, prevented it.

Two days passed into infinity. Michael, never the one to apologise, spent otherwise valuable time with his sullen wife. Anna had seen him do this once before—to a dog he had. He'd punished it severely and later had discovered it wasn't his dog that had killed every hen in Blackburn's chicken enclosure. So he tried in his own way to make amends. The dog cowered, wanting to approach but fearful of more pain. Not understanding why. And it slunk to Anna instead because it trusted her. She was then blamed for turning his own dog against him.

Anna was fearful of nothing now. She wanted him to suffer for his sins. It was simple.

The afternoon when he gently touched her hand she looked at him as if he were a dead cockroach found in the flour tin. He didn't say he was sorry. He never would. To him, sorry was an admission of defeat yet she always waited to hear it. 'Are you going to pan today?' he asked instead.

'No.'

'I see.' With a sigh, he walked off a little way and turned back. Something vague on his lips, too. It never emerged. He kicked a rock down into the muddy creek.

Sam Manning rode in a few days later. Anna watched him in conversation with his father. She didn't need to hear the words being exchanged. Sam even attempted to walk to where Michael was working, unawares. Tom stopped him. In anger, Sam rode away.

However innocently Sam had caused this latest drama, Anna wasn't pleased to see him go. She hoped he'd have the courage to walk up to her in full view of everybody.

She had lived in hope most of her life.

Later, Tom came to speak. 'Girlie.'

'Tom.'

'Can't stay like this forever.'

Anna's gaze slowly met his. Tom could have chipped the ice off her eyeballs. He honestly thought she'd gone and accepted Bitter Creek and its unending futility as her inevitable destiny. Life would never get better and if she kept this up, it damn well wouldn't. She couldn't sulk forever. Nor could Kate. 'You know,' he said, spitting his tobacco into the fire, 'if they said to me, Tom, you're dyin' and you got one week to live, do you know where I'd wanna go?'

Anna shook her head.

'Nowhere at all. I'd stay right here, girl, cos one week'd feel like two.'

A faint smile touched her face. Tom wiped his nose on his sleeve and began to cough. Eventually he had to sit down, and when he did he touched her hand. She tried to pull away, but he held tighter.

'Me and the boys been ignoring him but enough's enough. I think he knows he did wrong. Some men just can't say it, girlie.'

'Say what?'

'Sorry. He is, you know. In his own stupid way, he does love you.'

Anna looked into Tom's eyes. Yes, he meant it. No lie was present. Her eyes stung. Tom reached for some more tobacco to chew on. 'The sooner you get to smiling again, the sooner things'll be like they used to. Took us a while to get used to havin' a lady about, but we're used to it now. Least we was. We don't like too much change, girlie, so you best start smiling again.'

'There's nothing to smile about. I don't feel like smiling. I don't feel like anything.'

Anna expected him to say something. There was no sympathy from Tom Manning and there never would be. But his presence was a strange sort of comfort and it always had been. She held his hand a little tighter. 'Nothing will ever be the same, Tom. Nothing.'

'And where'd we all be if things never changed? Still be wearing fur coats and gruntin' at each other, that's where we'd be.'

'I hate this place, Tom!'

'Watch it don't start hatin' you.' He reached into his pocket and withdrew a doll that was carved roughly from wood. Crude, misshapen. He studied it before handing it to her. 'It's all right. You tell him it was a present from me.' Anna took it. She knew who had made it. The carved face was smiling. Best she study it now before she gave it to the teething baby. 'I never figured you was a quitter. Suppose I been wrong before.' With another squeeze, to her knee this time, he rose to his feet, turned and walked away.

'I'm not a quitter!'

Tom was deaf yet again.

'How dare you say I'm a quitter!' She'd never quit at anything in her twenty-two years of life.

Was he right? Was she really wallowing in self-pity or was it deep anger she felt? She wanted to pick up a shovel and hit Michael with it. She didn't really understand why. Revenge perhaps, for his lies at the beginning. The wily ways he employed when he was ill in the hospital. Marry me, Annabelle? The bright eyes implored her. We'll have a new life together . . . Oh, all those promises, indeed.

She watched him work for his piddling gold, not that gold would ever make him happy. She wished he'd die the same slow, painful way poor Dinny had. The wish became a desperate urgency until common sense prevailed. Death was no answer. I'll be a widow, she thought. An outcast, forgotten and left to manage alone. With a baby, too. Then I would have to make his imaginings a reality, just to survive. I would be the whore he thinks I am.

'I am not a quitter, Tom Manning!'

A few surprised faces turned to her. No one had heard the lady's yell from across the diggings for weeks now. Some of the faces grinned. Nudges and whispers abounded.

Anna poked savagely at the fire coals. Blue flame licked at the breezeless air. Her brass clip was still in the ashes. Burnt dreams. But dreams and visions that were still complete in her mind's eye. There were always new ones appearing. Always.

Anna searched the tent for the sheaf of yellowed, brittle paper. The pages were loose and there were hundreds of them. Two sketches to a page, perhaps?

What remained in yesterday anyway? Nothing that couldn't be recreated new and fresh with a different perspective, devoid of depression. Yesterdays were filled to overflowing with written memories which only inspired more recollections of tedium, of heat, of weariness and achings for something she could never have.

Now she was pleased the diary lay in ash. It couldn't hurt her any more. Nor could Michael.

Anna searched for something hard and smooth to rest on so the nib wouldn't tear the paper. To get what she wanted, what she'd dreamed of most of her life, would be a sole endeavour. She'd need no husband to help her reach her goals. He would only laugh anyway. Wasting time again? he'd asked more often than not.

She had hope. She had faith in that hope.

She began the drawing in stolen ink on stolen paper, on the metal trunk containing everything she owned. And it wasn't a hat she drew, it was her dream. The sign above the doorway bore the shop's name, Annabelle's Millinery. Then came the shop front.

She could see it now as perfectly as it had appeared in her child's mind. Oh, these dreams of yours, her grandmother would scoff. But it was here again— clear, sharp and bathed in sunlight.

Where the shop would be remained a mystery, but she knew it was a lifetime away from Bitter Creek.

Annabelle's Millinery.

Cobblestones on the footpath outside. Three stairs. A bell near the door. A bell which jingled when a customer entered. The smell would be of lavender, the walls a pale lilac. Hats of all kinds for all purposes and occasions would be arranged attractively in the window. And outside, a gas lamplight would illuminate her dream for all to see, even at night.

This is mine, she thought, and the thought brought tears to her eyes. One day, Annabelle's Millinery will be mine.

Anna looked down at her sleeping child. And one

day it will be yours, and your daughter's . . . 'I am not a quitter, Tom Manning,' she whispered as she found a safe nest for her future, a nest Michael would never chance upon—under the flour and tea tins.

He'd ruined enough of her life already.

That same afternoon, she filled her bottle with flakes of gold. She hadn't touched a pan for three weeks and three weeks felt like three years.

Bitter Creek had returned to its normal pace and the men's cursings filled her with a comfortable warmth. She even smiled at Michael. And, God help him, he smiled back. A huge weight had finally lifted.

Sam kicked the same rock in an ever-widening circle until his anger finally exploded. The rock curved high into the air and came down heavily in the creek. And now it felt like two toes were broken. The curse split the air and grazed his lungs.

For over a week now, the desire for revenge lingered in the back of his mind and surfaced too easily, the slightest thing its inspiration. His only satisfaction would come from beating the shit out of Michael Hall. There was no other way. And Sam didn't care if the man was six feet three and weighed sixteen stone.

He'd stewed long enough and kept away long enough. The time had come.

Quiet. Too quiet. A tingle he associated with fear rose and ebbed. Tom felt the flutter of unreasonable panic as an itching ache in his chest. He wondered where Anna and the baby were. Lately, she'd been taking off to meet the Chinawoman again. Asking for trouble. But what he felt was a different kind of trouble. No one else seemed to feel it.

Tom tried to discern the movement in the distance. Maybe it was the girlie coming back? No, he saw men. Billy Moonshine. But what was Billy doing with . . .

There was no time to voice a thing. No time to question.

Tom saw the rifles fire. Hands clawing at bellies, chests. The wide eyes. The surprise. The noise of chaos as the diggers ran for some kind of weapon. Screams of outrage blistering into screams of agony. Before he felt the searing heat, Tom recognised the man on the horse and suddenly realised that what Sam had been saying all along was true. Dammit, he'd never believed him. Never. Then came the fire in his chest. Fire from the sergeant's rifle.

Anna heaved the baby to her hip and traipsed up the hill. Lu Sun had definitely said Thursday. Something must have happened. The Chinese camp was without a sound except for the constant creak of a tree limb. Anna made it to the top of the hill and was swept into a nightmare.

Lu Sun's father was making that branch creak— the old man was tied by his ankles and swinging. Dead. Face covered in blood. It had pooled, drying now, on the ground. His throat had been cut. His long white plait was almost black from blood.

No sound would come although she wanted to scream.

She didn't remember very much of what happened, how she sidestepped around the body, how her eyes took in even more horrors. Had she screamed for Lu Sun, hoping against hope she'd somehow been spared? But her friend's naked body floated face down in the muddy, bloodied water.

Only then was she aware of the noise. Shooting. Distant. Coming from the south. From Bitter Creek. Baby in arms, Anna ran for a full mile and felt nothing except the terror, horror and disbelief.

Again, she was too late. She stood atop the hill near Dinny's grave and looked down on another sight her mind steadfastly refused to believe.

'Michael! Tom!'

She set the baby down heavily and ran, skimming the camp fires, leaping overturned machinery, bodies of people she knew. Tom's shack was nothing more than a few bent pieces of tin and splintered wood. But she couldn't find him. She was still screaming for Michael.

Lucas watched, amused for a little while before he dismounted from his nervous horse. He took the rifle from the saddle.

She was still calling.

Keep screaming, Anna Hall. They won't hear you now.

Lucas walked towards her. Anna slid down the creek bank and landed on her face in the fouled water. She scrambled to get to her feet and her husband.

Lucas stepped over the crawling, crying baby—he'd see to it later. Perhaps, perhaps not. And there she was, her husband's blood on her face and in her hair as she held his limp, heavy body, hoping her anguish could bring him back to life. No woman had that power.

Silly girl. This was no place for a woman, anyway. And certainly no place for miracles.

Anna heard the rifle cock and looked up into the blinding ten o'clock sun. Just a silhouette of a man but she knew the stance and she knew who it was without having to see his face. The sergeant slid down into the creek. 'He's dead.'

Anna held tighter. The man reached down, grabbed a handful of Michael's shirt and heaved the body into the water. Anna tried to scramble up the muddy incline but her booted feet had no hold and she kept slipping. One word clouded her mind, and she must have screamed, '*Why?*'

'Don't ask trivialities, Anna.'

She grabbed for a handful of mud and threw it wildly at his face. He only laughed and swung the rifle down. It ceased her blind attempts to scramble free. The hard barrel crushed into her chest defied her to breathe.

'Do you want your baby to live?'

Any reply she may have had was frozen.

'Bring the baby!' he called out.

And when she tried to move, the barrel of the rifle crushed against her ribs. In the distance she could hear Susan screaming. A glimpse of a couple of men, covered in blood. And one of them lifted Susan by the leg. All Anna could see of him was his bright red hair. All she could hear were Susan's screams. Her thoughts weren't on the rifle, or the sergeant or the death that surrounded her—her immediate terror was for her child. The youth walked towards them. Anna could see the knife in his hand. It glistened in the sun. It was bloody.

'Please don't hurt my baby . . .'

At first it was a whisper. Then it became a screamed plea, over and over.

'What sort of monster do you think I am, Anna?' the sergeant asked with a humourless smile. 'Whether your child here survives or not is entirely up to you.'

The red head holding Susan smiled.

'And what do you say, Anna?' the sergeant asked.

'Don't hurt my baby!'

'Anna, Anna, I have a daughter of my own. So you see, we do have something in common.' The rifle lifted and she scrambled away again, this time to her child. But the man holding the baby stepped back. He was still smiling. He was enjoying this. They all were. Anna counted six of them now. Four faces she had never seen before and two she had. She looked back to the sergeant and then to Billy Moonshine, but she knew there was no help from anyone.

'Please don't hurt my baby,' she tried to say, but her voice would not come.

The silence hit first. Under any other circumstance, Sam would have looked to the sky to see the approaching storm. There wasn't a sound, just a loud silence. Eerie, foreboding. His rehearsed words for Michael Hall filtered away into the sunset hush.

As he drew closer, faint wisps of smoke tickled his nose. Beyond he sensed something else.

Death.

He knew it well. He'd carried it with him for so long now he was too familiar with its presence. Death was there, twenty yards away, over the rise at Bitter Creek.

Nearly everything once standing was demolished; burnt, or still smouldering.

Sam's first thought was for Tom. And with the thought came a feeling of hope.

Hope that it'd been quick. He searched for his father. One of two places—Anna's, or his claim. He was at the claim, and he saw Michael Hall was dead. Shot.

Jesus!

Sam sat hard on the ground and checked the bile that rose. He swallowed his nausea so many times that he finally turned his head and threw up. And he sat amid the dead in the still dusk silence, the only sounds the steady hum of flies and the quick pounding of his heart.

He heard a noise. Faint, like a baby crying. The cries obliterated the echoing silent questions and he couldn't ignore the cries. It was Anna's baby.

He was on his feet and tracking the source before he realised it. How the hell it got over to the other side of the creek he'd never know, and he couldn't remember its name, either. It was crawling over a body. Crying. Sobbing. 'Jesus Christ,' he whispered. The baby looked up at Sam and chewed on its fist. Its face was covered in blood and mud and snot and flies. How it could cry in those long, deep, choking sobs and chew its hand he'd never know. Sam's eyes clouded for the second time and he tasted the salt of his own tears as the baby lifted its arms to him. It didn't have to talk to communicate.

Sam ran a shaking hand over his face and turned away from the sight. But he couldn't walk away from it.

He turned back. She still had her arms in the air, and was still sobbing. Long breaths ending in a hiccup.

He kept watching, frozen now, unable to move. It was trying to climb up his leg.

What am I gonna do? he asked himself.

Before he realised it, he'd bent to pick the baby up. She stopped sobbing and for that he was grateful. She was very wet and buried her fat little snotty face into his neck and started sobbing again. He held her tighter. 'Be all right,' he whispered. 'Be okay, little Suzie.'

Sam was surprised he'd suddenly remembered her name.

The images in his mind reappeared. He didn't want to look too far because he knew what he'd see if he did. Anna either strung up or staked out but, whatever, she'd be dead and it wouldn't have been quick. It rarely was for a woman in these circumstances. But he had her kid in his arms now and he had to make sure. For the kid's sake. He didn't want to, but there was no other choice.

This time it was easier because he had something to hold on to. He seemed less alone. The baby sucked at his buttons as Sam looked down at her mother. She was on her face. Naked. Covered in mud. There were footprints all around the shaker that had hidden her from view. Male feet. Boot tracks.

Blood pooled from her left side.

Sam crouched. The blood was stilling oozing slowly.

Dead bodies didn't bleed.

He put the baby down and turned her over gently. She'd been knifed in the ribs. She was trying hard to breathe. Bites and bruises and cuts on her shoulders, arms. Legs . . . How many were there? Sam thought. His quiet, broken voice interrupted the silence.

'Anna? Can you hear me?'

Her eyes opened for a fleeting moment, rolled and closed again.

Four

'Oh, you're back,' Daniel said and quickly removed his boots from the sergeant's desk. Lucas wondered what the boy had been up to. There was no mistaking the red face or the hideous bulge in the pants. He'd probably been studying dirty French postcards.

'Get off home, Brannigan.'

'Archie McMorrow's sleeping off —'

'I said get home!'

'Yes, sir.' Brannigan couldn't move fast enough. He wondered what had upset the sarge this time. Whatever it was, he wasn't staying around to be within reach of his boot.

Once the door closed, Lucas pulled off his boots and stretched his aching feet. He was about to reach for the rum bottle when Rose Keller flounced in. The perfume she wore was eye-watering in its potency.

'What the hell do you want?' he asked, trying to stifle the sneeze he felt coming.

'Fifty pounds should do.'

'What?'

'Playing deaf now? You'll be paying me fifty pounds. It should cover the damages your friends have caused me.'

'Rose, go away. I'm in no mood for your games.' Lucas caressed his aching feet. 'And you're in no position to be demanding money from me. One word, Rose, I can close you down.'

'And one word from me, Lucas dear, and I can watch you hang.'

He turned to her slowly. She was leaning over his desk, light amusement there in her eyes. She was still a striking, if hard-faced, woman in her late forties and Lucas knew she was quite serious. Threats were never used lightly where Miss Keller was concerned.

'One of Moonshine's friends let something slip before he passed out. Billy was quite upset. The poor boy almost turned white. What was said was something I'm sure Inspector Ritchie would like to hear when he gets back. But of course, I could just keep my mouth shut if I wanted to. I could pretend it was just the talk of drunks. Not to be taken seriously if you know what I mean.'

An intelligent calmness was strengthening her stare. There was no amusement there now. She straightened and stretched her spine like the dancer she'd once been. There was no grace in her eyes when she turned her head. What lay there was a simple warning. 'Thirty people if you include Chinese. Sorry Lucas, shall we make that fourteen? Chinese aren't people, are they? Come now, Lucas, my old friend, why aren't you talking?'

His huge hands fisted and his heart pounded, not from fright but from anger.

Rose moved away and studied the 'Wanted' posters as if she were interested. 'And of course, should anything happen to me my solicitor in Melbourne will be forced to open the letter I've already sent. It would be a shame to miss the hanging, though. Could we not discuss my licence application while we're at it?'

The silence was thick with two very different intentions.

'Fifty, you said?'

Rose thought carefully. 'Seventy. Seems fair, does it not?'

She watched as he opened a large locked cash box.

Rose enjoyed the sight of his eyes closing as he touched the money inside. Had she asked for his arm to be severed there'd not be as much pain visible.

Rose took the money and stuffed it down her dress. 'And the licence?'

Lucas closed his eyes. 'See me tomorrow.'

She touched his face. 'That's a nasty scratch on your cheek, Lucas love. Mind you get it seen to before it turns septic.'

And she left with money she had taken from a thief.

Sam upended the packing crate, heaved a blanket from his bed and stuffed it in. The baby was settled next. She could wail as much as she liked; his first priority was Anna, still outside, draped over the horse. She was probably dead by now. If the knife hadn't killed her, the six-mile ride from Bitter Creek should have.

Sam pulled her off the horse as gently as he could. She weighed as much as a full sack of wheat and was as helpful. She was still alive—he could feel her warm breath against his shoulder as he carried her into his shack and put her down as gently as possible on his narrow, creaking bed.

Sam took three steps back and looked down at her, a little terrified because for the first time in his life he wasn't sure what to do.

Tend her as best he could, he supposed. He wasn't a doctor but he knew how to stop bleeding. Her breathing was rattly and strained, not to mention the fine trickle of frothy blood escaping her mouth.

It was night. No moon. Sam could make it to Cormac's though, and Cormac would do what he could, which wouldn't be much more than what Sam could do here and now. The sooner the better.

The baby climbed out of the packing crate and

headed for the open door. Sam swooped on her, and her squeal of delight punctured the silence. He closed the door and cursed himself for not bringing in any wood. But he'd been in too much of a hurry to get to Bitter Creek that morning. With baby under arm, he somehow managed to add to the limited wood supply in front of his fireplace.

The baby tried to kick out of his grip—it was like holding a live fish. Sam supposed he could tie her up so she couldn't crawl into the fire.

The water bucket was empty. Sam cursed again, and with the cackling baby under his left arm he ventured to the creek for clean drinking water. A short time later he gave the baby a spoon to chew on, and hoped it would keep her entertained. The little squirmer should be asleep. It was night. 'Why aren't you asleep?' he asked.

She grinned at him and kept gnawing the silver spoon.

Sam turned back to Anna. He'd postponed the inevitable long enough. He reached for a bottle of spirits, washed his hands with it. Small cuts on his fingers stung like hell. He was furiously blowing on them when the spoon fell on the baby's nose and she started screaming. He turned and there she was, climbing out of the crate again.

'Jesus, Suzie —'

She crawled to him and, grabbing his leg, she started to chew on his pants. Sam put the bottle down and replaced the baby in the crate. 'You asked for this.' He took a loop of thin rope from the hook on the door and tied the baby's hands to her feet—not tight, she could still move about, she just couldn't go anywhere. 'Stay. Okay?'

Sam brought the lamp closer and unbuttoned the coat he'd covered Anna with. She was still unconscious, which made something easy.

Clean out that wound. Bandage it. Clean those bites, cuts. And hope she survived long enough to tell him what had happened. The thought sounded callous, but he'd seen men die from less than this.

When he'd washed the blood from his hands, padded the wounds and bandaged her securely, he sat back and looked at the woman once more. She was still alive, breathing with difficulty. There was nothing else he could do—she alone had to decide whether to live or die. The next couple of days would tell, if she lasted that long. Sam didn't think she would. He rubbed at his face. He needed a shave; his growth of four days was itching.

She looked peaceful. Innocent. She'd lost none of the loveliness that had captured him. She'd lost nothing except, maybe, her life. The baby wasn't too happy about her latest situation but Sam hadn't yet finished. He used some water and a cloth to wipe the mud and blood from Anna's face, arms and body before he covered her.

Then he turned to his other problem.

Susan Louise.

She was chewing on the rope. 'You can't eat your way out of those knots.'

Big dark eyes peered up at him and she grinned. Her smile was contagious. 'Think you're smart, don't you, kid. Okay, you're so smart, you tell me what the hell we're gonna do now.'

She blew bubbles at him.

The voice filtered in from the edges of a haze. Gone now the comfort of hands, the echoes of a heart not her own. Now, there was warmth to quell the cold; a tickle in her throat kinder than the bottomless ache in her heart. The voice again. Her eyes wouldn't open. The voice seemed familiar and there was no fear to associate with it. But just when she almost broke the surface, Anna felt herself falling into the grey depths once more. Here there was no pain. There was nothing at all.

The baby was bellowing. Angry. Sam took it personally. Aggravation set in. He didn't know how to put a nappy on or what he'd use for one. He found his towel and sighed. It had to be sacrificed. He tore it in half and pondered the problem. What next? 'Yeah, yeah, I'm new at this. Be patient.'

If she understood she wasn't about to co-operate.

'How can you suck on your hand and scream at the same time?' Sam asked as she kicked and wriggled. 'Be kind, kid. Please. I've had a bad day.'

He managed to secure the fabric. She didn't even appreciate that. Sam picked her up. Didn't appreciate that, either. The screams ceased when mouth found buttons, then she started again.

She's hungry, he thought. She probably hasn't had a feed all day. He knew the feeling well. Sam looked around his shack. There was some leftover stew in the pot. He tipped some into a dish and found the spoon she'd thrown on the floor. He took the first mouthful, not hot, not cold. Certainly not appetising either. He balanced Susan on his knee. 'Here, try it. You'll hate it.'

She wouldn't shut up. The screams were really disturbing him. Spoon touched mouth. Mouth opened. Sam shovelled some stew in. He knew his cooking was bad but hell, it hadn't killed him yet. The face transferred an unerring statement. The baby let the stew dribble out and she choked on her next lungful of revenge. Obviously, she'd never had this sort of stuff before.

Milk.

No cow for miles. Twelve miles to be precise— Lonnigan had a Jersey housecow. Twelve miles was twelve miles. It'd be this time tomorrow before he got back. There was no cow at the diggings. He'd have remembered if he'd seen one there.

Jesus.

Sam looked at Anna. She was either sleeping or unconscious, he didn't know which. He had no other choice. The spoon clattered into the bowl.

Sam took the baby to Anna and drew the bedcovers back. He rolled the mother to her side and put the baby down close, hoping she'd know what to do. She did. And that was all she had wanted from the start.

The sudden silence was sticky and deafening. Sam watched the two for a little while and finally retreated for some fresh night air.

The sergeant walked the short way home and was hit with a full recitation of how the neighbour's dog had finally killed the lemon tree. Maddy, his daughter, greeted him with this news, and a smile, as she placed a small glass of rum into his hand. Lucas looked down at Maddy and something in her eyes made him think about the baby. It would have been kinder to cut its throat. Billy, though, wouldn't be convinced. He must have had a couple of children himself. Lucas smiled at Maddy and looked away from her innocent eyes.

'You look tired, Papa.'

His smile was forced. 'Show me this tree, girl,' he said and was led away into the backyard where Maddy was attempting to grow vegetables with brackish artesian water. Her efforts at gardening were failures, too. The tree didn't look dead. It looked as it always had, ill. A dose of ratshot would cure Bartlett's pissing dog. 'Do we have any ratshot left, girl?'

'I used the last of it today, Papa,' Maddy said

proudly. 'I don't think he'll come back or sit down for a long time.'

'Caught him in the act, did you?'

'Got him fair up the—'

'Maddy!'

'Sorry, Papa. Mother's asleep. She has one of her headaches again.'

'Oh. I see.'

'What happened to your face?'

'Oh,' he said, touching the scratch. 'The horse bolted.' He finished his rum quickly, gave her the glass and walked toward the house.

'I made an apple pie for supper.'

'Not hungry, girl. Maybe tomorrow.'

The back door squeaked shut.

'I suppose you won't eat my apple pie, either,' Maddy said to the sleeping hens in the chook house. With a sigh she traipsed up the stairs. He'd been away a long time and it was always good to see him again, even if he was tired and cranky. It was light relief really to Mother's never-ending headaches and complaints about the heat. It wasn't even summer yet.

Sam threw the bundle of clothes into the rockpool and took the soap from his pocket. He only ever washed his clothes just before they walked to the creek by themselves. He didn't want to change his ways. He hated having no choices.

It would take his coat a couple of days to dry. All the frantic scrubbing hadn't removed the bloodstains. As for the rest of it, Sam did what he could. With any luck it wouldn't rain and most of it might dry by morning. These housewife-like thoughts took his mind off the day. If he stopped this train of thought he'd only start to ache. He kept his body busy in the hope that the nagging suspicions wouldn't rise again.

He wondered if Anna knew what had become of her Chinese friend. What they'd done to her. He'd ridden home via the shortcut through the Chinese camp. He'd seen it all. And her friend, the old man, everyone.

Anxiety began to fade, numbness set in. He still had the photograph in his pocket. He hadn't taken Tom's Bible. There'd been no time, no inclination. He didn't even know his father had a photograph of his mother. And to find it like that—discarded. Of no value. At least it hadn't been burnt.

Sam hung the dripping clothes over the porch rail and hesitated before stepping inside. All was quiet though, the baby asleep. Squeaking, but asleep against Anna. She was semi-conscious. The sight alarmed him. She was covered in sweat, her lips were parched and cracked. She couldn't move but her big eyes followed him everywhere. Sam dipped a mug into the drinking water. 'Here,' he said softly and helped her up a little. She choked. Spots of blood appeared on the bandages. Sam took the mug away even though her eyes begged him not to. He found the cloth he'd sponged her with, rinsed it a few times and gave it to her, dripping.

Anna sucked on it feverishly. Then she tried to say, 'Thank you.'

Sam smiled at her. 'It's okay ma'am, you take it easy with that.'

'Michael?' she asked next. It was like waiting for a stutterer to say hello.

'Try and sleep. We can talk later.'

Later. If there was a later. Death was surely swinging from the rafters, laughing, watching, waiting to take her.

'Dead. He's dead?' she managed to murmur.

82

'Don't talk.'

'Michael's dead,' she whimpered, emphasising the word.

Sam wondered what he should say. He wasn't too good with words, so he turned away instead. It was all he could think of doing, and when he next glanced at her she had passed out. Still he wouldn't be able to sleep. He'd lie awake wondering what the hell he'd say to her. But what about him? He was hurting too. It'd been his father out there. An old man with bad lungs, a bad heart and bad teeth, with not much time left anyway. It would have been quick, just how the old man would want it to be. One second alive . . . None of this getting sick or losing your mind. It was over quick. Sam wondered if he'd felt it, though. Wondering, wondering. All this was enough to send him crazy.

Sam leaned against the fireplace and rubbed his face. With a sigh, he took out the photograph of his mother. He never knew her. She'd died when he was a baby and that was all he'd been told. Well, almost. He looked at Anna and turned his attention back to the photo. And then he realised a lot of things.

Tom's mysterious friendship with young Anna made awful sense now, as did Sam's immediate interest.

The lady in the photo, his mother, had died years before Anna had been born. They seemed to be about the same age, though, judging from the photo, and they were mirror images. The same dark hair, same eyes. Same everything. But different people. Of course they were.

She was alone now. A widow. Husband dead, and with him died any security his name had given her. All she had was the kid. Little Suzie.

Sam balanced the photograph of his mother on

the mantelpiece. Next time he was in town, he'd get a frame for it.

He camped on the floor. His heart was alert to every squeak from the bed, every strained breath Anna took, every gurgle from the baby. He surprised himself in a way because it was a warm feeling to have others under the same roof.

Anna woke sobbing five times during the long night. The baby woke twice and he had to steer it to a nipple. Then there'd be silence broken by the loud beating of his heart. It didn't take long to discover that Anna didn't whimper as much if he held her hand. She was different now to the pretty girl whose book he'd ruined, whose hat he'd trampled, whose husband beat the hell out of her because a horse drank a gallon of water. Anna was different now because she was here with him when all the odds had decreed she should have been dead. What do I do now, Sam thought and with that he fell asleep.

Susan woke him at dawn. Sam sat bolt upright, wondering why he was on the floor and what was the noise, when all memory flooded back, hard, uncompromising.

Baby.

Baby. It was galloping across the bed, Anna vainly trying to reach it before it splattered on the floor. 'Hey, get back here,' and Sam was on his knees, grabbing the child by the scruff of the neck and swinging her high. She laughed and immediately grabbed a fistful of nose. The nails felt like razors.

Last night had he really believed he could survive this? 'Morning, ma'am.' He placed the baby back in its usual nest and closed his eyes. 'I'm not looking. I haven't seen a thing,' he lied and pulled the covers high.

She didn't understand his attempt at humour. Frothy blood was seeping from her mouth again. She was trying not to cough, trying to talk at the same time.

'Higher. Lift me . . . higher.'

He only had one pillow.

'Drown —'

'What?'

Anna closed her eyes. There was too much pain, inside and out. The baby at her breast didn't help either. 'Lift me higher . . . or I will drown.'

Sam pulled a chest out from under the bed and rolled a heap of clothing into a ball. A short time later, she was sitting the way she'd wanted.

'Drink?' she asked.

'Water or whisky, ma'am?' he offered with a grin and dipped the mug into the water again. She didn't choke this time—he stood by, just in case.

'Michael's dead.'

It wasn't a question this time, just a statement of fact. So how much did she see? Sam watched the eyes. 'It would have been quick.'

The dark eyes stared at him. No, not at him, through him. For a moment he thought she'd start crying, but no. Not yet, anyway. She held out the mug weakly and he took it in a shaking hand. 'Would you like some tea or something?'

She nodded.

Sam turned away. 'Gotta get some water for the fire. Wood for the water—gotta go,' he mumbled and groped for the door, pushing it open. Escaping. He breathed deeply of the cool mountain air, but he couldn't shake the feeling that she was still staring at him. He'd never felt anything like it. The air quelled his unease.

Fresh air always helped him think.

So what had she seen, apart from her dead husband, and how much would she relate? Sam knew it wouldn't be wise to hold his breath waiting.

Five

'Sergeant?'

'What?'

'The bath tub's gone, sir.'

Lucas closed his eyes. 'It's been gone since Friday, Brannigan.'

'Oh.' The tone was surprised. His news was not news at all. Daniel could have sworn it was there yesterday. Or was it the day before? What day was it, anyway?

'You and Billy get out to Mitchell's Hill. Camp if necessary.'

'Hell, Sarge—'

'Are you questioning me, boy?'

'I'm supposed to have tomorrow off, sir.'

'Would you like permanent days off, Brannigan?'

'Mitchell's Hill, sir. For Manning, I suppose?'

Lucas almost stood. He didn't have to. It was perhaps the quickest he'd ever seen Brannigan move. There was a collision with Maddy at the door.

Daniel tried hard to smile and politely dodge the enormous basket she balanced in her arms. 'Would you like a biscuit, Daniel?'

'Not right now, Maddy, I have to go. Maybe another time.'

She beamed, pale eyes effervescing at the promise she always held close. It added to Daniel's torment. He liked her. He'd like her more if she didn't try so bloody hard. Besides, he'd tasted her cooking. Let Lucas have it and choke. Tinned meat and open air were healthier.

'What is it, Maddy?'

Reveries shattered. Maddy had to tear away from the window where she'd been watching Daniel mount his horse. 'I thought you and Daniel might have been hungry, Papa.'

She heard the groan and pretended he was only tired, not cranky or impatient. 'What's in the basket?' he asked, trying hard to be friendly.

Maddy had felt these invisible barriers before. As he looked through the goodies in the basket, she studied him and wished he could be something else—anything but a trooper. He'd always been a trooper, ever since she'd been a baby and she blamed his job for being the sole cause of her friendless existence. All she ever got was torment—about him, about her mother whom they christened Lady Jane because she never spoke to anyone lower than her regal self, and when she did, Maddy shuddered from embarrassment. Boys teased her about her size, her red hair, the trouble she had with saying esses—they always came out as 'th' and her head ached from holding it high so often. She would pretend the torment didn't hurt until she'd get home and cry and even that she couldn't do very well. Mother cried like a lady, sniffing into a handkerchief whereas Maddy howled. Her eyes stung, swelled and her whole face blew up . . .

'Just leave it, Maddy,' was all her father said that morning and he returned to his work. He was writing something official.

'Is there anything you want me to do, Papa?'

'No.'

It was useless even to try now. Papa had no time to talk. 'Mama asked me to fetch the wash.'

'You know where it is.'

'Yes, Papa.' Maddy went through to the cells where one solitary, smelly drunk was snoring in a cell corner.

Maddy picked up the heavy drum of soiled linen. The drum itself would have beaten most girls her age, even some women older and more worldly. Maddy didn't think it was too heavy at all, but if Daniel was still here, he'd offer to carry it for her, possibly all the way home. He'd done that once or twice, usually when Papa was throwing a tantrum. Maddy pretended it was her company Daniel enjoyed, not any excuse for an escape. She was waiting patiently for an invitation to the dance at Yarrawonga Station. He'd almost said he would take her.

'Are you right with that, Maddy?'

'Fine, Papa.'

Out she toddled into the morning sun with the drum of dirty linen in her arms. A bunch of horrible little boys led by David Stills, who had rabbit's teeth, began following her as she crossed the street near Ryan's. Each time she stopped walking, they pretended to be playing marbles.

Monsters, she thought and was determined to make it home and slam the door in their ugly, leering little faces. Mother would shoo them away. Boys playing by her fence always shattered the dark security of her curtained sitting room and made her headaches worse. Lately, even a bottle of sherry a day wasn't helping.

'Big bum Hannaford. Big bum Hannaford.' The chant grew intense. Maddy kept walking as far as pride allowed until something hit the back of her head and knocked her hat off. Maddy put the drum down and turned to her tormentors. Boys plunged to their knees and scooted marbles over the dusty street. 'Who did that! Was that you, David Stills?' she called.

They all looked up, hiding laughter as best they could, all of then feigning innocence. Maddy stamped her feet. Sometimes that was enough to send them

running in different directions. A few baulked. David
Stills yelled: 'Why don't you send us to jail!'

'I wish I could!'

And they laughed at her anger.

Nothing ever changed and nothing ever would. Too
angry to cry, but with tears trailing down her face,
she walked on with her burden. Maddy had no free
hands to wipe her face. Mother would have a fit.

Had she been faster, she'd have caught David Stills
and beaten him fiercely. But it was unladylike to fight.
Ladies led extremely dull, boring lives anyway.

Why was I born a girl? That thought alone made
her howl.

The logs in the wall so close to her face were
horizontally laid. Within the gaps, spiders had woven
intricate webs. Anna watched a black spider close
in on a flying ant trapped there in the web. Anna
watched until the spider wrapped itself around its
victim. Could such a tiny thing feel terror?

Anna looked away. She wondered if the flying ant
was screaming as silently as she had screamed. She
couldn't remember very much at all, apart from the
voice which had warned her what would happen to
her child if she didn't co-operate fully. Perhaps it
was for the best that she did not remember too much.
Somehow her thoughts kept returning to Michael
and the feel of his limp, heavy body in her arms.
The rest seemed a blank, a terrible jigsaw of falling
pieces. Pieces she couldn't yet grasp and feared she
never wanted to.

Alone again. Her only companion, pain. She could
hardly move. Each breath was slow and deliberate
in coming, and agony in letting go.

Where had he gone this time? Come back, Sam,
please. Her throat was parched, her mouth felt like
fouled sand. Tasted like it, too. But there was no

sound at all, save for birds. Birds of the like she'd never heard before. Or had she? There'd been something similar as they'd crossed Cunningham's Gap—scores of green parrots. They'd been noisy but delightful. Cheeky things, too. What had happened that night? Hadn't one of the horses died of a snake bite? No. Of course not. That night, she'd finally given birth to Susan. The next night the horse had . . .

Anna closed her eyes. She didn't want to remember because she kept seeing Michael's face, his dead staring eyes.

Still she felt nothing, not even loss. Her heart's intense wish had been granted. Now he was dead and she was free. But what price? Surely she'd loved him once?

Her eyes closed. It was so easy to sleep now, so easy to wake, too. She turned to the sudden source of noise—her baby's cackles of laughter, the thumping from outside. Anna tried to move but her body was weighted and weak.

'Sh,' Sam said from outside. 'Not so loud, your mother's sleeping.'

He came in as quietly as he could. Susan was hanging upside down from his arm. Anna had never seen her child as dirty. Her newfound playmate was almost as bad. 'Oh,' he said. 'You're awake.'

'Water, please?'

Sam brought her some water, put Susan on the floor and went outside again. So much noise now. Anna could see his one leg holding the door open. The baby crawled towards him and got in the way as he dragged a huge wooden crate inside. The sides were high. Anna wondered what he was up to now as she sipped her water, watching curiously. Sam swooped on the baby like a bird of prey and in a moment she was out of sight, deep in the bowels of the wooden crate. 'See if you can get outa that.'

Two dirty, chubby hands gripped the top of the crate but nothing else of the baby showed. Sam stood there watching, smiling victoriously. 'Looks like I finally won.' Susan began to yell but the yells quickly faded to baby chatter. The hands disappeared and soon there was silence.

'She needs a bath.'

'She'll only get dirty again,' Sam said and glanced at Anna. 'Oh, okay. I'll take her down to the creek later. Will that be all right?'

Anna had no choice. She couldn't move to help herself let alone her child. She nodded and looked away from the thief's bright eyes. 'I don't know how to thank you, Mr Manning.'

'I do. You can call me Sam for a start.'

'Not proper.'

'Who cares about proper? I don't,' he said quietly. 'I think she's sleeping. Must have done something right.'

'She won't sleep for long.'

'Funny little thing, ain't she?' Ain't. Anna hated the word almost as much as Michael's annoying 'canna'. Ye canna do this, ye canna do that . . .

'How you feeling, ma'am?'

'Tired. Hungry.'

'You eat stew?'

Stew. After months of tinned meat he asks if she eats stew? Anna couldn't help it—she smiled. 'Yes. I like it. Very much.'

Sam thought it was funny and scratched his head. Anna wondered if he had lice. 'Some stew coming up, then.' He retreated to the open air and returned with two potatoes and a few carrots. 'Grow them myself,' he said, smiling at her as he threw them on to the rickety table. She tried to smile back.

His old red shirt sure made her look pretty today. He pushed the thought away and reached for a rifle on the wall above the door. She closed her eyes to block the sight of the weapon and a quick, sharp image burned her mind. The figure standing in the creek. The rifle . . .

'You be okay for a while?'

She nodded.

Sam looked down at his Spencer and wondered if she was frightened of it. 'I won't be long.'

And Anna was left to wait again, while the pressures in her body intensified and screamed for release. She waited so long for the shot that when it finally came as a crack in the distance the sound startled her. And what seemed hours later, Sam returned. He'd shot, skinned and cleaned a rabbit. The carcass dangled from his bloodied hands. 'Hope you like rabbit, ma'am. I can't do much about it if you don't.'

She nodded. 'Rabbit's fine, thank you.'

She tried not to watch him use that knife. She watched his face instead. He didn't enjoy this at all. He prepared his food as he prepared everything in his life. He was not very systematic or hygienic: throwing everything in at once and hoping for a successful outcome.

'Sam?'

He turned to her. Again, she had to close her eyes against the innocence on his face. He put the knife down quickly. 'I need to . . . I need to . . . ' Embarrassment seemed an insurmountable hurdle. He didn't know what she was getting at. She thought he might have showed a little intelligence—hadn't she seen some kind of spark in his eyes at some stage? He just stood there, regarding her in that same bored way Michael had. Waiting. Expectant.

'I need to—'

'What?'

'If I don't go soon, I shall burst.'

'Oh. Why didn't you say so?'

He wiped his hands on his dirty pants before he lifted her from the bed.

'Let me see if I can walk.'

'No.'

'Put me down.'

'Sorry. Maybe tomorrow.'

'Sam—'

'Sam—' he imitated as he carried her outside. The brilliance of the sunlight stung her eyes and she turned her face into his shoulder. She was dizzy, and the surrounding mountains bobbed up and down quickly. The movement made her feel ill.

Sam put her down after he'd kicked the outhouse door open and he held her steady. 'Think you can manage?'

'I'm sure I can.'

He guided her in. The door closed in his face. And he waited. He waited forever. For Sam, five minutes with nothing to do was eternity.

'Anna-ma'am?'

'Yes, yes. Must you do that?'

'Do what?'

'Stand there waiting?'

'Just making sure.'

'If I fall into this hole, I'm sure you shall hear the scream.'

Sam smiled. If she fell in, he wouldn't be fishing her out. He was quiet for a little while and drew abstract designs in the dust with the toe of his boot. A thousand questions were surfacing, but would the time ever be right to ask them?

'Sam?'

'Ma'am?'

'I can't open the door.'

'Stand aside. Tell me when.'

After a little while he heard Anna say, 'When.' Sam kicked the door in. Anna took two steps towards the fresh air and her knees jelled. Sam caught her. 'I told you you shouldn't walk.'

'You said no such thing. You just said no.'

'I did not.'

'You did so.'

'Are you arguing with me?'

'Stating facts.'

'Listen Anna, I know best.'

'You think you do. You need to shave,' she said quietly and shielded her eyes from the bright sunlight as she clung to his neck a little tighter. 'And bath.'

'You're gonna nag me, aren't you?'

'Just stating fact.'

'Fact is, lady, you won't win.'

Her silence was a loud reply. Once inside the shack seemed stuffy, and the one window looked as if it hadn't been opened in twenty years. 'I don't want to lie down.'

Sorry,' Sam said and deposited her back into bed.

'You're being unfair.'

'No, it's called sense.'

'Being sensible.'

'That too. You a schoolteacher or something?'

'No.'

'Thank Christ for that,' Sam muttered and went back to the stew. 'You'll never get better if you don't take it easy.'

'I can take it easy *and* sit up.'

'No. You'll only fall over.'

'Let me try?' Sam carried the pot to the fire. 'Nope. Maybe next week.'

'What happened to tomorrow?'

'Never comes, ma'am.'

'Please, Sam?'

He sighed. 'You always get your own way?' he asked.

'Eventually,' Anna replied quietly. Sam helped her

sit up in a fashion, and she gave him a tiny smile of thanks. He looked away quickly as if he were embarrassed.

An hour later it was his turn to smile. He wouldn't let her feed herself and Anna was too weak to argue. Sam fed her.

'You really like this?' he asked, amazed at how quickly she was eating his stew.

'Very much. Yes.'

'You sure.'

'Why aren't you eating?'

Sam glanced down at the bowl of stew. He'd ladled most of the meat into the dish for her and what remained now was no more than soup. The sight of it turned his stomach. 'I eat when I'm hungry, ma'am.'

'Living alone as you do, you are responsible for no one and I suppose you can do what you like, when you like. I'm almost envious of you, Sam. You do live alone, don't you?'

'Full of questions, aren't you—'

'Curious.'

'Maybe you shouldn't be.' He thrust the spoon into her mouth so she couldn't get the last word out. 'You won't win.'

Her smile was both contagious and unsettling.

She didn't have to say a thing.

She slept, and while she slept she couldn't nag or argue. She'd already said the baby needed a bath. Easy to say. It was true that the kid stank—noses rarely lied, but she didn't seem to mind. However, Sam couldn't postpone the inevitable, and now it was midday and hot enough to brave the cold water in the creek. He just hoped the kid didn't hate getting wet as much as he did. But if he did some serious thinking, maybe he wouldn't have to get wet.

Sam pocketed the soap. There wasn't much left. One cake usually lasted half a year. Now with the sudden company, a half year's supply was nearly gone in a few days.

The baby grinned at him.

'Don't make this any harder than it has to be, all right?'

She lifted her arms and Sam lifted her out of her new indestructible prison.

She liked the water and had no fear of it. In fact, she tried to drown herself a couple of times. Sam soon got used to holding a soapy baby. She even came out clean. She talked a lot. Sam didn't know if it was da da or dad dad she kept jabbering. But whatever it was supposed to be, it frightened him because when she said it she looked straight at him and grinned. With a clean, naked baby under his arm he said, 'Enough of this dad-dad stuff, Suzie. I'm doing you a favour, no more, no less. So don't get any ideas, right?'

Susan dad-dadded all the way back to the shack.

Anna had thrown up in her sleep. Sam smelt it the moment he stepped inside. He didn't know how much more of this he could take. This was going too far. If he'd half a brain, he'd have taken them both straight to Cormac and Sheila, wiped his hands of all this trouble. Right from the start.

He shouldn't have let her eat so much in the first place, either. Somehow he knew this would happen. The twinkle of a female eye, and a soft please, and what did he do? He gave in. Every damned time. Well, not again. No. Never.

I've had enough.

Sam had to change the bedding. He had one clean sheet left and it threatened to tear if he breathed on it. He had to dress her in his last shirt, too. Before long he'd have to change the bandages, not to mention carry her to the outhouse again.

By the time he'd finished the chores he felt sick and emotionally drained. All he wanted was some peace. The baby started bellowing. Sam recognised the tone. Communication lines were open wide. He did as he'd done for the last couple of days and waited for the yells to subside as they normally did. What made him expect anything would go right today?

Anna sweated and her skin glistened. She shivered in her sleep, her breathing was heavy again. The baby kept screaming. Sam was hit with the truth of the situation. It'd been too good to last. The well had gone dry, evaporated by the fever that had hit so suddenly.

He wanted to walk away from it all. He cursed himself for going to Bitter Creek in the first place. Damn his instincts and to hell with everything. Why couldn't the world just leave him alone? Was that too much to ask?

Maybe it was. He couldn't do this alone, not with some other man's baby screaming from hunger in his arms. Then *she* started. Was she dreaming? The screams grew intense. There was nothing but pure terror in the voice. Sam's spine chilled and his scalp crawled. Before he'd realised it, he'd put the baby back in her cot.

Anna, sitting ramrod straight, was screaming so hard she was bleeding again. Her eyes were wide open. It was as if she'd just seen a ghost or three. Lord knew there were enough hanging around to haunt her.

'Anna?'

Nothing. She kept sweating. Coughing blood. Screaming.

This morning she'd been good. But that happened to people close to dying. They suddenly got better and happy and bright and a few hours later . . .

'Jesus Christ, don't die on me. What the hell will I do with the kid? Don't die.' His frantic words frightened him because they felt very real. 'Anna?'

She was screaming one word, *No*!

'Anna!' Sam shook her and her eyes flickered with recognition. 'It's okay, ma'am. Nothing's gonna hurt you here.' More platitudes escaped him quicker than he believed possible. His mouth ran to overflowing and she seemed to drink in his words. The shakings eased but not the shivering or the sweating. 'You're safe here with me, no one's gonna hurt you here. You're with me now. Understand?'

'With you?'

The tension eased.

'Yeah. You're safe.'

'Dream—.'

'Dreams can't hurt, ma'am.'

They just terrify until you wake up. If you wake up. And if this is just a nightmare, God you better let me wake now, he thought.

'The sergeant—' Her voice trailed off to a whisper.

'The sergeant what?'

Her eyes glazed and all the fire died. Sam's grip tightened on her arms. 'The sergeant what?' he asked again, searching her face.

'Don't hurt my baby—'

'Baby's fine, Anna. She's fine.'

The flicker momentarily returned. 'Susan?'

'She's great. Just had a bath too. Just what you wanted, remember? The sergeant what, Anna? Tell me.'

No, it was gone. Whatever haunted her mind had dispersed. Anna slumped against him, extremely hot to touch, her teeth chattering from the cold within.

She's dying, he thought. She's gonna die and there's nothing I can do.

Sam held her for a little while and gathered his

98

thoughts. He had to get some kind of help, even if it was help for himself. He couldn't handle this any more and he was the first to admit it.

Six

Long before the riders approached the stone farmhouse, Sheila sent young Leonie on a quest to find Cormac. 'He's off planting by the creek. Go now.' The girl and her huge black dog bounded away to the south.

Sheila was pleased that her unexpected visitors were Daniel and the quiet Aborigine. She had no time for Lucas Hannaford and it was quite mutual. Daniel didn't have the sergeant's hatred of the Irish in his blood. Why should he with a name like Brannigan himself?

Daniel was pleased to see Sheila's smiling face. The last time he was here she'd upended a jug of water over the sergeant's head. The quiet chuckle he'd had then returned now, the memory spurred by Sheila's grin. 'Good day to you, Mrs Newberry.'

Billy Moonshine said nothing. He dismounted and sat under the shade of a nearby tree.

'I suppose it's a cool drink you'd be needing?'

'If it's no trouble.'

For you? No lad, not for you. 'Come on in out of the sun, now.'

Daniel followed her inside while Billy put his cap over his eyes and tried to doze. The young trooper took off his cap and received the cool drink in almost the same movement. 'Thank you, Mrs Newberry.'

'It's high time you called me Sheila.'

Daniel hid a smile and downed his lime drink. It was just as he'd expected.

'I suppose it's Sam Manning you'd be after again?'

'Yes, ma'am.' Daniel knew this woman knew Manning and knew him well. His calls to the Newberry farm were routine at the end of any mail coach week.

'He's not been here,' she said, no need to lie this time.

'Would you tell me if he had?'

'What's he done this time?' Sheila asked and poured another drink for the lad, who looked as if he hadn't eaten in a week. A few more pounds on the thin frame, a few more years . . .

'He's stolen a bath tub.'

''Tis a joke, no?'

'No. He's stolen a tub.'

'Not the sergeant's I hope?'

'Well, we don't know whose it is, yet. No one's reported a missing bath tub.'

'Daniel, have you nothing more to do with your time than chase Sam Manning about the hills?'

'Have you seen him, Sheila?'

'If only I had.'

Somehow, she meant it. Daniel knew that wistful look. He'd spoken to a number of Manning's victims; most were still starry eyed two days after their ordeal. If indeed it was an ordeal. 'Let us know if you see him,' was all he said, wasting his words as he usually did when confronting civilians over the disappearing bushranger. A legend around here, he was, and Daniel's secret hero. But he kept such secrets to himself. 'Thanks for the drink. I'd better be on my way.'

Sheila slipped two scones into his pocket and watched as he walked off into the scorching sun, replacing his cap, taking his reins. Tossing one of the scones to Billy, as she knew he would. With a wave, Daniel Brannigan was gone.

And Cormac had been called up from the lower

forty without reason. He'd be wanting a cup of tea to compensate his long haul. When he appeared, the afternoon feast was ready and Leonie was sitting on her father's shoulders, the dog circling them, barking happily.

'What'd the bastard want this time?' Cormac asked and put his daughter to the ground.

'Papa, you swore!'

'Don't hit your father, Leonie. Go and wash up now.'

And when the girl was out of sight, 'It was only Daniel. Sam's stolen a bath tub.'

Cormac wasn't suprised. 'Hannaford's, I suppose?'

'Is that all you can say? Don't you wonder he might be going crazy up there in the mountains all on his own?'

'Where's my tea, woman?' Cormac grunted. Sheila ignored him and continued in her normal way as she always did when she had something new to chew over.

'A bath of all things. He hasn't had a bath for years. You can smell him before he's seen.'

'That's because he has no nagging wife to contend with.'

'Don't you go saying that. You'd be lost without me. Talk to him, Cormac. He listens to you.'

'Ha. He pretends to listen. The head nods, nothing sinks in. He caught that habit from you, wife.'

Sheila thumped him, Cormac pretended to fall dead and Leonie watched, all the while hoping her father would hurry up, finish his game and take a cake before she starved to death.

'I'm serious now.' She was too. Hands on hips, mouth at full speed. 'Tell him if he let the troopers be, if he didn't cause trouble for himself, he'd be soon forgotten.'

'Mama, what if Sam doesn't want to be forgotten?'

'Mind your business, child. You should be seen and not heard.'

'Leonie's right. Hannaford wouldn't see it that way, either. Where's my tea, woman?' he asked again.

The tea duly came and Leonie ate most of the cakes she'd helped her mother bake. Both husband and daughter switched off from mother's monologue about the bushranger. Leonie's mind was actively planning the rest of the afternoon. She might try a special game with Dog—an adventure about the Indians Sam once told her about, or she might dress Dog in doll's clothes.

Cormac thought of Sam, who sometimes helped him fence or harvest and didn't mind being paid with Sheila's food.

'May I be excused?' Leonie asked. No one was listening. Her mother was still talking, her father in a daydream. 'May I be excused?'

Leonie tried four times, excused herself and ran off. Well, she'd been seen and not heard, how could she be in trouble now? As she tried to plan her latest adventure, Dog not co-operating, not sitting or playing dead when he was supposed to, Leonie decided for the ninth time that week she needed a brother or sister to play with.

'Oh, Dog!'

It had no intention of playing dead. He was barking at someone coming. Leonie watched, excited. Two visitors in one day? She couldn't believe it.

Sam?

The girl was elated. He'd give her a quick game of Injins like he always did. Sam was good to play games with. But something was wrong today. He was galloping his horse and he hardly ever galloped her. 'Leonie! Get your parents for me, quickly!' Leonie could hear a baby crying. She ran so fast she beat Sam to the house.

'Papa! Ma! It's Sam! Come and see what he's found!'

Cormac didn't have to see, he could hear it. There was a fight to be out of the door, and by the time both emerged into the sunlight, Leonie had her arms full of screaming baby. The grey horse of Sam's foamed with sweat, Sam was shaking, trying to speak, not able to.

'Lord Almighty,' Sheila whispered. 'Sam, get inside with you, quickly, there's troopers about.'

'Yes, I know. I've been waiting for them to go. I don't have much time. Can you help me? The kid's hungry. I need a cow or something. Anything—'

'Leonie, go and get Marigold, now.'

'Ma—'

'Now!' Sheila gave the girl a smack on the ear and she ran off, crying unfairness. She never got to see a real live baby, ever. And just when she'd ordered one, one appeared. Miracles did happen, and nothing in life was fair.

Sam looked frightened, hungry. A week's sleep would have done justice.

'Inside, out of the sun.'

Sheila was ignored. Sam and Cormac were studying each other, a thousand questions on each's silent lips. Sheila took the baby inside. Cormac didn't know what to say except for, 'What the hell is this?' as he followed Sam's gaze to Leonie, still running in the distance. 'Come in, it'll take the girl half an hour or more to get the goat. Come on, now.'

Cormac didn't notice how Sam settled into his chair. 'Will you be telling me what's happening? Where on earth did you get a baby? It's not Ginger-Lee's, surely to God—'

'For heaven's sakes, give the lad time to catch his breath!' Sheila called from another room.

It wasn't breath Sam needed, it was the right word

to begin with. So he made it infinitely short. 'They were the only ones left alive at Bitter Creek. The kid, its mother.'

'What?' Sheila yelled.

'I need your help. The mother, Anna, she was knifed. I think she's dying, I don't know. She's at home, alone. If you'd just help me with the baby—'

'She's dying? Are you sure?'

'For Christ's sakes, all I want is a little help!'

Cormac flinched from the angry madness in the eyes. No words could calm Sam, not now.

'Off with you, Sam. Get home, we'll be by tomorrow.'

Sam looked up at Sheila holding the baby like a prized jewel she'd never relinquish. 'You can't have her.'

'Will you let me worry about the baby? Just get off home and tend to the mother!'

Cormac followed Sam outside and grabbed hold of the horse. 'Take one of mine, I'll bring the grey tomorrow.'

Terror and indecision welled. Common sense was displaced for a little while. Sam didn't want to leave the baby with them, how the hell would he explain it to Anna? Maybe he wouldn't have to. Maybe she was already dead, and if she was the baby would have a good life with the Irish couple. They were the only friends he had. Of course he trusted them. He had no choice.

'You can't be seen with my horse,' was all Sam said, turning the grey and cantering off the way he'd come. The canter became a gallop and as he rode, he already felt as if half of him wasn't there. A couple of days and that damned kid had become a part of him.

Sorry Little Suzie, but I don't know what else to do.

Sam saw the traps first. It was always the way. He could hear Daniel's chatter as the two followed the creek downstream. Sam watched, torn between priorities. If they kept following the stream, it'd take two hours for them to reach Bitter Creek. Across country, fifteen minutes at the most. Sam figured the raid hadn't been reported—Sheila hadn't said a thing and she knew everything that happened within a twenty-five mile radius usually before the event even occurred.

Luck was with him. Hannaford wasn't there. It was only Brannigan. Sam had nothing against the lad, mainly because he knew Brannigan didn't shoot first and question after. He'd try to take him alive. He'd tried a dozen times. Nearly had him twice in fact. Nearly. But they'd gazed into each other's eyes, a smile touched each's lips and freedom reigned once more.

If Anna was going to live, another half hour wouldn't matter either way. The authorities had to know about the slaughter. If they didn't already.

No, they couldn't know.

Now was no time to argue with himself. Sam whistled and two heads turned. Brannigan didn't reach for his gun. Billy Moonshine did, the movement was stopped. 'No, don't shoot. He's worth more alive,' Daniel probably said. And again, Sam wondered why the kid always let him go as he turned his horse and bid them follow.

He made sure he kept in sight during the chase across heavily wooded and steep rocky hills, because if they suddenly lost sight of him, they'd stop like they always had before.

A few hundred yards from Bitter Creek, Sam was hit with Death. It was three times as ferocious now from the hot, still days. He didn't want to witness it again. He rode further, hoping the breeze's stench would slow the pursuit. When next Sam glanced behind, the two troopers had come to a complete stop.

Sam circled, his duty done. He was too far away to see the look of terror on Daniel's face, yet he was close enough to feel it. 'Sorry, boy, but it's part of the job,' he whispered to himself and wasted no more time in getting home to Anna.

Home to Anna.

What was he thinking of?

Billy Moonshine was spooked and he refused to venture any closer. 'No, they're dead. I'm not going up there, I know that stink. I know what it is.'

Daniel was frightened enough to threaten to shoot Billy, but still he refused to budge. Someone had to do it. Someone had to see exactly what was causing the stench. With heart in mouth and handkerchief over his face, Daniel took the final steps alone.

All thoughts of Manning's capture disappeared.

'Perhaps you would like my friends here to help you?'

Anna sees the red-headed one, his bright eyes flashing with more than laughter. And all she can say is 'Don't hurt my baby.'

'You won't hurt it, will you, lad?'

'Not unless you tell me to, Sarge.'

'There, you see? These boys will do everything I say. Take your clothes off, Anna, or these lads will do it for you.'

She opened her eyes.

Would this never stop? The terror lingered and so did the pain. It wasn't as bright any more, it had receded to a dull, infinite ache. But the jigsaw pieces were falling into place.

A speckled hen was staring at her from the

mantelpiece. There were no laughing eyes. No eager eyes.

All was quiet, no sound at all. There was no horse looking in the window at her, frightening her, just the hen to look at her now.

'Sam?'

Her voice was no more than a whisper. She tried again, louder this time. Nothing. No plod of heavy feet on the porch outside, no squeak of the door accompanied by the baby's laughter. 'Sam?'

He's gone, her mind said.

No, he can't have gone. He wouldn't leave me alone.

He's stolen your baby. He's going to sell her. He'll come back with pockets jangling.

No!

He's a thief. He'll tell you that just as his father told you.

No.

He's left you alone to die.

Tears came and the pain heightened the despair. Anna wiped her face but more tears filled her eyes. He would not leave me alone. He would not, there must be a reason.

Yes, he's off selling your baby.

No!

Anna rubbed at her eyes and saw a gunbelt hanging on the back of the door. There was a rifle near the fireplace and a shotgun on the wall, too.

He's taken Susan for a walk.

She repeated the thought until she believed it.

From the little filthy window Anna could see grey storm clouds devouring the blue of the sky.

They shall come home wet. *If they come home at all.* She closed her eyes.

The sergeant put his rifle down on the ground. Hold her.

She caught her fright with a sharp intake of breath,

108

and opening her eyes quickly she saw the hen again. A pretty hen. Quite benign. Still staring at her. There was no sergeant. There was no one. Just a pretty little hen inside Sam's house.

She almost laughed.

Almost.

Alone. So alone. Born alone, die alone. No one can share either with you. Like pain. No one can share that, too.

Anna pushed the covers aside and focused on the task of movement. It was slow, painful. It made her sweat so much she didn't know if her eyes stung from tears or perspiration. Bare feet touched earthen floor. Determination was winning. Anna rose unsteadily, undefeated. Her body screamed to be inert once more.

No. Savage thoughts ruled when she lay helpless and she would not be helpless any more.

She was dizzy. The rickety table kept moving but remained still when she grabbed it. The room undulated, steadied. Not far to the door. Six steps perhaps. Although she wanted to cough and she could taste blood, she ignored it all. The door seemed the most important thing in her life. Freedom, perhaps another world was waiting out there. Even though the sun was hiding behind the storm, the glare threw her off balance. Anna hugged the porch upright and either didn't see or misjudged the one step to the ground.

Someone called her name too late to stop the fall.

Sam was off the horse before it had skidded to a halt and he couldn't decide if it was anger stirring him—anger at seeing her out like this—or relief that she was still alive. Both seemed a miracle. He'd thought his emotional reserves had been tapped and completely drained until he saw her. Touched her.

'Come on, Anna-ma'am. Get back inside.'

'Where's my baby?' she asked in a tired, childlike voice.

There was a jolt of searing pain as she was lifted and held tight. 'Baby's fine.'

That wasn't the answer she needed. 'Where's my baby?'

All Sam heard was a very tired, aching anger, and he didn't blame her. It didn't feel right without little Suzie. It didn't feel right at all. 'Suzie's okay, trust me.'

'Trust you?'

'Yeah. It's been known to happen sometimes.'

Anna felt the bed greet her and she tried to protest. Her whimpers were drowned by the sound of the sudden, hard rain.

'Where's my baby? What have you done with her?'

'If you knew how worried I was, you wouldn't be so angry.'

She couldn't hear a word he was saying. He brought her a cup of water. Anna knocked it away, tipping it over him. Sam closed his eyes. Thunder boomed and the rain pelted down.

'What'd you go do that for?' he asked and took his shirt off.

'Where is my baby!'

'She's okay. I took her to a lady I know.' Calling Sheila a lady seemed strangely inappropriate. He should have said friend.

'You gave her away?'

'No, no, she'll be back.'

'You gave my baby away!'

'Anna, calm down, huh?' Huge red flowers were blooming across his last clean shirt. 'I didn't give her away.'

'No, you sold her!'

'Huh?'

Tears started. Christ, he thought, why me? He

sat close to her and tried to take one of her hands away from her face. 'Anna, listen to me. Suzie was hungry and I had no choice.'

She looked up into his bright bloodshot eyes. He was tired. Upset. She felt his fingers tighten on her hand. The rain lessened its sudden fury and the honesty she felt lessened her anger. 'What do you mean she was hungry?'

'You've got nothing there any more. Look, I'm sorry but I had to take her to someone who knew what to do. But she's coming back. I wouldn't lie to you.' And as if to prove it, he wrapped both his hands around hers.

'She's safe with this . . . lady?'

'Probably clean and dressed pretty and fed, and you name it, by now. But if this storm keeps up, it might take a couple of days for 'em to bring her home.'

'Days?' Anna asked, eyes filling again. Sam had to look away. 'But she's never been away from me, ever!'

'I know how you feel.'

'You don't! You can't know how I feel!'

Sam let go of her hand and stood up. 'I know enough.'

'I need her with me!'

'Well you can't damn well have her and that's all there is to it! I thought you'd be dead, right? Hell, I wasn't gonna risk that kid of yours goin' the same way! I don't like it much either, so can you just shut up and give me a little peace? Is that too much to ask?'

Wide eyes blinked and turned away to study the wall. Sam walked to the fireplace, grabbed the hen and threw her out into the rain. He hung his shirt on the hook near the door.

'You didn't sell Susan?'

'No. I didn't think of it. Are you happy now?'

Silence ruled for a little while.

'I have no milk for her?'

'Looks like it.'

'I'm sorry,' she whispered. 'I'm sorry for accusing you of stealing my baby, for imposing on you like this.'

Sam turned to her. Now *he* was feeling guilty.

'Yeah, well, I'm sorry too. And you're not imposing. I don't want to hear you say things like that again. If I thought you were imposing you wouldn't be here. I woulda left you to die.'

She looked up at him and burst into tears.

Why'd I say that? he asked himself and there was no answer.

'Don't you get any ideas, wife.'

Sheila looked up innocently. Cormac's face was bright red, redder than usual from the shadows of the lamplight. Sheila looked down at the baby, at the soft, tiny fingers clasping her hand. There was a towel catching any spills, and only her memory to catch the smiles.

From breast to a cup so easily. Hunger made the little one adapt quickly. 'She's such a pretty thing. Have you not seen her eyes? So large and so dark. Wise eyes to be sure.'

'Was I like her, Ma?' Leonie asked, the jug of warm goat's milk ready just in case more was needed.

'A little,' Sheila said quietly. 'All babies are special, child. Every last one of them.'

'I want a brother, Ma.'

'Want all you like, girl, it'll do no good.'

'Don't say that, Cormac. There's always a chance.'

'Do we have to give her back?' Leonie asked.

'Yes,' Cormac said quickly the moment Sheila said, 'No.'

Leonie glanced from one to the other. 'If she was a boy, you'd want her, wouldn't you, Pa?'

'Leonie, she belongs to someone else.'

'But if her mother dies, who will she belong to then?'

Cormac looked away from Sheila's inquiring eyes. 'Time I was in bed,' he mumbled. 'Kiss me goodnight, Leonie.' The little girl kissed him hastily and waited until he was out of sight. 'Ma, is it because I'm a girl that Papa doesn't like me?'

'Your father loves you very much and I don't want to hear such nonsense ever again.'

'Was I as pretty when I wore that dress?'

Sheila looked up into her daughter's Irish eyes, the round face covered with freckles, surrounded by curly fair hair. 'Prettier,' Sheila said. 'Now give me a hug and get to bed. It's late.'

The baby smiled at Leonie when the girl touched the tiny face before she went off to her room. Susan then talked to herself and didn't want any more of the cup. Sheila put it on the table, turned the child to face her, and strong legs kicked against her stomach. The baby smiled and reached for Sheila's face. Then her huge eyes searched the room. Sheila knew who she was looking for. 'She's not here, little one,' Sheila said quietly and Cormac's words echoed into her mind. *She belongs to someone else.*

Sheila rocked her to sleep. She had almost forgotten how it felt to have a baby in her arms again.

Sam wrapped a blanket around his half-naked body and lay down near the fire. The air was cool but not cold. All he wanted was to sleep. Anna hadn't spoken for what seemed hours. She just stared at the wall, sniffed back tears and suffered quietly. And the silence he was so used to seemed unnatural.

She was able to sit up without much help now;

she could even feed herself, and that added to his feeling of uselessness.

'Are you really a thief?' she asked a few minutes after he extinguished the lamp and ten seconds after he'd found comfort.

'I suppose I am.'

'Tell me why?'

'Why what?'

'Why did you bring us here?'

Sam raised himself on an elbow and looked at her. She was sitting up, watching him. So she wanted to talk, did she? Good. 'Even a thief wouldn't leave a baby out to die. Or you,' he added.

'Perhaps you should have.'

'I suppose I could have. Easy.'

He knew he hadn't convinced her of that, or himself for that matter. He settled down once more and his eyes closed.

'Do you think you're earning a place in heaven for this?'

Sam's face creased with a smile she wouldn't have seen. Heaven? What in hell was that? 'Sure I am, Anna-ma'am. A place in . . . in heaven . . . '

'Why don't you talk to me? You were making excuses to talk to me at the diggings.'

'I'm tired, okay?'

'Goodnight, Mr Manning.'

Sam winced at the sound of the 'mister'. How many times did he have to tell her?

Silence.

'Sam?'

'Mmm—'

'I'll be needing a bath tomorrow.'

He made a noise that sounded like, sure thing, and then he was asleep. There was nothing there to haunt him.

Not so, Anna. The darkness of the shack was

114

frightening enough but terror waited behind closed eyes—a terror she'd live with for the rest of her life, or so it now seemed. Those men. The faces. The bodies.

She cried so quietly Sam didn't wake. He woke later, from her screams.

Maddy sat on the front verandah and gazed up at the stars while her deaf white cat purred on her lap. She tickled the cat's chin absently until the last tiny space of clear night was obliterated by cloud. She could smell the rain coming, and the breeze turned into a wind which after such a hot spring day was more refreshing than a warm bath.

Woolly hated the wind. It turned him into a lion. She let him go before he scratched to get away. He bounded down the stairs and under the house without so much as a goodbye.

The town was very quiet.

Maddy loved this time of day–night. Mother was asleep, Papa asleep (the best place for him lately; he was so cranky he'd bite her head off for breathing). The whores were still working, though, and the men were still spending their earnings on drink.

She could never quite understand why, but it was a fact of life. So many smiles going into and coming out of the pub. Perhaps it was easier to be bad than good? She never saw too many happy faces at church on Sundays. So if the devil was alive and well and making people happy at Rose Keller's . . . She didn't understand it. She never heard the whores gossiping about the town ladies. Yet the town ladies gossiped non-stop about the whores, usually over the cups of tea and biscuits after church.

The whores would look at Maddy, and smile and say hello, and the town ladies never listened to a thing she had to say. Not that she ever said much.

Maddy was useful for pouring tea for the circle that surrounded Mother, and urged for more stories about Brisbane society.

Maddy sighed and wished she'd fit somewhere.

She stood up and decided it was worth trying to sleep again. She heard the sound of the horses as she opened the front door. Maddy turned back. It was Daniel, alone. But wasn't he supposed to be camping out at Mitchell's Hill? He wasn't due back until . . .

'Maddy, get your father, quickly!' He leaped the low fence and took the stairs three at a time. He was breathless, his eyes wide. She'd never seen him in such a state.

'Quickly!' he almost screamed.

Maddy was knocking on her parents' bedroom door before she realised it. Daniel's heated mood had been contagious. 'Papa!'

'What, what, what?'

'Daniel's here, Papa! Quickly!'

She looked back at Daniel, juggling his cap nervously. His face in the light was quite pale.

Maddy was pushed out of the way by her father's bulk.

'What the hell is it, boy?'

Crankier than ever now at being woken up and Maddy wasn't game to move. All she could do was watch. Daniel couldn't seem to speak and when he finally did, Maddy didn't believe what she'd heard.

'Bitter Creek, sir. Everybody's dead. Everyone is dead.'

Maddy, mouth open in shock, glanced at her father's face. Her father didn't twitch. Only his Adam's apple moved when he swallowed. 'Maddy get to bed. Now.'

'But Papa—'

'Do as I say!'

'Lucas?' Mother called wearily.

'It's fine dear, fine,' her father lied and, grabbing Daniel by the collar, he hauled him down the hallway and into the kitchen. The door slammed. Maddy remained glued to the spot. She hadn't even worried about Daniel seeing her in her nightdress, barefooted.

Everyone at Bitter Creek was dead.

What from? Fever? No, a fever wouldn't be so deadly as to wipe out a whole mining camp so suddenly. Why, only recently, Papa had been out there checking licences. She'd overheard him tell Mother about the young mother and baby out there. Maddy remembered because her mother started nagging, how it was no different than dragging a woman into the wilderness and giving her a house that was hot in summer and freezing in winter, and telling her this was home and she should be happy she had a roof over her head and food on the table . . .

The young mother and her baby had caused yet another argument.

Did that mean that the mother and baby were dead, too?

Maddy crept up the hallway and stood at the closed kitchen door. She could hear sounds as such, but not words, and not clearly enough to fully comprehend, either. But she did hear: 'Would you stop that snivelling and get the rum into you!'

And a moment later: 'Maddy, get to bed before I whip you!'

Oh God, she thought, heart in mouth. He can see through walls, too. Or could he? Maddy ignored the warning and stayed.

Another rum, he'd have fallen over. Daniel clutched his cap in one hand, the glass in the other. 'The Chinese, too, sir. Everyone.'

'Any sign of gold?'

'Nothing was left. Not a bloody thing. Days ago, it was.' His stomach was turning over again at the memory of the stink that still pervaded the air, his clothes. Daniel wanted to strip off and burn them, scrub himself until he bled. It would be the only way to properly cleanse himself.

'And it was Manning who led you there?'

Daniel nodded.'

'I see.'

Two words that chilled the spine. 'I'm only guessing he led us there. If he knew what was at Bitter Creek, he couldn't very well ride into town to report it, could he, sir?'

The sergeant said nothing. Daniel had seen the look in the eyes countless times before when a scapegoat had been found and used accordingly. And how often had Daniel turned the other way?

'You can't be serious. Manning's not a murderer.'

'He's wanted for murder.'

'That was years ago in another state!'

'Are you defending him?'

'No, but—'

Yes, he was defending him. If it had been anyone else leading him to a site of wholesale slaughter, he'd have been filled with questions, certainly.

'Anyone who breathes is capable of murder, Brannigan. You should know that by now.'

'There's no proof it was Manning.'

'Go home and try to sleep.'

Daniel wondered if his hearing was now impaired. How in hell could he sleep?

'Take this with you. It's the best company you're ever likely to have.'

The sergeant handed Daniel the bottle of rum, and Daniel took it because he knew he'd never be able to sleep unaided. Not tonight, at least.

118

The movement in the kitchen prompted Maddy to leave, quickly. She darted into her room and jumped into her bed with the agility of a mongoose. Shaking, she huddled deep into the covers.

Daniel had seen all manner of horrors.

So had Maddy, in her head.

Her father blamed poor Sam Manning. And now Mother would have her excuse to go back to Aunt Rachel's. Maddy was almost crying when her door opened and there he stood, in his underwear, his arms folded. 'How much did you hear?'

'Papa?' she asked sleepily and he seemed to believe her lie because after a little while the door closed and darkness fell.

Maddy didn't sleep at all that night.

Seven

He wanted to be the enamel mug at her lips. The thought took him unawares. Sam realised he was staring again. Anna hadn't noticed. She sipped her tea and, closing her eyes, she sighed. 'Today is what?' she asked.

'Sunday.'

'And it would be,' she paused and looked out of the window to the sun, 'about ten o'clock?'

Sam took a pocketwatch from his shirt and flicked the small instrument open. 'A quarter after.'

'I'm getting better,' she said with a tiny smile and sipped her tea again. 'When do you think—'

'I don't know.'

'Would you let me ask my question?' Her huge dark eyes cored him. He waited to hear her question. 'When do you think I could have my bath?'

Bath? What'd she want a bath for? 'I can get you some water for a wash.'

'No, Sam. I'd like a proper bath. I've seen the tub outside.'

'What if I told you it wasn't mine?'

'Please?'

Oh, that look. 'Can you wait for Sheila? She'll help you.'

'No. I need a bath now. It's been days.' Anna kept her demand as quiet as she could. She still wasn't sure how much will she could impose on this man, even if he seemed elastic compared to Michael.

'I can't smell you.'

'Please, Sam? A bath isn't too much to ask considering there's one outside.'

'Wait for Sheila, huh?'

She could feel the beginnings of the initial weakening and forged ahead. Quietly. 'Does the thought embarrass you?'

Sam couldn't look at her for very long.

'Really, Sam. Don't pretend you haven't seen me naked. Isn't that how you found me?'

But he couldn't be cornered easily. 'Wait for Sheila. She'll probably bring stuff for you to wear, and then I can have my clothes back.'

'Sheila must be the one you gave my baby to.'

'Why can't we just say she borrowed her for a while?'

'Perhaps I shall believe that if she comes. I do know one thing.'

'Seems you know it all, ma'am.'

Anna ignored him. 'I shan't last another hour without a bath.'

Sam studied her for quite some time.

'Even you said you had no idea when these people would bring my baby back. There wasn't that much rain to stop them. It's all a paradox, really.'

'A what?'

'You once told me no one knew where you lived and yet you wait for people to visit.'

'All right, I lied. Two people know where I live. Three now. You want a bath? You get a bath. Just stop nagging me.'

Sam picked up the tin bucket and went out, mumbling to himself.

Anna smiled. For the first time in her life, she'd been able to manipulate a man other than her father. A sad look, a quiet question, persistence. It was also easier to get out of bed today and shuffle to the door. Sam was taking great long strides towards the creek. Anna made it down the porch step, refusing to fall this time.

When Sam hauled the bucket out of the water and turned, she was right behind him. 'You look awfully tired,' she said quietly, stepping out of his way. 'I suppose I could wait for Sheila if that's what you really want.'

'Would you make up your mind?'

'You're angry with me,' she said and looked down at her hands.

With a sigh, Sam put the bucket down. 'No, I'm not angry. Just tell me if you want a damned bath or not.'

'I'll wait for Sheila. But you may as well put some water in the tub if you want to. Sam, you need to sleep. You're cranky when you're tired.' And off she walked, head low, shielding her eyes from the glare.

'You're right, you know. I am tired. When I'm tired I get edgy. It's hard to sleep when someone's screaming all night long.'

Anna turned to him and squinted into his face. 'What do you mean, screaming?'

'You. You scream all night, every night.'

'Don't be silly.' Anna turned and kept walking.

'Who's bein' silly? You shouldn't be out of bed yet. Look, the sooner you talk about what happened, the sooner I'll get some sleep at night.'

'I don't know what you're talking about.'

'Anna, if you tell me about it, maybe it won't come back and haunt you so bad.'

'Wisdom from someone who knows, perhaps?' she asked.

'Maybe.'

'Then you're not only a thief but a liar as well. You'll never know what haunts me or why. And as for not being able to sleep, you can have your bed back at any time. I never asked for it. I don't need your help. I'm not a cripple, nor am I completely helpless.'

122

She managed to walk back to the shack by herself. The door closed in Sam's face.

'You're not as tough as you think you are, lady!'

There was no reply at all.

Sam dragged the tub inside and began heating water over the fire. 'They're coming,' was all he said.

Anna couldn't hear anything unusual. 'How do you know?'

'I just do.'

Anna was sitting in the only chair, a fragile rocker. 'Tom knew of things before they happened.'

'Like I said, they're on their way.'

'You're a lot like your father.'

'Yeah? A thief and a liar. Trouble is, he never stole.'

'I'm sorry, Sam.'

'No, you're not. Never apologise for the truth.' He cast her a glance that could have cooled a boiling stream. To Anna, another knife would have had less damaging effect.

'Sam, I know you want to know what happened, but I can't tell you. I can't tell anyone.'

'Why?'

'No one would believe me.'

'You could always try.'

'I said I can't!' She tried to hide the fear in her eyes. Impossible.

'Anna, just remember I'm here if you wanna talk. And if Sheila sees you've been crying, she'll never let me forget it.'

Cormac, Sheila and Leonie Newberry arrived soon after in their rattling buggy. Anna could hear the Irishwoman long before she was seen, and she winced as the door opened and Sheila swept in. At first, all she saw was the flame of windswept hair, the fierce, hot face and Susan wearing pretty, unfamiliar clothing. But before Anna could speak: 'Here she

123

is and I didn't want to give her back . . . Why are you crying, lass?'

Sam, meanwhile, was trying to sneak out of his own house.

'What's this you've been doing to the lass, Sam? You've had her in tears with your heartless ways!'

'Please,' Anna begged. 'Give me my baby.'

And while Sheila handed the child over, Sam made his exit and Sheila followed. Hands on hips, she watched the goings-on at the buggy. One man to load the trunk, two to get it off? 'What's this you've been doing to the lass, Sam?'

'I told her not to cry,' Sam said quietly, wincing.

'So she's improving then?' Cormac asked with a grin.

Anna was reminded of her grandmother—a huge, overbearing woman who tended to take control of any situation whether she was needed or not. Where Grandmother had been forceful and intimidating to the unwary, she also lacked an ounce of warmth. Sheila, on the other hand, was lit with not just warmth, but a flame. Anna had never seen her baby as happy or as pretty, and she felt a curious mixture of jealousy and gratitude. Susan, it seemed, was pleased to see her.

Cormac Newberry was the opposite of Sheila— a short, wiry Irishman with mischief in his eyes. It wasn't hard to realise why he and Sam were such good friends. They carried the trunk in and set it down heavily.

'Out with you and stay away. Leonie, close the door and stand guard.'

'Yes, Ma.'

Once the door closed, Sheila warmed. She took the baby and set her in what looked like a cot. Sam must have made it. 'Good Lord,' she said. 'He expects a child to sleep in this contraption?'

'She likes it, Mrs Newberry.'

'There'll be none of this Mrs Newberry. You'll call me Sheila.'

Anna's head began to pound. Perhaps it was the voice. She wished the woman could speak gently. There was no need to yell in such a confined space. 'Do you know Sam well?' Anna asked softly.

'Does anyone know Sam well? Of course I do. You had him worried sick. Never seen him as flustered and worried. But he's fine now. And so's the little one. She'll be drinking from a cup now, and you're welcome to have Marigold as long as you need her.'

'Marigold?'

'The goat. She's outside. Just you watch Sam's vegetables. She's already seen them.'

'Oh. Perhaps you'd better tell him.'

'What's this I hear about Bitter Creek?' Sheila asked. Anna looked up into Sheila's eyes and a thick silence hung in the air.

Was she so heartless to ask such a thing?

'I remember nothing of Bitter Creek. Nothing at all. I was hoping you would help me have a bath because it's been days and I feel so unclean—'

'Oh, lass, I'm sorry. Sometimes I don't know what I'm saying until after I've said it. It comes from not seeing a soul for weeks and weeks—' Sheila, lost for words now, reached for Anna's hand and held it tightly. 'I brought you some clothes and some lavender water, pet. I had a feeling you'd be needing them more than I.' Sheila squeezed Anna's hand. A fine hand, too. Soft, as her hands had once been.

'And half as much again if you please,' Cormac said to the sky. 'I'll be in trouble if there's no decent rain by Christmas. It's been a bad winter.'

Not being a farmer, Sam wasn't preoccupied with

the weather. Nor did the weather play much of a role in Sam's chosen occupation of harassing and breaking the law on occasion.

'Tell me something,' Sam said after a thoughtful swig from Cormac's bottle, 'what drives a man to murder?'

'Hate?' Cormac offered.

'Something's not right here.'

'By Jesus, I wouldn't have known if you hadn't told me, like.'

'She knows, Cormac. She knows who's responsible and she's not saying a thing.'

'And would you if the boot be on the other foot?'

'Depends how scared I was. Depends what the circumstances were, what really happened.'

'So exactly what is it you're thinking of, Sam?'

'I don't know. I'm hoping she might say something to Sheila. You know, tell her what happened. Do women talk about things like that?' Sam asked.

'Why ask me such a fool question? I suppose if she tells Sheila, Sheila'll tell me, and if she does, I'll let you know.'

Silence ruled again.

'She's a pretty one, no doubt about it. What is it you plan to do?'

'I don't know,' Sam said softly.

'Is there anything at all you do know?'

'Maybe I'll wait until she gets a little better and decide then.'

Cormac watched Sam draw circles in the dirt. 'I can see why you're a worried man.'

Sam laughed. 'Worried? Me? Have you ever seen me worry about anything?'

'If I was you I'd be bloody worried. One day a free rover and now a sudden family man.'

'Bullshit.'

'You can't look me in the eye and tell me she's

not the one you told me about weeks ago, now. The married one. The one with the pretty eyes and the dark hair and the big—'

'Okay, you've made your point.'

'Now can you see what you've done?'

'You'll tell me anyway.' Sam grabbed the bottle from Cormac's hands.

'This is punishment for all your sins, Sam. You wanted her, now you have her.'

Sam rolled his eyes and took an almighty swig. It burnt his toes, or so it seemed. All was quiet for a little while. Both men were watching the door of the hut.

'You say everyone was dead at Bitter Creek?'

'Except these two.'

'Tom?'

'Everyone, Cormac. I led Brannigan to it yesterday.'

'Was that wise?'

'Probably not. All I know is there's a lot of bodies out there that needed burying. And I don't wanna talk about it.'

'Perhaps you should.'

'What good does talking do? It's never done me any damned good.'

'Perhaps you should stop and think then.'

'Yeah and that's worse.'

'I know what I'd be thinking of if I was you. I'd be thinking about whoever it was stuck the knife in her. He'd be expecting her as dead as the others, you see.'

'And when he finds she's not dead . . . Yes, it's crossed my mind. She's alive, she's a witness.'

Silence hung in a heavy cloud.

Sam studied the door and wanted to be a part of the knowledge that hid behind that wood. 'How do you get a woman to talk to you?'

Cormac shrugged. 'Be kind, maybe. Love her. Earn her trust . . . how should I know?'

'You're a great help, Cormac. Anyone ever told you that before?'

Cormac sighed. 'Seems to me it would have been easier to leave her where she was. Turned a blind eye, so to speak.'

The stick Sam was toying with suddenly snapped. He glanced at Cormac. 'And could you have done that?'

'No,' Cormac said with a smile. 'This is what you get for wanting another man's wife.'

'You're asking for a punch in the nose, friend.'

'So I'll be keeping my ear to the ground instead, then.'

'Thanks,' Sam said absently.

Tranquillity arrived within moments of the Newberrys' departure. The silence was so loud it was almost deafening. Susan was sleeping on her stomach, thumb in mouth. She seemed longer, fatter, her hair was starting to curl. Anna touched the soft, fine hair. She felt whole again now the baby was back with her. For a moment, she didn't blame Sheila for wanting to keep the child, either.

Anna didn't bother to turn when she heard the footsteps.

'I missed her too, you know.'

'I know, Sam. I was just worried.' Anna turned to him. 'I tried, but Sheila wouldn't let me thank her.'

'She's like that.'

'You were right. She brought clothes for me to wear and she gave me all of her baby dresses.'

'Don't forget the goat.'

'Yes, Marigold.' Anna sat down and tried to fight her exhaustion. 'Something's missing, Sam. Something is still missing. I don't know what it is. I feel only half alive.'

Sam had the overwhelming urge to touch her, hold her, tell her everything would work out fine. But she didn't need lies. He reached out and touched her cheek. Anna flinched from the touch and moved away.

'The dresses she gave me are big, but at least you can have your own shirts back now. After I wash them of course.'

'Anna?'

On his lips the silent question: Who was it?

But something in her eyes prevented him from breathing for a little while. He turned away. 'Why don't you get some rest while Suzie's sleeping?'

'Her name is Susan.'

'Yeah, right. Susan. You have a sleep. I'm going for a walk.'

And he took his rifle for company.

For supper they shared the last of Sheila's baking. Anna seemed to eat a little more, and she didn't complain much. How could she complain if she didn't talk? No matter how hard he tried, Sam couldn't deny it was good to have company, even if it was silent.

Sam poured the last of his whisky. A slug before bed always helped him sleep, or that was the excuse.

'Tom and I used to pretend it was tea we shared in the afternoons. No one realised what it was we were drinking,' Anna confided.

'Sounds like Tom.'

Anna watched Sam sit. Perhaps he thought ladies didn't drink whisky?

'I'd only have a little, of course. I found it helped me sleep.'

'You too, huh?' Sam asked but it wasn't really

a question. His face creased with a smile. 'All you have to do is ask, you know.' He gave her half of his whisky. When she caught his eye and hands touched, an unfamiliar shyness leapt inside him.

And there they were, two strangers trying to find conversation to fill the gaps. Sam said nothing. This was going to be tortuous because now she was clean and looking half alive, she was very, very attractive. The whisky was helping him feel it in more ways than one.

The baby squeaked in her sleep and while she slept she was no excuse. Sooner or later, Anna would have to face the onslaught. Sam glanced at her, at the way she sat, holding the cup, staring into the fire. It seemed to be now or never.

'Anna, who are you protecting?' The question was out. Finally.

'Protecting?'

Anger rose. Sam fought it. 'The one who tried to kill you. You're protecting him.'

'I think I'll go to bed.'

'I think you'd better stay where you are and talk to me, girl.'

'No.'

'Yes.'

'No! It's none of your business! It's over!' She tried to walk away.

Sam made a hasty grab for her arm and he wasn't expecting her reaction. She honestly thought he was going to hit her. He let go quickly. He'd never hit a woman in his life and he probably never would, but seeing her cower stunned him. Damn her. What sort of man did she think he was? He took her arm again, gently this time. 'You're wrong, Anna. It is my business because you're here with me and it's not over. What if he finds you survived? Huh? What then? He sure as hell won't want witnesses. So don't

130

you tell me it's over. It hasn't even started yet.'

Her face contorted. Tears blurred her vision. 'Please don't say that.'

'Maybe it's not what you wanna hear but I can't help it. Anna. Who is he?'

'Everyone is dead, why can't we just—'

'Just what? Let 'em all rot out there? Or go on pretending nothing's changed? My father was murdered for what he dug outa the ground and you know who's responsible!'

'No, I don't!' She tried to loosen the tight grip on her arm but it was futile. Her legs were shaking. She had to sit down again. Tears wouldn't work now. Nothing would.

'What's going to happen if he comes looking for you?'

Terror touched every fibre of her being. 'Don't say that!'

'You're the only one who can hang him, Anna.'

'Them!' she spat. 'It wasn't just one. They all . . . they—'

'You think I don't know what they did to you? Who is he?'

'I don't know!'

'What'd he look like?'

'Which one!'

'The one that stabbed you.'

'None of the others are important?'

'Anna, I'm trying to help. I know it mightn't feel like it or even sound like it but—'

'If you wanted to help me you should have left me to die!'

He wondered if it was the whisky talking. She couldn't mean it. It had to be the whisky.

'I'm tired. I just want to forget.'

'You won't unless you talk about it.'

'To a stranger? I barely know you!'

'Sometimes it's easier to talk to somebody you don't know. You hardly ever get judged that way.'

'I don't know who he was and I don't remember what he looked like. Now please, Sam, let go of me.'

Sam let her go and stared into the fire. He heard the sounds of the woman getting into his bed—the covers being pulled back, the creaks. Then he heard her quiet breathing.

'Give me time, Sam. Just some time.'

'I would if it was mine to give,' he replied.

He slept soundly that night, feeling more than hearing her wake, reaching out to touch her in sleep as if knowing the touch would calm her back into her safe, dreamless void. He caught two words again: Sergeant. Sergeant.

The words filtered through his brain, and lay there below the surface. Just like yesterday, he was back at Lambing Flat, sitting on his horse. Luke was there on the ground, searching the body of a white man this time. 'What the hell are you doing now?'

'They sure as hell can't take it with them, Sam. Better me than someone else.'

The memory was like a nightmare in colour.

Before dawn, Billy Moonshine rode in. Lucas was waiting. He could smell the fear. For a while he thought it was his own. He'd had a restless night, blaming it on the heat of course. He'd spent hours fighting off the vision of that baby dying slowly amid the dead, or of dogs taking it, fighting over it. 'She's not there, Sarge.'

'What?'

'There was everybody 'cept her and the baby. I searched all over. She not there.'

Lucas's mouth went dry.

'Hear me, Sarge? She not there.' Billy spat the words as he dismounted and began to unsaddle his horse. 'You said she die for sure.'

'Shut up!'

Billy balanced his saddle over the railing. 'What now, sarge? What the hell we do now?'

'Get back out there before the burial party arrives.'

'What for?'

'I want two graves, Billy. You hear me? One for her, one for the baby. This woman is dead, do you understand me?'

Billy said nothing.

'When I get out there, I want to see two graves. Is that understood?'

It took a moment before Billy smiled, and with a quick nod he took Daniel's horse. As he tiredly swung on, he said, 'Too bad they be empty.'

'If she's alive, she can't have got far. We'll wait until the burial's over then we'll find her.'

Ten men volunteered to help with the mass burials— Harry Ryan couldn't accommodate all the bodies. The sergeant told Daniel to organise the party of gathered men, put them into some semblance of order.

Daniel knew it would do no good to complain about Billy taking his horse. The animal had a soft mouth, Billy was too hard. And he wondered why the sarge had sent him out again, but the thought passed quickly.

'Mr Michaels, are you sure you want to come?' Daniel asked as he gave the sixty-year-old blacksmith a leg up. The old man wouldn't be denied, even if he looked too frail to walk across the street on his own. But the more hands, the quicker the mess would be buried. Daniel didn't want to face it again. He'd rather be involved in the daunting task of apprehending those responsible, even if he didn't know where to begin. With any luck, the news would reach Brisbane within the week, and the inspector would return. The pressure would be off Hannaford and therefore off Daniel as well. He was tired of being the only one left to kick.

Daniel, leading the pack for the five-hour journey to Bitter Creek, noticed Maddy standing on her verandah, her cat in arms. Watching. Always watching. Daniel looked away before she waved. Even the sergeant was abnormally quiet. Maybe he was preparing himself, too. No one, not even the sarge, was made of iron. 'You right there, Mr Michaels?'

Daniel received a grunt in reply.

'She's too small to be drinking like that.'

'It's not whisky.'

'She needs me, not you.'

'She's not complaining and you need to rest.' Sam went back to concentrating on Susan, who was balanced precariously on his knee. He was showing Anna how Sheila had taught him to feed the baby, and Sheila had a knack of making hard things appear easy. More goat's milk was lost down the dress and on to his lap than was swallowed. And she choked a couple of times too. Maybe that was worrying Anna. Too bad. Sam had strict orders not to allow her to attempt anything for at least another week.

Having to sit there and watch the unkempt thief feed her own child set Anna's teeth on edge. Her jaw ached. Susan was far happier with Sam, and Anna didn't like it at all.

It was betrayal.

Lately, she was feeling so much better that she refused to stay in bed, and would not admit that a short walk to the outhouse and back was exhausting. Worse, Sam followed her everywhere. His innocence and helpfulness was aggravating.

'You better start taking this in with you,' he said, holding Susan under his arm, indicating the long stick leaning against the outhouse door.

'Thank you, no. If any snake intends swallowing me, he asks for all he gets. Now leave me alone. Go away.'

'You really want me to go away?' Sam asked.

'Yes!' came the snap from behind the closed door.

'Okay.'

Anna didn't see Sam or her baby for over an hour. Panic soon surfaced. Where had he gone? Why would he leave her alone for so long? Imagination needed no assistance. He didn't answer her frantic calls, either.

Sam eventually returned when the baby grew restless and hungry. Anna was sitting on the porch step, angry and upset. He didn't know why. She'd told him to leave her alone. He had.

'What're you upset about?'

'Where have you been?'

Sam looked suitably innocent and stricken. 'We took a walk. She gets bored.'

'Don't ever do that to me again! If you want to get lost, fine, but don't take my baby with you!'

'Want her back?' he asked. 'Here, she's all yours.' Sam thrust the wet, crying child at her and loped away. Then, as if remembering something important, he stopped and turned. Anna studied him cautiously. All her anger had disappeared. Perhaps it was the silly look on his face which helped. 'You prove you can manage all day on your own tomorrow, I'll go to town on Wednesday. We need supplies.'

'I thought we had enough to last another two weeks.'

'I need some news. I need to find out what's going on.'

'You won't tell anyone I'm here, will you?'

He walked back to her, and the baby reached for

him. He tried to ignore it. 'Someone in town you're scared of?'

'You won't corner me, Sam, so stop trying. And don't lie to me, either.'

'Lie? Me? When did I lie to you?'

Anna rose up off the porch. 'I know what you do on Wednesdays. That's the day the mail coach goes into town.'

'Oh.'

'I know what you are, Sam Manning.'

She walked inside and Sam smiled to himself. Before she closed the door in his face, she said, 'There is no need to make me the centre of your excuses. If you still wish to hold up mail coaches that's your decision, but the time will come when you will have to pay for what you do.'

His smile faded.

Bitter Creek's decaying residues of humanity were wrapped in canvas as quickly as possible and rolled into one long, narrow hole after another.

'Who were these, Billy?' Brannigan heard the sergeant ask. He turned to see Billy Moonshine patting down the top of a grave with the back end of his shovel. Moonshine had had a sudden change of mind and belief. Now he was with the others burying the dead. One of the first here in fact.

'Who was that, Sarge?' he asked.'

'Here. Who was it?'

'Mick Hall's missus and the baby. Something wrong?'

Daniel stopped shovelling. If he opened his mouth to voice his immediate question of, 'Where were the bodies?' he'd probably taste the rotting meat and throw up again. There was nothing left in his stomach to lose except perhaps his stomach itself. He hadn't been the only one to throw up a few times and that

136

was a slight comfort. The woman and her baby? Why hadn't he seen them? And as if to answer his silent question, 'They were over there in the scrub. Crows had 'em. Not much left of the baby.'

Daniel looked to where Moonshine was pointing. North. Nothing else was said. Daniel had not seen them because he hadn't looked over there. The body he was burying received another load of dirt.

Revenge, he thought. Spent their lives digging in it and in the end it always claimed them.

'Brannigan!'

'Sir?'

'What was her name?'

'Who, sir?'

'The Hall woman.'

'Anna, I think, sir.'

The sergeant was writing a list of all the dead in one of his notebooks. 'The baby's name?'

'Don't know, sir.'

'Does anyone know?'

There were a few shrugs.

Lucas wiped beads of sweat from his forehead. It was working. She must have crawled off to die somewhere in the vicinity. Daniel hadn't mentioned seeing the woman or the child and he was obviously none the wiser. It was working. Now to be patient a little while longer. Brannigan would take the detail back to town and the search could begin in earnest. Lucas moved to Harry, who had a handkerchief tied about his face. 'Any idea who this was?' he asked.

'Tom Manning. Poor bastard.'

The sergeant was calm throughout, expressionless, thoughtful, busy with his register of names and busy with the monotonous chant of the same Biblical verse Daniel would be hearing in his sleep. No one said very much. What was there to say that was appropriate? For some reason, Daniel thought the sarge looked almost happy.

Something's wrong, Daniel thought. No, not quite wrong, something wasn't right. He was left to take the others back to town and thought little of it. He was pleased to be away from the stinking damned place. But he went alone. The sergeant stayed to inventory what belongings were left and to burn everything otherwise destroyed. Daniel was to take everyone to the pub for well-earned drinks.

Lucas Hannaford and Billy Moonshine searched in a radius of one mile from both camps and they found nothing.

Nothing at all.

'Someone found 'em,' Billy said and, as usual, Billy was right. 'Might be Sam,' Billy said.

Lucas said nothing. His thoughts were on fire.

Eight

'I shall miss you, Papa,' Maddy said quietly from her seat on the coach. Lucas was too busy calming Jane to say any more than, 'And I shall miss you, Maddy. Take care of your mother.'

She glanced at her mother's dramatics and wanted to say: If I see her.

She could imagine her with Aunt Rachel already. Never home. If it wasn't shopping in the city, it would be a succession of luncheons and garden parties to which Maddy wouldn't be invited. She'd be made to stay home with Ronald the Rat, her fourteen-year-old cousin. If he dared mince another frog and put the remains in her underwear drawer again, she'd beat him to within an inch of his horrible life.

Still, being in Brisbane for a while would give her plenty of time to finish her tablecloth. There'd be nothing else to do but embroider. And she'd have some water to look at, too. Rachel lived close to the river but not as close to the governor's house as everyone, including Mother, liked to think. Why, the house was within walking distance of the city, too. Not that Aunt Rachel ever walked. No, no, she took cabs.

Maddy expected the dramatic change to take place at any moment now. Ten years would instantly peel off her mother's face. It always happened when her father wasn't about. At home being a martyr, she looked and acted her age. Forty-three. But with Aunt Rachel . . . the thought alone was embarrassing.

Maddy didn't want to go away. If she was a boy,

she'd be allowed to stay. She could shoot better than any boy she knew, anyway, but no, her father had decided it best they leave until the mess was cleared up and any danger, whatever that was, had passed. Did he expect a horde of murdering robbers to take over the town?

Mother's departing performance was admired by the two gentlemen on the coach. Papa, though, was embarrassed at the way her nails almost drew blood on his arm. 'Be careful, darling,' Mother moaned. 'For me, please be careful?'

And she looked at him like she'd never see him again. She was probably planning how not to return, anyway. It was all a lie. Maddy knew Mother spent half her life hoping for news that Papa had died on duty. It was the only chance she had to escape back to the city where she belonged.

Maddy wanted to jump out of the window, and she would have, too, if Daniel hadn't been there watching, ready to wave her goodbye. Even he was pleased to see her leave. It wasn't fair.

The coach finally pulled out. The seats were hard, uncomfortable. The ride was already rough and jarring and they hadn't reached the end of the street yet. Maddy looked out. Her father wasn't watching. It was no use waving. He was talking to Daniel and the other trooper, who'd been sent when the news of the massacre at Bitter Creek had been made public.

His name was James. He wasn't even handsome. What help was one extra man? No one knew when Inspector Ritchie would come back from Brisbane.

And home for Christmas? That was just another lie. Another broken promise which amounted to the same thing.

Maddy sighed. Mother was already in full conversation with both male passengers. Something about how dangerous it was to be married to a senior trooper. Senior? Oh Lord, Papa's only a sergeant. Then Mother began on the terrible threat that Sam Manning had become. He's a murderer, you know.

Maddy groaned and wanted to scream at them to leave Sam alone, but no one would hear her. No one ever did. Ahead lay a long, boring journey unless Sam Manning decided to adjourn the proceedings. Maddy was cheered by the thought.

Sam watched the coach rattle down Mitchell's Hill. He swore to himself. Since he'd found Anna he'd lost track of the days. It wasn't Wednesday at all. It was Thursday, dammit. The coach was going, not coming.

Just as Maddy had given up hope, she thought she saw Sam Manning high on the hilltop, watching. Her heart skipped and fell into her boots when the figure turned the horse and rode away. The wrong way! Oh no, no, no! Prove to them you're not a monster, Sam! Come and rob the coach, please? Let them see how friendly you really are!

The coach continued on its rough journey.

He was no murderer. Why, she used to sit on his knee when she was a small girl and he would tell her all about California. Then Mrs Manning died, or was killed—something like that—and she never saw Sam again. He was supposed to be hanged but he escaped. Papa had been terribly worried for a long time. Mother too. Sam seemed to always be wherever the family was. It was as if he followed Papa all over the country. And sometimes in the early hours of the morning, her father would wake from a bad dream. He'd yell something about Elizabeth, and Mother would tell him it was all over, he mustn't worry about it now. Maddy heard a lot through the wall. She remembered, too.

Sam's wife who died was named Elizabeth.

Mother refused to speak of her and she dared not

ask Papa, either. But one day she knew she would meet Sam Manning again. She would look into his eyes and ask, 'Mr Manning, did your Elizabeth have beautiful golden hair and deep green eyes? Did she bake the most wonderful shortbread?' And he would say, 'Why?' And she would say, 'I think I remember her, Mr Manning.' And he would say, 'Maddy, you're too old and too pretty to call me mister. Call me Sam.' And he would kiss her. Just like Daniel had kissed her once.

Sam crept into the Establishment via the back door—he'd seen the troopers still in town. As he slunk down the red-carpeted hallway the floorboards creaked in protest. Ginger-Lee's door was open, welcoming. He peered in. Empty. She'd got herself new curtains. Apart from that, nothing had changed. Sam felt no sudden anticipating heat, his mind kept seeing Anna with the baby in her arms as she waved him goodbye. Though nothing had shown on her face, Sam felt she was pleased to see him go. She must have had something planned.

He didn't like that, he wanted to get back, quickly. But he had to wait. He couldn't venture downstairs, not now. He recognised Ginger-Lee's approaching footfalls. As she wandered in, humming a song under her breath, Sam grabbed her from behind and covered her mouth with his huge hand. 'It's me,' he said. Under ordinary circumstances, 'me' could have been anyone. Her struggles ceased and Sam let go, finger to mouth now, closing the door quietly.

'What're you doing, Sam? Trying to scare me to death?' she whispered. Before he had time to reply she asked, 'What're you doing here? Haven't you heard?'

'Heard what?' he asked as he scanned his favourite whore from her dyed red hair to her painted toenails.

All thoughts of Anna disintegrated.

'Sam, you shouldn't be here. There's traps looking everywhere for you.'

'Yes, I know,' he replied, nuzzling her neck, slipping his hand into her dress for a delicious feel.

She pulled away, surprising him. 'It's true?' she asked, wide eyed. Sam pulled her to him and tried to slip her dress off her shoulders. 'Sam, no!'

No?

'What's wrong?' he asked, shocked at her rejection. Ginger-Lee turned away and rearranged her clothing.

'Have you ever lied to me?' she asked.

'You're my only girl, Ginger-Lee. You know that. I never want anyone but you.'

'I don't mean that.'

Sam looked dazed.

'You once said you'd never killed anyone. Is it true? Is it still true?'

Sam reached out and turned her to face him. He liked to see eyes in situations like this, but he saw only fear and affection in hers. His blood chilled. 'Is what true?'

'They're saying it was you, you the ringleader.'

'Ringleader for what?'

'All those miners at Bitter Creek. Tell me it's not true. Tell me it's a lie, that you didn't murder men you knew for their gold?'

'Jesus Christ,' he whispered and had the sudden need to sit down. 'They're saying it was me?'

'The whites, the Chinese, the woman and the child. Everyone.'

Sam looked up into the woman's pale eyes and saw the tears emerging, but his shock had become a cold, sick feeling. 'I didn't kill anyone. Who's saying it was me? Luke?'

Ginger-Lee sat with a thump beside him on the bed they'd shared so often. This time she only groped for his hand and strong fingers curled over hers. It wasn't true. But why did she listen? 'Yes. Lucas is saying it was you. He says he has evidence of it, enough to hang you. By God, he will. I never thought I'd hear myself say this, but you have to go back wherever it is you came from, Sam. Go away and don't come here any more. If Lucas finds you've been here, I'm the one who'll suffer. No friendship is worth fifty pounds.'

'Fifty pounds? Is that the reward?'

She nodded. Sam made no move to go. Not yet. 'Talk to me, Ginger-Lee.'

'All I know is what's being said. Like how you got together a pack of murderin' thieves and took to the Chinese diggings first before you raided your own father's camp.'

'Well, that's different,' he whispered. 'I'll give him that much.'

'Don't you see it's because you've been seen there at Bitter Creek, Sam?'

'Yeah, taking my old man his tobacco. That's what I was doing at Bitter Creek.' Sam rubbed at his eyes and didn't let go of her hand. 'You said a woman and a child?'

'A team went out there yesterday and buried them all.'

'Did they? . . . You don't believe it?'

'God strike me for lying if I said yes, but Lucas is doing a mighty fine job of convincing half the district you're dangerous now. Go, Sam. Go as far as you can away from here. I don't want you to die.'

He held her tight and planted a small kiss on her forehead. She knew it would be the last time she'd feel his touch, smell him, see him. Then he was on his feet. His face had drained of colour but his eyes were still summer blue and bright.

'If I never see you again, you remember one thing,

girl. I'm no murderer and I never have been.'

'God be with you, Sam.'

'God forgot me a long time ago.'

And he was gone.

'Psst. Ryan.'

Harry Ryan thought he was hearing things as he was tucking into his sandwiches during a lull in trading.

'Psst, Harry, you there?'

The ageing storekeeper and undertaker went to investigate the source of the sounds coming from the back of his shop. He found Sam Manning crouched behind a display coffin. The face was pale, the eyes wild. 'Sam, what the hell are you doing here?'

'I need supplies. Sugar, flour, tea, tinned meat and—' There was a pause as Sam pulled a tattered list from his breast pocket. Coins and a couple of pound notes soon followed. 'Bandages and a hairbrush if you've got one.'

'Sam, there's no need to whisper. You can come in. No one's about.' For the first time in two years, Sam wondered if he should trust old Harry Ryan.

'Come on, Sam. If the traps find you here I'll be measuring you for one of the finest and no one wants that. Do you not trust me?' One of the finest? He was surrounded by coffins and had hardly noticed. He followed Harry, watched him turn his Open sign to Closed. He even offered Sam one of his sandwiches. Sam declined with a shake of the head. Still eating, Harry attended to the list, while Sam's gaze stayed mainly on the door.

'And so you should be scared.'

'I'm innocent, for Christ's sakes.'

'I know that. Even Elsie doesn't believe it. Neither do most of the town. That's on your side if nothing else is, lad.'

Sam dived for cover when footsteps were heard on the verandah and a glimpse of uniform appeared. It was Daniel wondering why the door was locked. 'Get on out to the wagon and hide under the canvas. I've to take an order out to Mrs Sellar. Get off with you, quickly.'

When Sam departed, the door was unlocked. 'Morning, Harry,' Daniel said. Harry consulted his timepiece. 'You're behind yourself, Daniel. 'Tis afternoon.' The young constable pushed his cap back on his head and fished in one of Harry's huge glass jars for a peppermint. 'No one's been in for bandages or infant things?'

'No one injured or newly birthed, no. Why?'

'No reason. Thanks for the sweet.' With a smile, Daniel left, duty done. The doorbell jangled in closing and Harry looked at the scrawled list. Bandages. Small cup. Hairbrush.

For a moment the old storekeeper wondered just what was going on.

'Elsie?'

After a soft, incoherent mumble, Elsie Ryan appeared at the top of the stairs. She was up to her elbows in bread dough. 'What?' she snapped.

'Mind the store for me, lovey.'

'You said two o'clock.'

'Elsie, don't argue with me.'

'Two o'clock and not a moment before,' she snapped and Harry sighed. Sam could wait another half hour. He'd send a boy to fetch Sam's horse and ride it to Sellar's, no questions asked or answered for a pocketful of sweets.

The baby slept. Anna soon tired of chatting to the staring goat, and had tried to sweep the floor. After a great deal of exhausting effort she discovered the floor was wooden. Sam was right, she wasn't that strong. She tired quickly. Thirty years of dirt could wait a little while longer before it was evicted.

And Susan slept on, thumb in mouth, dreaming whatever it was babies dreamed of. Anna tried to sleep unsuccessfully. It was too hot, too still. Too quiet. She sat by the clear sandy creek, half listening for the baby to wake and give her something to do. Perhaps Susan sensed this; perhaps that was why she slept so deeply. Memories drifted back as Anna watched a myriad of smooth river stones toss and tumble down the tiny waterfall.

Michael's beard, already greying. His voice, one she once found comforting, now replayed in her mind as a curse. Tom was there too, so close she could almost smell him. Tobacco and sweat and old age. 'No, no, you're tippin' it out the . . . dish.' Funny how he never swore when she was nearby. And his gnarled old hands snatching the pan from hers, picking leeches from her arms and ankles. 'No, no, when I say shake it, I mean like this!' The voice of a cranky, impatient old man. But she loved him. And he loved her. She could see it and feel it in his eyes.

But now there was nothing but the clear water, rippling, foaming, bubbling. She looked around her, a complete circle of mountains. A lifetime in distance from the mud and blood of Bitter Creek.

Aptly named.

No place for a woman. Or a man. Let its gold lie unclaimed for all the good it would do; no amount was ever enough. Gold. It turned a placid creature into an hysterical monster. Gold. Let it rot in the hell it causes. It's over, it's gone.

'It never happened,' she told the water. 'I've nothing now. Nothing at all. No husband, no home. Not a penny to my name.' Nothing now, except for Sam. A bushranger. You take it easy, he'd ordered.

I shall try, she'd replied. And off he went to pillage, or if stories were true, relieve someone of a small burden.

'This is what I get for needing another man, for wanting something I couldn't have. I had forty-three ounces of gold, not including two nuggets, and now I wear someone else's boots and even they are too big. What has this gold done for me?'

She rarely felt silly talking to herself; at times it was the only voice she managed to hear. A voice was slower to emerge than thoughts. Thoughts took all manner of shapes and directions and lately, Anna felt her mind had a better chance of killing her than that knife ever had. Sam had swept her away from death when it was close enough, so close she could feel its icy touch. She felt deprived because everything she once had was gone. Yes, it would have been better if he'd left her to die. Surely there was no pain in death? Surely there was freedom?

Anna looked up into the afternoon sun.

Susan slept on, there was no sound at all except the bubbling water. Anna dipped her fingers into it. Neither warm nor cold. Perhaps she could take a swim? Just as she had with Lu Sun? Lu Sun. She closed her eyes and tried to see the Chinese girl's cheeky smile, the dark sparkling eyes. Nothing came except emptiness. Not even a tear was left. There was nothing to feel, just a scab which stuck the bandages to her side. How it itched. On yes, the water looked wonderful. She needed to feel it caressing every part of her body.

Sam had said he'd probably be late and there was no reason to doubt him. Also, the bright sunshine would help the wound heal.

Anna decided to sit in the creek. She peeled off the dress Sheila had lent. It was far too big and so were the bloomers. The bandages beneath her breasts were sticky from congealed blood and wouldn't come off easily. Persistence won. It brought a sharp, hot sting and the warmth of fresh blood tickled her side. Anna stifled a curse—Lord knew, she'd learnt a few good ones of late. She'd torn the scab off. Don't get it wet, Sheila had said.

'Get it wet indeed,' Anna said quietly. The damage is done on the inside. She could feel its scorching heat with every breath she took.

I won't give in, Sheila. I won't give in.

So it takes more'n this to kill you, does it, lassie?

Anna tried the rocks, slippery under tender feet. She almost fell four times. With impeccable timing, just as she'd immersed herself in the water, stark naked, enjoying her freedom, she heard the sound of the approaching horse.

Uttering a string of colourful obscenities (not knowing what they meant), she clambered back to where her clothes lay. She'd time to don Sheila's dress and nothing else when Sam came into view.

'There's leeches in that part of the creek,' was all he said, giving her an odd look as he went by while Anna tried to hide the bloomers and bandages, and tried, too, to pretend she wasn't wet while her hair dripped in her eyes.

'I thought you said you'd be late?'

'And I thought Sheila told you not to get wet. You're bleeding again.'

'I needed—'

'Don't tell me. Another bath.'

'No. I just wanted to get wet.'

Sam dismounted and sent her a look that proved just how crazy she was. He unsaddled the grey. He seemed to rattle when he walked, too.

'What did you get?' she asked.

'A headache,' he replied and removed the bridle. Sam put the saddle on the porch. The horse tried to follow Anna into the shack. 'Close the door or she'll come in, too.'

Anna closed the door on the curious horse and while Sam's back was turned, she put the bloomers on. Sam was emptying the pockets of his coat. One thing after another was put on the small table. Flour, tea, sugar, bully beef, potatoes already sprouting. (He put those aside.) Matches. A bottle of whisky. A small enamel cup and a brown paper bag.

'Goodness, you rode with all of that?'

She expected him to say something funny in return. Something witty perhaps. Sam wiped his forehead and took off his coat. Anna stepped aside as he hung it on a nail behind the door. He poured himself a whisky from the new bottle.

Something was wrong. She could sense if not see the dark cloud hovering over his head.

'You all right?' he asked, standing by the window, looking out at nothing.

'Yes, I'm fine.'

'I told you to take it easy. You promised me you would.'

'I did.'

When he turned, the look in his eyes belied any innocence she could have mustered, or any excuse for that matter.

'I had nothing to do.'

'So you swept the floor. No wonder you're bleeding.'

'Sam, what's wrong?' she asked. In reply he took a swig of his drink and took a hairbrush from his trouser pocket.

'Here, I thought you'd be needing this.'

She took the brush. 'Did you steal it?' she asked lightly.

'No. I didn't steal it,' he snapped and went outside.

Yes, something was indeed wrong. Was he ill? He

didn't look ill. Anna was concerned more than curious. He returned with water and then again with kindling. Though he appeared to be relaxed now, something intangible betrayed the image.

'Thank you for the hairbrush, Sam.'

He said nothing.

'Are you feeling yourself?'

'I'm tired. Don't fuss.'

'I'm not fussing. Yet,' she added.

Of course not. That's what they always said. One way or another they poked and prodded till they hit bottom. Women were all the same. Let her try. See how far she gets.

Anna began to brush out her tangled hair. Wincing, ouching.

Sam wondered why she wasn't asking questions. 'I got some new bandages,' he said. A revelation.

'Oh. Good.'

He walked out once more. Anna pretended she didn't know he'd gone. But she went to the window and watched as he loped off towards the mountains at the back of the hut. Not mountains exactly, but boulders of granite balanced percariously on little rocks half the size of wagon wheels. Sam disappeared behind one such boulder. Swallowed whole it seemed, like the Pied Piper disappearing into rock. That story had given her nightmares as a child.

He took no gun so he couldn't be hunting.

She waited to see him again. Nothing. Sheila's dress fell off her right shoulder. Wearily, she rectified it. The other side fell. Anna sighed and wondered if he had a needle and cotton. Susan slept on. She'd be awake half the night, demanding entertainment other than hiting two spoons together.

Still no sign of Sam. Did he ever stay in the house for a moment?

Anna turned to the purchases and looked up at

the dusty cobwebbed shelves along the wall. Tins, empty bottles. Rags, three dishes, two mugs. Knives. Knives not meant for polite culinary usage, these were knives with one purpose—to kill.

Especially that one. It had a savage curved blade. Anna stepped away from it. She could tell by sight alone it was razor sharp. She well knew the agony such a thing could inflict. Anna put a plate over it quickly. She peeked into the brown paper bag. Bandages.

She thought of Dinny; Tom holding him down while she wrapped up his foot. The screams were only strengthened by the rum someone poured down his unwilling throat. Late at night she was still there, whispering to him to let her go because his grip was sending her arm numb.

Don't leave me.

She hadn't. She'd endured the same terrifying loneliness when giving birth to Susan. Days in which she thought she would surely die. Anna rubbed at her arm where for a moment she still felt Dinny Masterson's touch.

Bandages.

Sam would have to dress her wound again. He wouldn't say what he was thinking. He wouldn't have to.

Where on earth had he gone? The quiet was oppressive here after the ceaseless noise of Bitter Creek. Quiet terrified her. Death crept in with the stillness, death was silent.

She tried to sing Molly Malone. A sad little song which always made her feel a little better. Her voice came as a whisper, shaky, barely a song at all. From the window she glimpsed Sam. She saw he was dragging something.

Bright. She must be bright. Happy. Cheerful. It would be the only way to find out what was wrong with him. Anna built up the fire into a neat A-shape so that when all was alight and crumbling, the small log on top would collapse and ignite fully. Michael used to laugh at her fires but they rarely failed, even after rain when the kindling was wet.

Sam dragged the chest in and threw his shirt over the rocking chair. 'Some stuff here might fit you,' he said. 'I remembered it a bit late. The things Sheila gave you don't fit. Don't suit you much either.' He looked away from the dress, which had fallen off her shoulder again, and he chose a key from one of many on a ring taken from his pocket. There were keys of all shapes and sizes and one he knew well. It instantly opened the rusty padlock on the battered chest. 'There you go; it's all yours if you want it.' Sam stood back.

Anna, curious, opened the chest and couldn't believe what she was seeing. It was full of women's clothes. She looked up at Sam. He was scratching his nose. He seemed a little embarrassed by this.

The first dress was dark maroon in colour, heavy, thick. The next was a deep yellow, almost saffron. It was a ballgown. Anna rose from her knees unsteadily and held the dress against her body. Lost for words, she looked at Sam again. He was having another drink now and his face was expressionless until he held the bottle out to her and asked, 'Want one?'

Anna shook her head. He turned away, dismissing the question on her lips. *Who did these clothes belong to?* Anna carefully folded the ballgown and put it on the bed. A faded blue gingham dress appeared next. It was light and cool and would definitely fit better than the heavy green one Sheila had given her.

There were five dresses in all. Anna kept the gingham aside. There were no shoes, but there was a full-length cotton petticoat and a bottle of rose scent, rancid with age. It made her eyes water, or was she crying?

Then she saw the uniform coat. It was dark blue with red braid epaulettes. Under the coat were once-white breeches, now grey. The dresses lost their magic. 'What on earth is this?'

Sam turned to find her holding up the uniform jacket. So there it was. He thought he'd burnt it years ago. 'It's a trooper's uniform, what's it look like?'

'Is this yours, or did you steal it?'

'It was mine,' he replied quietly.

'You were a trooper?' she squeaked.

She was full to the brim with curiosity and disbelief. The 'you' was almost a giggle.

'Yes, I was a trooper.'

'But you're a thief. A bushranger.'

Sam pulled a face. 'Bushranger, trooper, just names for convenience.' He was very aware of her deep interest. She was itching for more information and there was no way in hell he would tell her a thing unless she talked first.

As if reading his mind, Anna put the coat back. She said, 'My wound needs dressing. Could you help me, please?'

Sam put his whisky down.

'You'll have to use the spirits.'

'It'll hurt.'

'Nothing changes, does it.'

Anna let Sheila's dress fall to her waist. She caught it and lay on her right side as she'd done many times. The fire from the spirits was still agony. Her dependence on Sam was even worse than the tears stinging her eyes. He helped her sit up and she turned her face away. He wrapped those new bandages around her.

154

'You were a sergeant,' she said quietly.

'Maybe I was.'

'You don't want me to know, do you?'

'There's things you don't want me to know, so I guess we're even. You can put your arm down now, ma'am.'

Anna dressed and lay down on the bed. 'Will you tell me what's wrong?'

'Nothing's wrong,' Sam said and tried to smile. Something was very wrong when he had to force a smile.

For Jane Hannaford the overnight stay in the coach-house was as unavoidable and as horrid as the heat and the incessant flies. She relieved the situation by extolling her virtues as a trooper's wife, and verbally shaking everyone awake with her news of how she'd be invited to meet the Duke of Edinburgh when he visited next year.

It was certainly news to Maddy. Her father didn't know Commissioner Seymour although Aunt Rachel probably did.

Maddy kept eating. Mother complained about the food, but that was normal. To Maddy, anything she didn't have to cook tasted wonderful. And of course, conversation turned back to Bitter Creek. Rumour was rife, curiosity bubbling. Everyone was taking precautions against attack now.

What Mother was saying about the atrocities came from her own imagination. Papa always thought her too fragile to be told truths. What Maddy had overheard was the truth—people had died. No, died was not the word to use. Slaughtered perhaps? Now Papa had enough evidence to hang Sam Manning. But it wasn't true. None of it was true.

Maddy left the table after finishing her meal and walked out into the darkening air. She gazed out to the mountain range on the distant horizon. It had taken all day to travel over the mountains, all day for so few miles. Sam lived up there, somewhere. Somewhere in Girraween.

Maddy kicked at a rock. What evidence, Papa? How do you know it was Sam?

It was probably her father's way of blaming the one he thought was responsible. He did that often enough, guilt or innocence made no difference to him. Why, she'd even cornered Daniel in the stables to ask him. Daniel didn't think Sam was responsible— he said as much. Why, he'd even kissed her, but was too much of a gentleman to do anything more.

Maddy kicked at another rock and let her gaze drift to the distant hills again. They were smothered now in a rich purple glow. She imagined Sam Manning standing beside her. She imagined so much. It seemed her only happiness. She was so captured by her dream of what would happen if the coach left her behind that she didn't hear the calls.

The boy who tended the horses while his parents tended the people tapped her arm. Maddy jumped in fright. 'Hey, Miss? Your mother's stuck in the bath tub and my mother can't get her out. They need you.' Maddy wanted to strangle her mother for having the audacity to interrupt another brilliant fantasy. She looked down at the skinny, scabby youngster. He reminded her of that Stills boy.

'You really the sergeant's daughter?' the boy asked as they walked back to the coach house.

'Yes, I am. Why?'

'Did Sam Manning really do it?'

'Am I a Police Magistrate?'

'Oh, come on. You can tell me.'

Maddy stopped walking and so did the boy. What she said though, he didn't want to hear. Not many people did, it seemed. 'Sam Manning is not a murderer.'

'How do you know?'

'Perhaps, little boy, I know more than I should. Go away.'

'Make me.'

Maddy stomped her black-booted foot and the boy ran off into the night. He wasn't about to hang around and torment her, she was built like an outhouse— twice as big and three times as strong as all his schoolmates combined.

The boy waited in the dark before slinking around to the room that served as a bathroom—a rough shed tacked on to the kitchen. He climbed noiselessly onto a rusty feed bin and peered in through his gouged spyhole, smothering his giggles at what he saw. He liked it better when there was a pretty lady in there. But no doubt about it, this memory though would keep him silently smirking for weeks. Mrs Whatsername had her fat behind stuck, all right. Grandpa Johnson's favourite sow was pink like that. Not as hairy though. The noises were nearly the same, a lot of grunting and groaning. He nearly choked trying not to laugh.

The edges of sanity were slippery. The outhouse door slammed shut as she came out. With the sudden bang came a montage of memory. It wasn't Sam walking towards her, it was Lucas Hannaford. Screams hit the twilight; startled parrots added to the uproar.

Sam threw the shotgun to the ground and sprinted toward Anna. The galahs screaming above accentuated the sudden terror he felt as he heard her screaming: 'Don't hurt my baby!'

Sam caught her easily and swung her about. 'Anna, it's me. It's Sam.' She didn't seem to hear. She was stiff, he didn't think eyes could open so far. And for a moment, she was Elizabeth. For a fleeting moment, that familiar terror ate right through him. Again.

'Anna, it's me!'

And slowly the animal fear died in her eyes. She whispered his name, still shaking.

'I didn't mean to scare you. Maybe I should wear a bell around my neck.'

If she heard his attempt at humour, there was no reaction.

'Are you okay?'

She tried to nod. Another lie.

'Oh, Anna, talk to me? I'm not gonna hurt you, you know that.'

She slumped against him and hung there, silent. Hesitant at first, he enfolded her in his arms until he felt her gradually relax. 'You're gonna have to talk to someone, girl. This can't go on.' He held her for an eternity.

Her breath scorched his bare shoulder. 'You'll think I'm insane.'

'So it'll be one crazy talking to another. Anna, you're just scared.'

'But it's over.' Anna pushed away and searched his eyes.

'No, it's not over. It won't be over until you talk to someone and the only person around here is me.'

She said nothing for a long time but there was an improvement because she didn't fight to get away. He could touch her lately and she wouldn't flinch. Cormac was right. Maybe she was starting to trust him now she knew there was no danger, not from him at least.

'Look, I know what they did. I know it wasn't one. You damn near died and you're thinking maybe it would have been better if you had. But you're not dead. Anna, things like this don't go away on their own. The sooner you get it out—'

'It was the sergeant. Hannaford,' she whispered, expecting him to walk off, laughing. But he didn't. There was no trace of disbelief anywhere. 'He's a little older than you and he has pale eyes and a scar on his face. A scar on his cheek. It was him. He stabbed me and you have a knife just like his.'

'Luke. I thought so.'

'You knew?'

'Well, let's just say it makes sense now.'

Sam ventured back to retrieve the shotgun. This time her mind didn't play with illusions. 'How can anything make sense? Why? Why Michael? And Tom? Everyone. Why me? What did I do?'

Sam turned to her and tried to keep his gaze on her face, but that damned blue dress made it impossible. His mind, his heart and his gut all seemed volcanic, but as usual, nothing showed on his face or, he hoped, in his voice. 'Why you? Why me? I've been asking myself the same thing for most of the day. Trouble is, I never got any answers. You really wanna know why? I think you were in the wrong place at the wrong time. I think you should never have gone to Bitter Creek.'

'I never wanted to go!'

'You think I don't know that? You think I never saw that in your eyes the first time I seen you? Huh? I do know something, Anna. You're dead and they're blaming me for killin' you. For killing everyone at Bitter Creek. So I guess now it's a case of, why us? Suzie's crying,' he added quietly and scratched his nose.

Anna couldn't move. The only sound she heard was the pounding of her heart. Surely he was joking?

'Anna, Suzie's crying.'

'I am dead?' she asked, disbelieving.

'Yep. You were buried at Bitter Creek with

everyone else. Suzie's dead too, and that's the story, ma'am. You're looking at a mass murderer.'

'No, it can't be possible.'

'Anna, the kid's driving me crazy. I can't stand it when she cries.'

'I am not dead! How can they say that!'

Sam sighed. 'Okay, you're alive. Why don't you get on my horse and gallop off into town and tell 'em all you're alive? Why don't you walk right in, look old Luke in the eye and say, "I'm not a ghost no more. Look at me, you thought you knifed me, well you didn't kill me." Try it, Anna. See how far I'll let you get.'

Sam paused, allowing his words to sink in.

'Luke'd like to see you again. You stick a knife in someone and it's nice to have them call in and say, howdy. Specially when they're supposed to be dead. When he's countin' on 'em being dead.'

Anna's face, if it were possible, paled even further. Sam touched her arm. She didn't flinch.

'He'll be looking for you, girl. He won't want any witnesses. If a knife in the breast didn't kill you, a bullet in the head sure as hell will.'

'You know this man?'

'Yes, unfortunately, I do.'

'But—'

'Don't go looking for reasons. Just makes it harder to understand.'

'How dare he?'

Fire sparked her eyes. Sam let his hand fall from her arm. 'Anna, getting angry is not going to help.'

Slowly she turned those firing eyes to him. His blood iced. 'He won't get away with this,' she said calmly.

'Yeah? And what are you gonna do about it?'

She didn't know, that was obvious. 'God forgive

me,' she whispered quietly. 'Forgive me for these thoughts.'

Sam believed if he was God he'd probably forgive her for anything. Unfortunately he wasn't God, just some fool who should have kept his mouth shut and his eyes off someone else's wife.

'Supper will be ready when you are,' Anna said quietly and turned away.

Nine

Under normal circumstances, the realisation that there was now a woman residing under the same roof would have scared him enough to sprint in the opposite direction.

Supper's ready when you are.

Already roles were being played. The only thing missing was conversation.

Anna stared at the tinned meat and boiled potato as if they were something unmentionable. Sam had finished his and hoped she'd push her plate away so he could have hers, too. She fiddled with the food, rearranged it on the plate while his stomach growled. Finally, her fork clattered down and she held her head in her hand.

For too long she'd been in a stony, deep silence filled only by darkening thoughts.

'I wasn't gonna tell you,' he said. 'I thought you'd . . . oh, I don't know. Forget it.'

'Is that your solution to everything? Forget it? What do you think I am, Sam? Haven't I endured enough without this?'

'I never said that.'

Anna knew from his face that he was suffering too. Suddenly she wanted to apologise and stopped short. Apologies made him angry and what was she sorry for? It was none of her doing, nor was it his. 'Why is he doing this?' she asked.

'He doesn't want to hang.'

'Hanging! Ha! It's too quick for the likes of him. He deserves much more!'

'Like what?'

'Castration,' she snapped as Sam casually stole her plate. 'All I need is a blunt knife. Oh, don't look at me like that, Sam Manning. How else am I supposed to feel?'

Sam said nothing at all. He was too busy eating. He acted as if he didn't have a worry in the world and Anna couldn't comprehend it at all. 'How can you sit there so calmly!'

'No use getting upset,' he said softly while he picked the skin from the potato. Susan crawled across the floor, grabbed a handful of Sam's pants and made the effort to stand.

'Upset? After what that man has done?'

Sam put a tiny piece of potato in the baby's mouth and she sat with a thump on the floor and pulled faces at the foreign substance in her mouth.

'And what exactly did he do?' Sam asked softly and glanced at Anna. The anger and fire suddenly died. He knew then she would never tell him. She possibly couldn't tell him or anyone for that matter. He gave the baby some more potato. She ate more than she spat out this time. Talk to me, Anna, he thought. Talk to me.

'I had a friend, you know.'

Sam glanced up but Anna wasn't looking at him. She was staring at her hands.

'She was Chinese. Michael never knew.'

'Oh, one of those friends,' Sam said quietly and lifted Susan to his lap.

'Your father knew. He'd warn me to be careful of them. We would meet twice, sometimes three times a week.'

At the waterhole, Sam thought.

'We'd swim in the waterhole not half a mile from the Chinese camp site. Michael thought I was fetching water.'

She was quiet for a while. Sam dared not breathe too loud in case she stopped talking. He'd learnt the value of listening. If only he'd listened to Elizabeth like this, heard what she was trying to say, things might have been different. Her death might have been avoided. It was too late now for might have beens, should haves and if onlys.

'Lu Sun never came to the waterhole that day. That Thursday. I waited and waited and in the end I went to see what was wrong. I knew something had happened, Sam I knew. Everything that is within me warned me, said, don't go up there. Don't. I didn't heed it. For the first time in my life, I didn't heed it.'

Sam seemed to understand. The baby wetly chewed on his wrist, her incoherent babbling breaking the quiet.

'Did you see what was left at the Chinese camp, Sam?'

He nodded. Tears welled in her eyes and her face trembled a little. One deep breath cured it all.

'They were more of a family to me than my own.'

He understood that, too.

'I remember hearing the shooting, so I must have run back to Bitter Creek. I don't know why, perhaps I thought I could stop it, something, anything.' There was another pause. She was reliving too much too soon. She changed direction.

'My scalp crawled when I first saw him. It was as if I knew he was . . . ' She searched vainly for the word. A thousand sprang to Sam's mind. She continued, 'He frightened me, Sam. It was the way he looked at me, the way he spoke to me. It was only a feeling, and how do you prove a feeling? He was in his uniform the first time we spoke.'

For a little while there was absolute quiet. Come on, Anna, he thought. You've come this far.

'I can still hear them. I can still smell them. I can still see them. I can still see everything and I want it to go away and leave me alone. That's all I want.'

Sam looked down. The baby was suddenly heavy. He'd forgotten he was holding her and now she was asleep. Anna's voice was but a whisper as she haltingly continued. 'They were dead. Dying. I found Michael and he was dead. There'd been no time, no warning.' Anna absently reached for her fork and fondled it while tears welled in her eyes. She looked across the small table and into Sam's eyes. 'I know it was him, Sam.'

'Who?'

'Hannaford. The one you say you know. The sun was blinding me but I knew who it was and what he wanted. What they all wanted.'

'How many men were there?'

'Four I didn't know. And Billy Moonshine,' Anna whispered. 'And the trooper.'

Only one? Sam thought.

'What about the other trooper?' he asked, thinking of Daniel and hoping it wasn't possible the boy was involved.

'No. I only recognised Billy and the sergeant. And if I didn't do what they wanted, Susan would . . . ' The fingers touching the fork started to shake. 'I had no choice, Sam. And when the others were done, he came back. The sergeant came back and he had that knife.'

Sam was unsure whether to touch her hand or not. He decided not to. A touch might break the spell. 'I heard him say, "Leave the baby". Just leave it. He looked at me and he said, "I'm not a monster".'

Sam needed another drink.

'There was the pain. They argued about making sure I was dead. But they went away. Animals. I was nothing. No one. I wondered how long it would be before I finally died. Susan was crying so far away, and I couldn't move. Such a long time. Then I saw your face—'

Sam thought she was going to throw up. He was right. Anna jumped to her feet and ran out into the darkness. For a while, he sat where he was, unmoving, listening to her vomiting. He put the baby into her cot and went out into the night to find Anna.

She was leaning against the rickety fence which bordered the vegetable patch. Her arms were folded against the pain of the obscenity revisited, but finally confronted.

Sam looked up into the brilliant night sky. The stars were close enough to touch. From beside him came her soft, shaking voice: 'He cannot say it was you.'

'He has.'

'What will we do?'

Sam reached for her. She didn't pull away. She clung to him. 'I'll think of something.'

Her sniffles were moist, and his strength somehow melting, being absorbed by her. He didn't mind, he needed something to hold almost as badly as she did.

'You are so calm, so strong,' she whispered.

'Yeah, well, it could be worse.'

'Do you really think so?'

Sam pushed her away and looked down into her eyes. 'We're not dead, yet.'

And he smiled. In his reassuring squeeze lay an unspoken promise. Anna felt it and took strength from it. And it seemed as if an immense weight had lifted. Even if the aching remained, it was, by far, less intense.

'Do you feel better now?' he asked.

'Yes, I think so, although my side still hurts.'

'I didn't mean that.'

'Oh,' she said. 'Yes, Sam, I feel much better now.'

'I told you you would,' he said quietly, his voice almost amused. What was there to be amused about? Anna didn't know and nor did she care. She rested her head against his shoulder once more, and felt his hand stroking her hair.

Anna listened to the baby's steady breathing, to the creaks and groans the old shack made in the wind, to the occasional pop and fizz of the dying fire. Sam was talking in his sleep, nothing she could understand of course. He seemed restless down there on the floor. Was he planning something? She thought she'd seen something in his eyes, in his tiny smile as he blew out the light. His repeated promise, *I'll think of something*, echoed into her mind.

If he'd used the past tense, perhaps she would have believed it. He had thought of something. But like any man, he wouldn't tell her until he was ready, if he decided she needed to know. And whatever he was planning or had planned was for her, a stranger. She thought she knew how men reasoned. She wondered if he, or any man for that matter, felt the same emotions for their thought processes were certainly different. Women weren't supposed to think or worry, women were supposed to accept and not question a man's wisdom.

A man's wisdom?

It certainly hadn't felt wise when Michael had sold off most of her things to finance the expedition to Bitter Creek, or Paradise as he'd called it then. No companies to work for, what a man dug from the ground was his and with it he would accomplish . . .

With it he would die. Because of it he would die.

Anna had begged him not to sell the music box. It had been her grandmother's. The pleas were ignored, so were her tears. He'd promised to buy

167

her a hundred music boxes, perhaps her own orchestra. But gold was of no use to him now.

Anna rolled to her side, and tried to block the image of the little girl who walked down the front path, winding up the small, gold-embossed box. Faint tinkles of 'Für Elise' faded and so did Anna. She dreamt of nothing, and woke tired with sunlight across her eyes.

Sam was singing in a booming deep voice, *Way, hey and up she rises early in the morning*.

Susan was cackling with laughter.

Anna rose from the bed and peered out the door. They were both stark naked in the creek. And a smile lit her face.

'Good morning,' Anna chirped to Sam's deeply tanned back and very white behind. The sound of her voice alarmed him. He spun around, joyous baby shielding privates. Anna had seen men blush before but nothing was comparable to this. For a moment, she wondered what he would do if she took Susan away. The thought coerced an inward grin and a feeling of wonderful devilish amusement.

'Morning, ma'am. When she woke she was covered in . . . yeah, well, this is the easy way of givin' her a bath.'

Anna could have waited there for a long time if she'd wanted to; his embarrassment was extreme. 'Would you show me how to make those things we had yesterday morning?'

'What, flapjacks?' Sam asked, wishing she'd go away.

'Yes. I liked them.'

Jesus, Sam thought. She's going to stand there all day. Any other lady would blush and run off, but somehow he didn't think she would. 'I was thinking,' he said and wished he hadn't because she came closer. The baby was slippery as hell and squirming to get back into the water. 'I've got paper and stuff if you want to use it.'

'Is it stolen?'

'Well, depends what you mean by stolen.'

'That would be nice, Sam. Thank you. Are you sure you're managing there? I can take Susan and finish her bath if you like.'

'No, no, it's fine. No problem. We've done this before, haven't we, kid?'

With a grin, Anna turned and walked away. His relief was overwhelming.

Anna watched from the seclusion of the hut as Sam put the baby on the grass and dried himself. He almost fell over three times while trying to squeeze his pants on over damp flesh and stop Susan crawling away as well. His modesty amused her. Michael had had none at all. Oh, he'd been attractive in a strange way, but Sam? She wondered if all the stories were true. Of course they were. She recognised what she'd felt the day she first saw him. Any woman would have secret cause to wonder what his touch would be like. He'd touched her hand and had stolen her heart with his eyes.

Something about him was instantly pleasing.

There was nothing of that, now. Not on his part, anyway. She was here because for now there was nowhere else to go and he knew that. When she was well again, would he send her away?

They were coming inside now. Anna turned away and pretended to be busy. She was becoming very good at that lately.

'So you wanna know how to slap up a flapjack, ma'am?' he said. Susan was hanging upside-down under his arm, his shirt was around his neck, his feet were bare. His damp chest glistened. What was mirrored in her eyes to make him smile at her like that?

'I only need to be shown once, Sam,' she said and reached for Susan, damp, heavy, pudgy, naked and dribbling. Always dribbling.

'She bit me,' Sam said as he slipped his shirt on and didn't button it. 'You should have called her Gator.'

'Gator?' Anna asked as she dressed the baby and brushed her wet hair.

'Yeah, it's short for alligator. I nearly got ate by a twenty-footer in the Everglades when I was a kid.'

It would have spat you out, she thought. 'What on earth is the Everglades?'

'Remind me to tell you one day,' he said, and went about concocting his flapjacks.

Anna watched. He cooked as she did—a handful of this, a bit of that . . . Mostly, she watched his face, rather serious when he thought she wasn't watching, and the opposite when she was. You're a strange man, Sam, she thought. There's a lot more to you than you want to show the world. When are you going to show me?

Susan loved his flapjacks. The little monster accepted everything Sam put into her mouth. A little jealousy rose yet again. Why did this man take more interest in the child than her own father had? He seemed to love her, yet he shouldn't.

'You look tired,' Sam said quietly as Anna took his empty plate away. He was still fussing. Would he never stop?

'I'm fine, really.'

'I'll go get that paper for you. I don't think I got a diary, won't know till I have a look.'

'A diary?'

'Yours got burnt, didn't it?'

'How did you know?'

'I know a lot about you, ma'am. More than I should I guess.'

Before she could question him he was gone, disappearing into the mountainside again. Not for the first time did Anna wonder just what was up there.

While he was away, she changed her dress and tidied her hair. It still hurt to hold her arm high for any length of time, and in the end she admitted defeat and left her hair down. Who was here to see such impropriety? Sam wouldn't notice if she were bald, barefoot or naked.

He wondered why he was doing this. Perhaps it'd give her something to do. Sam dragged out the stolen box he'd in turn stolen from Spencer's Brook and he studied the contents in the half light of the entrance to the cave where most of his treasures were hidden.

Two years ago it all looked new, smelled new. Not now though. Two years ago, he'd wondered where Luke had got it and what use this stuff would be to him, and then he'd heard about the wagon that went over the side and ended wheels-up in Dun's Gully. It was probably an order going through to the store at Callandoon.

People helped themselves in situations like that.

By the look of the stash at Spencer's Brook, Luke was helping himself to a lot lately. Then again, Sam didn't know why he decided to steal this box instead of the jewellery. He looked down at the collection of brushes, oils, papers and inks. At least someone would be using them.

Sam carried the box from his cave. Getting down the hill was a hell of a lot easier than climbing up, especially when he slipped and rolled most of the way.

He'd expected her reaction, but not his. She was speechless, and so was he. All he'd seen was the hair, so dark it was nearly black, and it cascaded all the way to her hips. She was wearing Elizabeth's pale green dress, and Elizabeth had never worn it as well. Ever. He swallowed his heart before it burst. He couldn't take his eyes off her.

'Oh, Sam you startled me. What's this?'

He opened the box and stood back.

For a minute or two he was sure she'd leap up and kiss him, so he retreated to the door and watched as she rummaged through the wares like a kid at Christmas.

'What sort of stuff do you draw, anyway?' he asked.

'You'll laugh.'

'We could both use a good laugh right now.'

'Michael used to say I was wasting my time.'

'I'm not Michael.'

'Promise me you won't laugh?'

Smiling, Sam promised.

'One day, Sam Manning, I'm going to have my very own shop.'

He didn't see anything funny in that. 'What sort of shop?'

'Annabelle's Millinery.'

'Hats?' he asked.

'Oh yes, hats. Hats and more hats. I see them. I draw them. All I need is someone who can make them, but I shall find that someone one day. Some of my best designs were burnt. I kept them in my diary. They're still in here, though,' she said and tapped her head.

'So you'll make hats and sell 'em, right?'

'Do you think it's silly?'

'Hell, no. Why should I? I just never met anyone who wanted to make hats before.'

'And I've never met a bushranger before. Especially one who used to be a trooper.' Here we go, he thought.'

'Why is it the traps haven't found where you live?'

'I'm smart and they're lazy.'

Anna resumed unpacking the box. 'I think it's because you used to be a trooper, and you know how they think and what they're likely to do.'

'Yeah?' he asked, hiding a grin.

'Why won't you tell me very much about yourself?'

Sam squatted by the door and studied his hands. 'Maybe you shouldn't know. Maybe it's safer that way.'

'For heaven's sakes, Sam, I'm dead. How much safer do you want?'

'Maybe it's not the first time I've been accused of murder.'

'Are you having a joke with me?'

He shrugged but in his eyes lay the truth. He was not joking at all.

'I used to be married, you know.'

'Yes, I've seen her photograph. There.' Anna pointed to the mantelpiece.

'That's not Elizabeth. That's my mother.'

'Oh. I thought—'

'Sometimes thinking can be bad for your health.'

'But these clothes are your wife's, are they not?'

He nodded.

'Where is she now?'

'She's dead. That's why I'm here. Doin' what I do.'

For a moment there was silence.

'You were accused of murdering your wife?'

'Aha.'

'Did you?'

'Did I what?'

'Murder your wife?'

'I don't know,' was all he said.

'Sam—'

'It's a long story, Anna.'

'And we have nothing left but time.'

'Maybe not a lot of that, either.'

'What do you mean?'

'It's all happening again. It's time it was over, girl,' he said quietly and stood up. 'He's pushed me a bit too far this time.'

'Who?'

'Luke Hannaford.'

Her face paled at the mention of the name. 'How well do you know him?'

'We used to be friends. We used to work together.'

'Elizabeth knew him, too?'

Sam was terribly quiet. Such an innocent question hurt him so much. 'You're better off not knowing, ma'am.'

Sooner or later, she thought, I shall discover what you refuse to tell me. I can wait patiently. She turned her attentions back to the box of artist brushes and paints.

'Sam, I've been thinking. Surely there's someone who can help us?'

'An escaped murderer and a dead woman? Yeah, of course there's someone who can help us.' He was being sarcastic.

'Perhaps if I sent a letter to the Commissioner of Police in Brisbane?'

'And tell him what?'

'I'd tell him exactly what happened.'

'Sure, Anna. That'd be good. Luke'd be made officially aware you're not dead, and the search'd be intensified.'

But she had a good idea. Commissioner Seymour was new to a new position, but what sort of man was he? Anyone's guess. A letter, signed, dated, chances are it wouldn't even arrive before Christmas. No return address. Cormac could post it next time he went to Warwick. A miracle might occur and Anna Hall might be believed, even if she was never found.

If she said she was supposed to be buried at Bitter Creek, it might even mean an exhumation of a body from an empty grave. It might mean a lot of things. Would they take it seriously at Headquarters?

'Sam, what do you think?'

Sam turned to her. 'The Commissioner's name is Seymour. That's all I know. But you better write that letter soon, girl. They'll be gettin' ready for the Duke.'

'Pardon?'

'The Duke of Edinburgh's comin' next year.'

'You live in this isolation yet you know about that?'

'I don't steal the mail for nothing,' he said with a grin.

'Sam, are you asleep?' The question filtered in through the murk.

'Aha,' he mumbled.

'Sam, I didn't know what to say.'

'Huh?'

'In the letter. I tried, but all I could manage was, "My dear Commissioner Seymour".'

'Oh.'

'Sam, I've never written to someone like that before.'

'First time for everything,' he mumbled and rolled over.

'Do you think he'd believe me?'

No. 'Of course he will. It's the truth.'

'But I was thinking, if the Duke of Edinburgh is coming, the Commissioner may be too busy to take much notice. He might think it's a joke. And take no notice at all.'

'At least you'll know you tried.'

'I don't think I have that much faith any more, Sam.'

'Makes two of us, Anna.'

There was silence for a long time, and again Sam was woken by her soft voice.

'Sam, are you asleep?'

'Aha.'

'Is the floor very hard?'

'Aha.'

'You could sleep here if you want. I can move over.'

His eyes opened wide. Had he heard right? He rolled over and in the dark he could see her, staring at the ceiling. She turned her head to him. 'I won't mind, if you don't. I've already rearranged your life too much, the least I can do is give you your bed back.'

'It's okay, I don't mind.' A lie of course. His back was breaking.

'Yes, you do. You wish you'd never seen me.'

'That's not true.'

'Doesn't your back ache?'

Against his better judgment, Sam brought his blanket with him. Anna rolled to her side and faced the wall with a sigh. Sam lay on top of the covers and faced the opposite way.

She smelled so good.

'Goodnight, Sam.'

He made a noise that could have meant anything. Sleep now eluded him completely. What'd she think he was? Made of steel? What'd she want by this, anyway? Was she expecting something to happen here?

Anna rolled over and flung her arms across his side. He froze. But nothing happened. Time passed slowly. He wasn't game to move at all. Soft snores now. Easing his tension.

And he wondered what was wrong. He'd imagined this the first time he'd seen her. He imagined her beside him, curled against him, quietly sleeping. The snores ended when she changed position yet again and curled into his back. Her body heat was intense. It matched his. Breasts pushed into his back and he was rising to the occasion. Sam smiled to himself. He could, if he wanted to.

He rolled to face her. She didn't frighten but she didn't wake either. Even when she was sleeping she trusted him. She knew he'd rather die than hurt her. She cuddled closer. Her breath was hot against his shoulder. He put his arms around her. Still she didn't wake. But Sam wouldn't have known if she had. He was already asleep.

Until she had another nightmare.

Sam woke, heart thudding from the scream in his ear. 'Anna, it's okay. It's all right.' He was used to this. It happened every night, but tonight she reached blindly for him in the darkness and his touch eased her panic, the shaking. Within moments it had all faded. 'It's okay now, it's gone.'

He pulled her closer, his body was hot and hard, yet soft and comforting, too.

'S'okay,' he whispered sleepily, hot breath in her hair. 'You're not alone any more.'

Anna whispered his words in her sleep.

Ten

It took a week to write the letter and Anna tested every word of it on Sam. 'But why tell him where I used to live in Brisbane?' she'd asked.

'So it's easy to check.'

'Oh.'

The letter told of the journey to Bitter Creek, the baby's birth date, how much gold they'd recovered. She named most of the diggers, but no, Sam didn't think it neccesary to tell the Commissioner in three thousand words how Dinny died. She had to keep it as short as possible. 'But why?'

'If he's like me, he hates reading, and writing's even worse.'

'Oh.'

'Just the facts, Anna.'

But it was all fact and she thought every detail was all important and relevant, until she had to account for the day of the raid. It took her three silent days to write of the nightmare that had almost killed her. She hadn't read any of this section out to Sam. Rather she gave him the papers dated 28 October 1867, and went for a walk. She didn't return for a long time. As he read, he knew why.

He hoped against hope her efforts wouldn't be wasted and burnt along with the rest of the week's garbage.

When Anna did return she asked if he was able to get fabric for curtains. He said he already had some. On hearing that she lost interest in curtain-making and took down to the creek the easel Sam had made for her. She spent the rest of the day on her own, drawing. She didn't want to talk. Again, he knew why.

Mid-afternoon, Sam took her a mug of tea. Sketched on the paper he saw Girraween Mountain. Three hours later when he came to tell her Susan was awake, the mountain had been discarded for a shop. The sign on it read: Annabelle's Mil

'Is that it?' Sam asked.

'What?' she asked, her concentration broken, and suddenly tired. She looked exhausted. He had the urge to touch her hair so he plunged his hands into his pockets.

'Your dream. Is that it?'

Anna looked down at her drawing. It wasn't quite what she could see in her mind when she closed her eyes, but it was as close as she could make it. 'I don't know, Sam. Do dreams come true or not?'

Sam couldn't stand it any longer. He reached for the mass of hair that hung to her hips. It was soft, shining. He wanted to brush it for her, not answer her question because he wasn't qualified. None of his dreams ever came true, but that didn't mean hers wouldn't. 'It's getting dark.'

'I won't be much longer.'

'Okay.'

Anna watched him walk off; a casual impish walk, neither hurried nor slow. She wasn't used to this, being brought tea, being offered encouragement, being brought back to reality so softly. It felt good. Very good. There was no hurry, no pressure, no guilt. He let her be what she wanted to be.

When she finally came in, supper was ready. Guilt rose automatically. 'You're not angry?' she asked when she sat. The sight of the tinned meat didn't whet her appetite at all.

'I figured you needed some time to yourself but—'

'But? I'm wasting my time living in dreams, correct?'

'Suzie needs you. Sometimes dreams have to wait.'

'It won't happen again.'

'What?'

'I won't do it again. I won't go off to draw or paint or think. I lose track of time, I'm sorry.'

'If you don't stop saying sorry all the time, I will get angry. It's not for me to tell you what to do. You wanna draw? Go for it. I'm just saying Suzie needs you, too.'

'Do you need me, Sam?'

Sam looked at her as if she'd hit him with something spiky. 'Well, I'd probably miss you if you weren't here,' he said after careful consideration. Trouble brewed if a woman didn't feel wanted. 'I gotta go away again tomorrow, so if there's something you need, you better write it down now. I'll be gone before you wake.'

'Is it Wednesday again?' Anna asked, eyes not matching the innocence in her voice.

Sam kept eating. It was best to ignore her little pokes even if they were barbed.

'If you find the fabric for me, there'll be curtains when you come home.'

'Curtains?'

'Don't you want curtains?' she asked, and because of the question he knew *she* did, and come hell or high water she wouldn't stop nagging until she had curtains.

'I suppose this place needs something.'

A fire, Anna thought, but asked: 'Is the fabric blue?'

He shrugged.

'Is it in the cave on the hill where you go so often?'

He nodded and kept eating.

'Can I come?'

'Where?'

'When you go to get the material for the curtains.'

He shook his head.

'Why not?'

'You'd break your neck, that's why not.'

'You don't want me to see what you've hidden up there.'

'Exactly.'

'You don't trust me.'

'Anna, no. Are you hearing me? No.'

It sounded very final so she let the silence brew for a while. Unfortunately, Sam didn't notice it. He was too busy eating to see her hurt expression. It was wasted. 'Sam?' she asked. He looked up in instant recognition of the tone. She wanted something again.

'Please be careful tomorrow and don't do anything too strenuous.'

'Who, me?'

'Helping beautiful ladies from mail coaches would be strenuous, would it not?'

'Where'd you hear things like that?'

Anna smiled and kept silent.

'It's just gossip,' Sam said and couldn't look her in the eye for long. 'Stories. What folks don't know they make up.'

'Promise me you'll take care.'

'I'll try.'

'Sam, you may not have as many friends as you think.'

'I'm not used to people fussin' over me. I'm not dead yet.'

'It's not fuss. It's concern. I like you. I always have.'

Her offhand remark was planned to hit hard. 'Don't say things like that.'

'Why? You told me to keep it factual.'

'Anna, everything, everyone, I get close to either gets hurt or dies. You understand?' There was silence for a moment. 'I'll be leaving early. I'll try not to wake you.'

'Mama! It's Sam!'

Oh Lord, not more trouble, Sheila thought and stopped hoeing. Sam swung Leonie up onto the horse and she clung tightly. 'Any sweets for me, Sam?'

'Sorry, sweetheart, not this time. Give me a kiss instead.' Leonie was set back to the ground after a quick peck on the cheek.

'How's the lass, then?' Sheila asked.

'Sheila, you taught her how to nag.'

His bright smile told her all was well, very well apparently. More than casual interest arose.

'Is Cormac around?'

'Down by the creek.'

'Good.' Sam turned the horse towards the south.

'Sam, you get back here!'

The horse came to a halt. Sheila walked to Sam and grabbed the reins so he couldn't escape so quickly. 'Would your lass be feeling like some female company?'

'She's not my lass, Sheila.'

'You know what I mean.'

'I think Anna might appreciate a visit. See you later.'

Off the horse walked once more.

'I don't suppose it's wise asking where you'd be heading this fine Wednesday?'

'Is it really Wednesday?' Sam quipped and rode on to find Cormac and ask him to deliver the favour that sat, neatly addressed, in his pocket.

Cormac wasn't 'down by the creek' at all. Cormac was nowhere to be seen. Sam was already late. Far too late. Dammit, he thought. I'll come back on the way home.

Daniel glanced at the time and scratched his leg. Damn the mosquitoes. James wasn't getting eaten alive. Daniel had long since lost concentration on the trooper's conversation. He'd have talked if he had company or not. Daniel filled the gaps with noises of appreciation for courageous efforts—secretly he thought most of the anecdotes were fantasy or plain stupidity. No wonder the sarge didn't come on this wishful escapade. Daniel doubted Manning would show anyway.

James Smith-Johnson had been sent south-west for one reason, perhaps two. He was a walking disaster and his constant talk gave everyone a headache. Daniel didn't say much and he was a quick learner. Smith-Johnson was a corporal and outranked him marginally. And Billy kept well clear of them both.

Daniel sighed. He'd rather be out walking with Maddy Hannaford. At least she didn't talk a lot, and what she had to say usually made some sense. Daniel wondered how she was, as he chewed on a stalk of wire grass.

'Daniel, I don't want to go.'

'You'll be all right, Maddy. It's not forever.'

'You've never met my aunt,' she'd pouted. He'd ruffled her hair. 'Will you still go to the dance at Yarrawonga?'

'I'll probably be working.'

He'd wondered why she'd beamed so. If he wasn't on duty that evening, he'd take Nelly providing Rose set her free for one night. Did Maddy think he would take her to the dance? The thought frightened him.

'Will you miss me, Daniel?'

'Of course I will.' He didn't say why. He'd rather muck out the stables than the cells. She always offered to do it for him. He did like Maddy. She seemed the sister he never had. She knew her place in life, she was easy to talk to and never, as far as he knew, betrayed a confidence. Perhaps the coach carried a letter from her today?

Funny how he missed not having her about.

'What's this Manning bastard really like, Dan?'

Daniel closed his eyes. Nelly called him Danny, acceptable only from Nelly's little mouth during their heated copulations on paydays. No one, but no one, called him Dan. It was Brannigan, or Daniel or Constable or 'Where the hell are you, you little snake-eyed bastard!' when the sergeant needed someone to kick.

'I don't know what Manning's like,' Daniel lied. True, he'd never spoken to him. Their meetings had been from a distance, yet Daniel was sure he knew the man. Manning's destiny in life was to torment the police, and with his torment came a mountain of paperwork. Whenever something went missing, Sam was automatically accused, convicted and, when caught, he'd surely hang.

Especially now.

The sergeant's evidence was closely guarded, under lock and key. Or otherwise, non-existent. He prayed the Sub-Inspector would be coming back very soon. Sanity might return. The tension at work was getting unbearable.

'How did Manning kill his wife?' James asked.

'I don't know. He's wanted in Victoria, not Queensland.'

'You don't think he did it, do you, Danny?'

'Did what?'

'Bitter Creek.'

'No one gives a pig's fart what I think, Corporal.'

Corporal? James pulled a face and rolled a cigarette, asking, 'What's the sarge's problem?'

'Sam Manning.'

'No, it's deeper than that.'

'Look, James, I gave up trying to understand Luke

184

a year ago. Thinking about it just gives me a headache and so do you.'

Daniel watched the road for signs of the coach. Usually there was a cloud of white dust first, then the horses were heard. And in the sudden quiet, Daniel sensed a presence.

Sam was nearby, waiting, too.

His heart thudded. Daniel was torn. The revelation hit. He was getting as bad as the townsfolk and squatters who protected Manning, who saw him as some kind of hero or saviour. They were misguided poor creatures, all of them.

'Here it comes,' Daniel said.

James looked up.

'It's late again,' Daniel observed and made no move to rise.

'What are we waiting for?' The corporal rose quickly and, checking his pistol for the hundredth time, he walked to his horse.

'No, James. If he stops the coach we wait until he has a mailbag, then we attempt to take him. Those were the orders.'

'Orders be damned. The reward's mine.'

'I wouldn't if I was you.'

'You're not me. Get your horse and move. Now.'

'This is a mistake.'

'He's mine.'

Sam covered his face with his scarf and kicked the grey into a canter the moment he saw the coach crest the hill and slow with a squealing of brakes for the rough crossing. There was a new driver, the lookout was armed. The coach must have been carrying something or someone very important indeed.

'Just the mailbag, friend,' Sam called and pointed his pistol at both men on the coach. A heartbeat of time would decide their fates or their reflexes would decide for him. Something was wrong. He knew that now. He should have let the coach go on its way. He should have trusted his instincts. Troopers. They were troopers. Anna's gentle warning echoed in his head. He turned the grey and fled.

The driver reached for another weapon as the first bullet hit Sam's left arm. He fell forward. The letter dropped from his pocket. Sam kicked the horse into a canter down the creek, turning, firing blindly, pain filling senses. His right side took a second bullet. Volleys of hot lead fizzed by. Sam kept as low as he could, knowing if he came off now he was dead. The survival instinct outweighed all terror.

'Is he dead?'

Smith-Johnson's body lay in a tangle, still. Very still.

'I didn't mean to shoot him. I didn't mean it, he got in the bloody way.'

Daniel looked up into Porter's face. He'd known something like this would happen. The new boy, Porter. It was the sarge's idea he pose as the driver. The idiot couldn't pose for a photograph. Useless. Proof lay at Daniel's feet. Smith-Johnson, shot in the back. There was no heartbeat. Daniel hadn't expected to feel any life. Daniel looked about for Billy. He wasn't there. 'Where'd he go!'

'After Manning. I think he was hit.'

'Get the body in the coach and get out of my sight.'

Daniel waited for the coach to pull out and continue on its way. He picked up the dirty letter, stamped now with the imprint of his boot. The others hadn't seen it drop from Manning's coat. Daniel had. He looked at it now.

The Commissioner of Police.

Headquarters.

Brisbane.

There was a small, bright bloodstain on it. So the

Phantom of the Mountains did bleed after all?

Daniel cursed and angry tears welled. He tucked the letter into his coat pocket and called for Billy. There was no reply except his own echoing voice. There was nothing but silence, total, stark silence. He looked at the blood on the ground. One day, he thought, someone will listen to me.

Sam felt the warmth of blood trickling from his hips down into his boot as he clung tightly to the horse's neck.

Blood also dripped from his elbow on to the horse as she weaved her sure-footed way through the thick, rocky scrub. He heard another shot. Bark splintered inches from his face. He had no energy to return the fire. He was almost giving up. Almost.

Then came the memory of Anna's voice. *Do you need me Sam?*

Her voice was so clear in his head.

He felt the next bullet fizz past his nose. He felt its quick heat. Sam turned, lost his balance and fell, heavily. Eyes closed, he heard the horse's breathing, the squeak of the saddle as his pursuer dismounted. The cock of the pistol, the footsteps drawing nearer. Nearer.

As he opened his eyes and lifted the rock at his fingertips, Sam thought of Anna getting raped while this bastard watched. Maybe even helped.

It was over in an instant. The rock hit Billy's happy and then surprised face. The cheek and nose shattered, blood sprayed and he came down heavily across Sam.

Sam wriggled out from under the weight and lay quietly waiting for the others. But there was no sound at all. The grey and Moonshine's horse were both hunting for grass. Sam whistled, the grey obeyed the call. She nuzzled him but Sam lay on his side, barely able to move for a little while. He pulled his scarf off and gasped for air. The horse nuzzled at him to get back on. Sam touched his right hip. His belt was torn, holed. The flesh felt cut, scorching. Pain incinerated his entire side as he tried to get up. He couldn't move the fingers of his left hand. Somehow, he managed to tie the scarf around his bicep and, finally, he reached for the dragging reins. Sam pulled himself to his feet and stumbled. Concentrating all efforts, he slumped into the saddle once more and tried to focus, to get his bearings. He sighted the hazy outline of Girraween Mountain to the north-east. It was unmistakable. It was home, and in a couple of hours he'd either be home or dead.

Anna didn't hear the buggy or the woman enter. If the baby's rhythmic breathing had altered in any way, she'd have been awake instantly. But she was so tired, lately. She'd only wanted to take a short nap while Susan slept after lunch.

Anna woke with a scream from the hand on her shoulder. The scream frightened Sheila as well. 'Lordy girl, it's only me.'

'Oh, Sheila . . . I must have fallen asleep.'

'With this heat it's no wonder. Sam's been telling me you're fit now?'

'Oh, you've seen him?'

'Aye. But this morning, lass.'

'Is Cormac with you? Young Leonie?'

'No, no. Think I'd bring them along to hear them whine and moan about wanting to go home again? I came to chat and have a cup of tea. I came to see if it was true that you're better now.' Basically, she'd come for a gossip.

'I'm fine, Sheila. Really.'

'So I see,' Sheila said, glancing around the interior of Sam's ramshackle house. It was easy to see a woman resided here now. 'You'll be doing too much too soon, lass.'

'I can't be doing nothing all day, Sheila.'

'Ha, you even sound like Sam.'

Horror crossed Anna's face. 'Tell me it's not true?' she begged.

Sheila didn't reply but she did smile, teasingly. 'Where's my tea, then?'

Anna set about making tea. She did have one cake to offer, unless Sam had eaten it for breakfast. Anna searched in vain. Sam had found it. 'Oh dear—'

'Don't you be worrying over food now, lass. I brought along a basket of baking for you all,' Sheila said and looked down on Susan, who was sleeping thumb in mouth, bottom raised high. 'My, she's a pretty little thing. And isn't she growing, too.'

'She has Sam running all the time.'

'And how is he?'

'With Sam it's hard to tell. He doesn't say much. I fear there's an almighty temper there somewhere, Sheila. No one can remain as calm as he can for very long.'

'I've not seen a temper yet,' Sheila said.

'And how long have you known him?' Anna asked.

'Long enough,' came the reply. Sheila settled into the rocker. Anna hoped it would hold her bulk. 'And what might your plans be, lass?'

'Plans?'

'Lord knows you can't stay here.'

Surely that's none of your business? Anna wondered but didn't voice her thoughts. Sheila meant no harm. 'I try not to think of tomorrows, Sheila. Do you think Susan is fat enough for a baby her age? Should she be trying to walk? She's nine months old.'

'Baby's fine. It's you I'm concerned about.'

'Please don't be.'

It was becoming harder to stay polite.

'Do you not think it's time to talk?'

'About what?'

'Losing your husband of course. I can't sympathise for I don't know what I'd feel if I lost Cormac.'

'I feel nothing,' Anna said quietly and simply.

'Oh, you will in time. You will. It happened so quickly, lass, you've had no time to mourn.'

'Mourn? How can you mourn the death of someone you barely knew? I didn't like my husband at all. Perhaps in a way I loved him, but there's nothing left to mourn. If there is any sadness it's from the brutal, Godless way he died.'

Sheila didn't know what to say. She certainly hadn't expected this. 'Anna, surely you should be thinking of your future? What about your baby?'

Anna thought the question was amusing. 'My baby? Sam's a better mother than I am or could ever hope to be. Lord knows, she likes him better anyway. Perhaps I should just go away and leave them both together. Perhaps he should never have found me. Everything that's happened is because of me. How do you have your tea?'

'However it comes.'

Sheila watched as Anna's shaking hands poured strong brewed tea from a billy tin.

'Oh, if only I'd never set eyes on Sam Manning, none of this would have happened!'

Sheila took the tea Anna gave her and gazes locked. 'You worry about the things you can change, lass and only that. You have more than you think. You have Sam.'

'Of course. Sam. Sam who's been accused of the slaughter at Bitter Creek when it was none of his doing. Such is justice.'

Sheila's mouth opened wide.

'You didn't know? Sam hasn't told you?'

Sheila shook her head.

'Then you wouldn't know that I'm supposed to be dead and so is my baby. For all of this, we have Lucas Hannaford to thank. Perhaps now you'll see how futile it would be for me to make plans for myself and Susan.'

'It's Lucas Hannaford's doing?' Sheila asked, her voice a squeak, her eyes even wider than before. 'And Sam knows of this?'

'Yes,' Anna whispered quietly. 'Yes. But how to prove his innocence? It's as if he doesn't care. He tells me not to worry, he'll think of something. And he keeps smiling. How can he? If he's caught, he'll hang.'

Sheila sipped her tea and sighed. ''Tis a mess, to be sure.'

Anna silently agreed.

'So old Luke says you'd be dead, then? I never thought he'd go this far.'

'You know him, too?'

'Ah, who about here doesn't? 'Tis the worst criminal who wears a uniform, Anna. Perhaps that's why we love Sam. At least he's an honest thief. My God, you must be special.'

'Me?'

'You're wearing Elizabeth's dress. Has he told you about her yet?'

'Only that he was accused of her murder.'

'Another lie from Hannaford's tongue.'

'Do you know what happened? Sam won't tell me.'

'Perhaps no one will ever know what really happened but let me tell you something, now, and you'll swear it wasn't me who told you. Months ago when Sam came to visit, he told us about the most beautiful woman he'd ever seen. How she was married to a man who beat her and made her wear man's clothes while she dug in the dirt for gold he'd probably claim as his own. Besotted, he was.'

'Sam talked of me?'

'Constantly. He loved you then, he loves you now. And if he could hear you talking the way you've been talking, his heart would break. He's a good man, Anna. Deep down, he's a good man. Confused and perhaps misguided, but good all the same.'

'He's a thief.'

'Aye, he's a thief. For a reason. We all have our ghosts. If you're destined to run and hide for the rest of your life, so be it. You'll not be alone if Sam's claimed you, and claimed you he has. You're here are you not? He didn't have to take you in but he didn't think twice. Call him what you will but he's a good man. And it's not for me to tell you things which will certainly come from him when he thinks you should know and not before.'

Anna's head was swimming with confusion. 'I feel such a fool.'

'Don't we all?' Sheila's eyes were smiling now.

'Do you think he's handsome, Sheila?'

'Now that's an obvious question with an obvious answer, lass.'

'The first time I saw him I thought my heart would explode. It pounded so hard I was sure he'd hear it.'

'He probably could,' Sheila said with another smile. 'Funny, though, he said the same thing to us. Tell me, is he still sleeping on the floor?'

Anna didn't reply. She smiled into her tea instead and winced when Sheila's huge, calloused hand slapped her knee, hard.

'You little devil,' the Irishwoman cackled.

Susan woke from the thunder of laughter.

Lucas was sipping on a watered rum, and meaning to have a word to Rose about the quality of her liquor, when the coach rattled by and two of the new troopers jumped down and hurriedly approached. Lucas finished his drink, hid the glass in his desk drawer and met them at the door. Porter was very nervous, his face was white.

'Smith-Johnson's dead, Sergeant. Shot in the back. It was Manning.'

Lucas closed his eyes. The tale began—disjointed, excited. He held up his hand to halt the bombardment. 'Where's Brannigan?'

'He went off to find the tracker.'

'Moonshine isn't a tracker.'

'Sorry, sir.'

'Where's the body?'

'In the coach, sir.'

'Well, don't just stand there! Surely to God you know where to take it!'

Lucas sighed and returned to the relative cool of his office. Some time later, Bert Whipps came waddling in. 'Your mail, Sergeant.' A bundle of letters plopped to the desk. 'What's happening?' he asked as he watched from the window while the two new traps carried what looked to be a body across to Harry's.

'Manning again. Together, we'll watch him hang, Bert.' The postmaster left with a smile of satisfaction on his face.

Lucas sorted through the mail. Official, most of it and divided into two categories—that which could wait, forever if possible, and the rubbish. There was a letter in Maddy's neat hand for him and one in the same hand for Daniel. Lucas picked it up. He smelled it. Scent.

Scent?

He turned it over and was almost inclined to tear it open but no. No. There was a simple way to rectify this: kick Brannigan in the arse and threaten to castrate him if he ever, ever touched Maddy.

Lucas threw the letter onto the other table and opened his. Had it been from Jane he wouldn't have read it, not that she'd have time to write, thank God. Rachel would keep her busy enough. The thought of Jane's elder sister made his skin crawl. He could see them sitting on the huge verandah of the house overlooking the river, sipping dry sherry until they were both politely drunk. Rachel would spend every available moment reinforcing the notion that Jane should leave her husband, telling her relentlessly that she was not suited to be a pioneer's wife or a trap's for that matter.

Lucas knew exactly what Rachel Long needed. A man, preferably one who was blind, deaf and oversexed to give the haughty bitch what she needed. Give her something else to think about other than her little sister missing the good life.

He unfolded Maddy's letter.

Dear Papa,

I miss you terribly. Mother has told me I should write in case you are worried that we never arrived. The axle broke at Ipswich and we stayed in a wonderful hotel. It was much nicer there than here. Aunt Rachel hasn't changed at all, but we never expected her to, did we? They are rarely home and Ronald is not here to annoy me, either. He is away being taught how to build bridges.

Papa, I am a prisoner here. I want to come home, desperately. Christmas is close now and I don't want to spend it here alone. Lady McTaggart has invited Mother and Aunt Rachel for Christmas dinner, and there they shall all discuss some new charity. I would rather be with you at Christmas time for I love you dearly.

*I shall ask Mother if she will allow me to travel
alone so I can be with you at Christmas. She is so
busy I know she will say yes. Please do not worry
about me, Papa. I am not a child any more. I do
not need an adult to hold my hand.*

> *Until I see you again, soon,*
> *Your loving daughter,*
> *Maddy.*

PS Please give Daniel my regards.

Hannaford folded the letter, put it back into its
envelope and shoved the thing into his pocket. He
was on his way to Rose's for a double serving of
steak and kidney pie when he saw Brannigan coming
in. Alone. Lucas didn't go to meet him. The boy
looked as if a week's sleep was needed.

Daniel dismounted tiredly and waited for the
inevitable blast. Nothing came. 'Manning was
wounded. Billy's still out there somewhere tracking
the blood, I suppose. Although judging by how things
have been today, I wouldn't be surprised if
Moonshine's dead by now, too.'

'Have a drink with me, boy.'

'Yes, sir.' Daniel was relieved there wasn't any more
said. 'Sergeant?'

'What?' Lucas asked tiredly.

'Smith-Johnson. If he'd listened to me, he'd still
be alive. If he'd stopped to think about anything
except the bloody reward Porter's bullet wouldn't
have found him.'

'Porter's bullet? That's not what I was told.'

'Excuse me, sir?'

'It was Manning, Daniel. Manning killed Smith-
Johnson.'

'No. No, that's not—'

'Are you listening to me, Constable? Manning's bullet killed Smith-Johnson. That is what your report will state, too. Understood?'

Daniel led his horse away. He was suddenly deaf.

'Is that understood?'

Anna had felt this before—a dull-edged despair which had no apparent reason to exist. The sun was setting in bright red hues, spreading its bloodstain over the hilltop, flaming the trees, the mountains, the clouds. The very sky.

She sat by the creek on the huge rock she found comfortable, and from there she could, if she wanted, see for a full three hundred and sixty degrees. She would see anyone approaching, and the person she needed so badly to see right now was not coming.

'Where are you, Sam?' she whispered. Susan, bouncing up and down on her knee, turned at the words and she chewed on her fist and grinned at her mother. Anna closed her eyes and held the baby tightly. Susan sucked her thumb and rested her head against Anna's chest.

The despair welled again. Something had happened, there was no doubting it.

Anna waited until the sun was shielded by the granite surrounds. Tears filled her eyes for no apparent reason. Suddenly she was aware of the reason.

She'd been asleep when he'd left. She hadn't said goodbye. She hadn't said she didn't want him to go, that the precious letter could wait another week. Trust me, Sam, she'd have said. Please don't go. Not today. Something bad is going to happen. Don't go . . . Instead, she'd woken late to find a roll of moth-eaten blue cotton on the table, as well as a jug of goat's milk. Apart from the one cake left, he'd had no breakfast. And he'd taken all his weapons except for the shotgun. All this was hours ago.

Blue curtains now hung on the small window, and his favourite food was waiting. Feed him well, Sheila had said. Feed him well, he'll come back for more without fail. Look after him, he'll look after you. Most of all, be his friend.

Be his friend.

The table was set. She'd taken a bath, washed her hair. And waited.

She waited so long her imagination started going wild. 'Where is he, baby?' she whispered and cuddled the child closer still to find Susan was alseep. She'd spent all afternoon awake, trying to walk, and was exhausted.

Anna put her baby to bed, lit the lamp, stoked the fire and tidied the small table. It, too, was covered in blue cotton. The same blue as his eyes, well, almost. The colour of the cotton had faded with age. Sam's eyes only grew brighter with each passing day.

'Sam?'

Had she heard something? At last, he's home! She ran to the door and leaped the porch step. And didn't want to believe what she was seeing. She screamed his name.

The voice came to him from the edges. He tried to reply. Her scream chilled his blood. What was left of it. The cloud surrounding his eyes was grey and red, and he tried to relinquish his grip on the horse's mane but his fingers had locked.

Anna was running towards him, yelling things he couldn't understand. All he knew, he was home. Safe. Depending on how far behind Billy Moonshine was. Fingers let go and he slid off the horse.

'Oh my God, Sam—'

The strength she needed came from panic alone.

Anna dragged him across the hard ground, up the porch and, finally, inside. His heavy, limp body left a red smear across her clean floor. Anna didn't notice it. 'Talk to me, Sam, please talk to me!'

His eyes rolled. His voice was incoherent even to himself. He tried to tell her not to yell but his words were a slur of pain.

Anna, on her knees, managed to take the coat off, then his shirt. She looked at his side, the chunk of flesh that had been burnt away by the bullet. So much blood! Anna tried to sit him up, but he kept toppling over. 'Forgive me,' she whispered as she pulled his trousers off. He was in too much pain to object.

Anna scrambled for the spirits bottle, the bandages and one of Susan's clean nappies. She pressed it tightly against his side, the material flowered a bright red. She tipped a liberal amount of spirits into the raw bleeding wound. There was no scream. He caught his breath then passed out. For that Anna was pleased. And she didn't realise she was crying, not for a long time. She packed the wounds as best she could and balanced him so that his shoulders rested against the bed. He seemed to be breathing evenly enough. His eyes opened and tried to focus on her face.

'I told you to be careful. Why couldn't you be careful? Why didn't you listen to me, Sam?'

She untied the scarf which was soaked with blood. Anna peeled it off and closed her eyes momentarily. 'Oh, God.'

Sam mumbled something again. Why was he talking about the moon? 'Sh, be still and quiet.' Anna took her attentions back to the bullet wound in his arm. It seemed as though the bullet had hit from behind and had passed right through his arm. The hole at the front was twice as big as that at the back of his arm—raw, gaping, black. For a moment she thought she could see bone. She felt nauseous as she reached for the spirits again. 'Oh, Sam, forgive me.'

When the alcohol entered the wound, Sam hit. His right arm came from nowhere and he pushed violently as he screamed. Anna rolled three times and came to rest against the wall. Undeterred—she'd suffered far worse from a man and lived—she crawled back and grabbed his face between her hands. 'Sit still and let me finish this!' she yelled. 'If I don't help you, Sam you will bleed to death!'

He opened his eyes. Whose voice was that?

Anna?

He tried to say her name, tried to tell her Moonshine was following him.

'Sam please, if I don't stop this bleeding, you'll die! I don't want to hear about the moon!'

He didn't settle at all. Anna leant across him and grabbed another nappy from the dwindling pile. She folded it and wrapped it tightly around his arm. 'Can you hold this?'

Sam held it. 'Moonshine's comin'. Shotgun, get the shotgun.'

Anna secured the makeshift bandage. 'Is that too tight?'

'Get the shotgun! I'm being followed!'

Anna ran for the shotgun. 'What's happening, Sam!' she cried.

Sam tried to get up but the most he could do was fall onto the bed.

'Sam, tell me what's happened!'

There was no reply. He had passed out.

'Sam!'

Susan started to cry the moment Anna heard the movement outside.

Eleven

With effort and a lot of pain, Billy Moonshine got off the horse. The wad of rag he'd pressed to his face wasn't helping. Occasionally he saw double but not now.

There was the grey. Still saddled.

From inside the old hut, he could hear a baby crying. It was familiar, he'd heard it before, that cry.

Manning and the woman were here.

He saw where she'd dragged him in. Saw the blood.

The sarge'll promote me for sure, he thought.

Billy took his pistol out and moved quietly around the back of the hut. Through a slit in the curtains he could see her in there. Manning was face down on the bed. Bandaged up. Not moving.

Probably dead.

The thought made Billy smile.

Anna felt the stare from behind her. She turned and saw the silhouette. Swinging the shotgun to the window above Sam's head, she closed her eyes and pulled both triggers. The force sent her backwards into the wall. Glass shattered, a bullet cracked into the wall near her face.

Then there was silence.

Stark and echoing.

Her ears rang. She felt as if a horse had kicked her. Anna dropped the shotgun and covered her face with her hands. Only now was she aware of what she had done.

Susan had stopped crying. Her eyes were huge, her mouth was open.

Anna looked down at Sam. He wasn't moving but he was alive. She could see him breathing.

Have to see. Have to see . . . Anna took one hesitant step after another towards the door and she opened it. Barefooted, she stepped outside, past the bath tub, the woodpile. She peered around the corner.

In the twilight gloom she saw what was left of the Aboriginal trooper. His head was at an angle to the rest of his body. The shotgun's blast had caught him in the throat and had almost torn his head off. His eyes were open and staring at her.

Anna gagged. She couldn't even scream. Something momentarily died inside her, until common sense prevailed. If one had found them, how many more would be following?

Anna ran back inside, bolted the door and leaned against it, shaking; crying now, begging forgiveness.

'That was lovely, Mrs Macauley.'

'Did you have enough, Peter? Are you sure now?'

'Positive. Goodnight.'

Daniel, in his dressing gown, left the table and walked down the hall towards the room he rented from the old, senile widow Macauley. Sometimes she thought he was her lawyer son from Sydney, the one who never visited but sometimes sent money. Mainly it was Daniel's rent which kept them both eating. When she called him Peter, he knew it made her old heart happy if he played along with the role.

'And where's my kiss?'

Daniel turned, walked back and kissed the old woman's forehead. She pinched his cheek in return, and with a smile they went their separate ways, she to the kitchen to wash dishes, he to his room to read.

It had taken half an hour of fast talking to convince the sergeant he had no romantic notions about Maddy. At least his lies calmed the storm before it appeared. Lately, Daniel thought he was becoming a pretty good liar.

Since late afternoon, he hadn't had time to scratch his nose let alone read his mail. Maddy's letter seemed lighter than the one he'd picked up out of the dirt at Mitchell's Crossing. Daniel took off his dressing gown and put the lamp nearer the window. He was sweating again. A breeze caught and cooled his skin. Daniel opened Maddy's scented letter and quickly read it. He had a quiet chuckle at her grizzlings about her aunt and life in general, and he was glad the sarge hadn't read it when he got to the part that said, *So for Christmas, all I want is a kiss in the stables.*

If she said some funny things, she wrote worse.

By now, everyone in town would know Maddy Hannaford sent perfumed letters to Daniel Brannigan. The gossips would have them married before much longer. Daniel put the letter back into its envelope. He'd write back tonight, he decided, and give her something to anticipate when she came home. If she wasn't on her way back already.

He put thoughts of Maddy aside and picked up the letter addressed to the Commissioner. This was the one he'd been busting to read all damned day.

Curiosity overcame guilt. It was an offence to open other people's mail but Manning had dropped it. It could be crucial, he told himself. Crucial to what, exactly?

The handwriting seemed to be a female's. Neat and precise. Daniel swept over the words and frowning, he flicked through the six pages of the letter for the signature at the end.

Anna Hall?

Hall . . . Bitter Creek? His heart leapt to his ears.

The words were digested, sentence by sentence, paragraph by paragraph. The light flickered in the breeze and he turned all the pages face down.

Finished. Daniel rubbed at his unshaven face.

He pictured Anna Hall in his mind. He remembered her very well—how could he forget? The licence check, a month before the massacre. She was panning, oblivious to the leech on her wrist. She was sunburnt, dirty but somehow very attractive. Twenty-three at the most. Before her confrontation with the sergeant she'd smiled at Daniel shyly and his heart had turned a full circle in his chest. Oh, yes, he remembered Anna Hall.

And Bitter Creek. But Billy and the sarge with four others?

Daniel chewed on his thumbnail and stared out into the night.

So she was raped and stabbed.

The sarge gave the orders.

It was more than possible. Nothing that man could do would surprise Daniel. But no. No, it had to be some kind of fantasy.

Anna Hall is dead.

Is she? Did you see the body?

No, but Billy . . . his thoughts froze.

Billy. It'd been Billy who'd buried her body before the burial detail even arrived out there. Billy, who'd acted like a dribbling idiot when Manning had led them to the slaughter of the Bitter Creek site.

Manning had led them there because Manning knew what was waiting over the hill. And Billy had hid himself away. A quick word to the sarge, and like a miracle he was back at Bitter Creek, burying a body Daniel never saw amid all the other dead.

If she was alive, if this letter was hers, that would make her the only witness apart from a bunch of renegades who'd never be believed.

Are you listening to me, Constable? Manning's bullet killed Smith-Johnson. That is what your report will state, too. Is that understood?

Daniel rubbed his neck before he picked up the last page. The woman stated that Sam Manning had saved her life, and her baby's life, and he did not deserve to be accused of a wholesale slaughter which he did not commit. She was positive the Commissioner would act immediately on receipt of this letter and she was hopeful that justice would be done.

'He'd better bloody act,' Daniel whispered.

And he recalled Maddy cornering him in the stables the morning before she left, grabbing him as he saddled his horse. Her hand was like a claw against his shoulder. 'Hell, Maddy. Don't scare me like that.'

'You don't think Sam's responsible, do you, Daniel?'

Daniel searched for any eavesdroppers. He shook his head. 'No, it wasn't Sam.'

'You like him, too, don't you.'

'Perhaps, but if you tell your father, he'll shoot me for treason.'

Maddy grinned. It faded to become something he'd seen too often of late. 'You like me, don't you, Daniel?' she asked.

'Of course I do, what sort of question is that?'

'Prove it.'

She stood there, puckering up, eyes closed. Daniel tried hard not to laugh. Maddy with hurt feelings was a dangerous thing indeed. He had two choices, frighten her back to her senses and therefore stop this nonsense, or give her what she expected. Daniel had hesitated.

'Maddy, no. Not here. Someone will see.'

'Let them see, I don't care.'

'Maddy, you're too young.'

She opened her eyes, realising he wasn't going to kiss her. 'How old must I be?' she asked, whining.

'At least . . . at least seventeen,' Daniel said quietly,

trying not to hurt her feelings, but kissing her forehead anyway.

'Oh. Then there shall be nothing to do but wait for Christmas.'

'Christmas? Why?'

'I turn seventeen at Christmas.'

The glow was back in her eyes. Oh, no, he'd thought.

Daniel decided he wouldn't write to Maddy that night. He found an envelope in his drawer and re-addressed the letter to the Commissioner. He would slip it into the outgoing mail and no one would ever know of his treason.

To him the letter bore the truth and the revelation of such a truth kept him awake all night long.

So did thoughts of Maddy.

Anna stared past the speckled hen she could not relocate to a nest outside, no matter what she tried. She knew the pillow of her body was soft, that her heartbeat lulled Sam into a nothing she envied. How many more deaths would there be before this was over? She held Sam a little tighter.

He didn't remember sleeping. He didn't know how she held him all night long, the loaded shotgun beside her, hoping she wouldn't have to use it again, ever. Now and then a soft weeping filtered into his consciousness but he was powerless.

At some stage, it was day and her hands were cool and comforting. There was a voice asking how he felt, a moist cloth cooling his body, cooling the intense fires for a little while only. And somewhere in the haze, he thought she was Ginger-Lee. Her name emerged thickly, choked.

Ginger-Lee?

'I'm here, Sam,' Anna said.

She could make no sense of his ravings. He couldn't

hear her anyway. Touch alone gave comfort of knowing he wasn't alone. Hadn't he done the same for her?

Ginger-Lee?

Eyes searched her face and found someone else's. 'Yes, Sam, I'm Ginger-Lee.' If it helped, she'd be anyone whose presence might ease his pain. She knew what it was like, the pain, the need, the emptiness of solitary suffering.

A curious look passed over his face as if something in his mind had registered that this woman wasn't Ginger-Lee or, if she was, she sure had changed. A light of recognition flickered in his eyes. He tried to move.

'No. You must lie still.' Like a child he obeyed, too weak to argue.

After two nights and one day, the feared became a reality. Sam became violently feverish. Anna found it impossible to hold him any more.

'Don't trust him, girl. You never seen me.'

'Of course,' Anna said, squeezing his hand.

'Don't trust him, Ginger-Lee.'

Who is this Ginger-Lee? Her mind screamed. As far as Anna knew, there was only Elizabeth's ghost to haunt him.'

'Promise me—'

'You can trust me, Sam.'

He pulled her hand down hard and squeezed it against his chest. Obviously, he didn't want to let go of this Ginger-Lee. An insane jealousy rose. Sheila was lying, she thought. I am not the most beautiful woman he's seen. This Ginger woman is. And then she remembered where she had heard that name. She'd heard it on her very first night at Bitter Creek.

Ginger-Lee. The men had been talking about a prostitute. There had been a Rosie mentioned, too. Rosie. Didn't she own the hotel? Weren't they talking about stuffing and mounting poor Dinny above the bar at Rosie's? Ginger-Lee is a whore!

Anna wrested her fingers from his hand. Sam opened his eyes and focused on her face.

'Anna?'

'Try to sleep.' She tried to, but couldn't keep the hurt from her voice or her eyes.

'Moonshine—'

'He's dead, Sam.'

Lucidity was returning, perhaps those cold words helped.

'How?' he asked, confused.

'I shot him,' Anna said quietly. Please God, do not let me cry again. Please.

There was no shock. What played across Sam's face was relief. He smiled and Anna ached. She watched him drift away into sleep once more. Free now, fingers aching, she wondered what he'd say when he was better and discovered she'd had to bury the body. She only hoped she'd dug the hole deep enough, and that the heavy rocks she'd gathered were enough to stop the wild dogs from digging the body up again. She'd even said a prayer for him but to whose God she'd directed her offering she didn't know.

Anna wasn't sure of anything now, except that she'd killed a trooper, and Sam Manning loved another woman. A whore. And his love for another seemed more painful than the death of Billy Moonshine.

'Where the hell is that black bastard?' the sergeant yelled.

Daniel turned away, swallowing his doubt. Without looking at the sergeant, he said quietly, 'He's probably dead. If he was alive, he'd be back by now. At least I think so.'

'You think? You tell me it's possible for you to actually think?'

Daniel chewed on his inner lip, closed his eyes and dared not face the man. He'd never felt hate quite like this and worse, he was enjoying the feeling.

'Where was he last seen?'

'It's in the reports.'

'I asked you, Brannigan! You! What the hell's got into you lately, boy?'

'Nothing.' But it'll be a pleasure to watch you swing. A smile touched Daniel's mouth. 'He was last seen chasing Manning south from Mitchell's Crossing, Sir. As I said, it's in the report.'

'Bloody Girraween!'

'Possibly.'

'Take Porter with you and find him.'

'Find who?'

'Billy, you idiot!'

'I doubt there'd be a body left to retrieve. It's been three days and Porter's useless in the bush. I'll probably lose him.'

'You were just given an order.'

'I would like to attend Smith-Johnson's funeral.'

'Are you frightened of Manning now?'

'No. But I feel I owe James something.'

Lucas studied the boy. Come hell or high water, the lad would not be convinced to change his statement that Manning had not shot Smith-Johnson. He would not budge from his story of crossfire. Lucas felt something was amiss in the lad. He didn't like the feeling. 'Tomorrow then.'

Daniel was surprised his request was granted. He retired to the stables to think and hate a little more. There was no justice. There never had been nor would there ever be. Enforcing the law was just another term for revenge.

Sam woke to the baby's 'dad-dads'. He opened his eyes and turned his head. Susan was holding on to the bed, grinning at him. He smiled weakly and lifted his good hand. The baby watched the fingers rise, cackled and fell flat on her behind.

'Up you get. Try again, Suzie.' Sam offered her his finger, she clutched it and stood up again, knees buckling but better this time. More confident. Sam smiled at her efforts and felt a breeze coming from an unexpected direction. He looked up. The window above his head was devoid of glass. What happened to her new curtains? He gazed around the familiar room. There was a bullet hole in the wall near the door.

Anna was askew in the rocking chair, a mug of tea at an angel. Spilling.

'Anna?'

She woke quickly and turned. Her smile was instant.

Sam sat up higher. His side hurt like hell, his arm was heavy and useless. He stood up. One step became two. He looked down. The pants that felt so odd were his old regulation whites.

'I'm sorry but they were all I could find.'

'No problem,' Sam said and shuffled past.

'Sam?'

He turned too quickly and nearly fell.

'Welcome back.'

A true smile touched his eyes. 'Good to see you, too. You don't know how good.'

Outside, the fresh air hit like a wave. The goat bleated at him. 'Watch your mouth, Marigold. You're living on borrowed time.' He realised what he'd said. 'We all are.'

Sam saw the mound of dirt covered in rocks. A grave. Moonshine. Soon came footsteps and Anna appeared. 'You shall have to start working your hand, Sam.'

'Can't do eight things at once, Anna. I'm not a

woman. The damned thing won't work anyway. Fingers won't bend.'

'That's what I mean. You have to force yourself. You have to try. I shot a rabbit this morning. I'm making up a stew.' Instead of wanting to throw up, Sam said, 'Great. I could eat a horse.'

'You nearly had to. That grey of yours follows me everywhere. She ruined two perfectly good shots. Does she understand English? When I said she would be next, she trotted away.'

Sam smiled down at her for a little while until his pleasure at seeing her again had faded. 'When did you bury him?' Sam asked. He was in no mood for small talk, not when heavier things lingered unspoken.

'Thursday.'

The body had stiffened overnight. It had been a nightmare, the worst day of her life. Perhaps, perhaps not.

'How deep's the grave?'

'As deep as I could manage,' Anna replied softly and studied her feet like a schoolgirl in trouble again.

'No others came?'

'No, why?'

'There were three of them. Maybe four. Hard to tell. I think I got one.'

'Got one?'

'Shot him. I just hope it wasn't Daniel.'

'Daniel?'

'Brannigan. He's just a kid. I don't think he'd follow me too far. He's got more brains than to come get lost up here. When did it rain?'

'Yesterday. There wasn't a lot of water here, but there was enough in the mountains to make the creek rise.'

'Good,' Sam said, relieved. 'I think we're safe a little while longer yet.'

'What do you mean?'

'I left a trail of blood. What'd you do with his horse?'

'Pardon?'

'The horse. A big bay stallion. Where's the horse?'

He was referring to the trooper's horse. Anna's face paled. 'Oh, God. I never thought of a horse.'

'You had your mind on keepin' us alive. It's okay, girl. I know.'

Anna glanced up into his face once more. 'I thought you were going to die, just like Dinny. I was terrified, Sam.'

He touched her face. There was so much he could have said then, but nothing emerged except a soft, hoarse, 'Thank you.' She looked different, somehow. Weary. Worried. A bit older.

'You haven't slept much, ma'am. You look worse than I feel.'

'Surely it's not that bad?' Anna asked, smiling, until a movement caught her attention. She'd come outside and had forgotten to close the door. Susan was crawling off. 'Oh, no. There she goes again!'

Sam turned. The baby was heading for the creek, attention suddenly diverted by the discovery of a stick to chew on. Anna moved for the rescue. Sam grabbed her arm. At that moment he almost told her he thought he loved her but her eyes were too full of questions, so he kissed her instead. Maybe that would tell her more.

Anna stepped back, surprised. She hitched skirts and sprinted. The baby saw her coming and crawled off, fast. Very fast. Sam watched and thought it all a little funny. 'You little horror, Susan Louise!'

The baby laughed as her mother saved her from suicide. Again.

Sam had never seen Anna do anything like this before: lifting the baby and swinging her around.

She was getting better. A lot better. She'd be wanting to leave soon. There was nothing here for her. She'd want to go back to Brisbane. Where she came from. So far away. He didn't like the thought at all. It wouldn't be the same here without her. Without them both.

'Come on, Sam! Let's have something to eat!' Anna called. He made his way back to the house, but first he kicked over the makeshift wooden cross. Two sticks tied together. Good thought, Anna, very bright. Show the world there's a trooper buried here. He turned and saw Anna, baby on hip, watching, horrified at what he'd just done.

'They got their own God,' was all Sam said and hoped she'd believe it. Anna said nothing.

He ate so much she thought one more mouthful of stew or bread would see him explode. He finally sat back with a groan. Sam looked at her shoulder— the black and purple bruise extending from her collarbone down into her blue dress. She wore the imprint of the butt. 'Shotgun, right?' he asked. She nodded and used a spoon to entice the baby to open her mouth for more broth. The kid was more interested in eating the spoon. Anna put her to the floor. She crawled to Sam and chewed on his thigh. 'You never used one before right?' he asked, absently caressing the baby's head.

'Right.'

'Did it send you through the wall?'

'I don't remember. I suppose it did.'

'Both barrels?' Sam asked cautiously.

'I shot him in the throat, Sam. He was by the window, he was going to kill us all,' she whispered and wouldn't meet his gaze. There was quiet for a little while.

'Does that bruise hurt?'

'Yes.'

212

'Can I kiss it like you kissed me?'

'Oh, Sam, don't.'

He smiled at her. He liked watching the way she blushed. 'It was your kisses that mended me.'

'You behave yourself, Sam Manning.

He picked up his cup and sipped on his tea. His eyes were sparkling, telling her things she shouldn't know.

'It was my birthday yesterday,' she said softly, hoping to change the line of conversation. Perhaps she hoped he'd say something more appropriate or perhaps he'd lean across the table if his stomach allowed it, and kiss her again?

He just sat there, lazy, full, a curious expression on his face.

He said nothing except, 'How old are you?'

'Twenty-three.'

There was nothing else. She should have been used to it by now. Birthdays, anniversaries, Christmases meant nothing to Michael, either. 'When is yours, Sam?'

'My what?' he asked, caught in a daydream.

'Birthday.'

'Oh, that. June. Thriteenth or fourteenth, can't remember.'

He can't remember his birthday? Perhaps there's never been anyone who cared enough to help him celebrate?

Give him space, Sheila had said in all her wisdom. So when he rose from the table, Anna didn't ask where he was going or how long he was likely to be. The door closed and she was alone again. The baby was protesting because he'd gone.

Anna smiled to herself. Can I kiss it, indeed. She looked down at the purple bruise on her shoulder. Too much of her body showed when she wore this dress. She knew what he wanted to kiss.

Susan toppled and hurt her head this time. 'Oh, Susan, please be careful—' Anna picked her up and soothed the tears.

And there was wood to be cut and brought in, a goat to be milked for the night. Anna sighed, settled Susan for the evening and pushed her thoughts of pleasure aside.

She dropped an armload of split logs to the floor and began to stack them. Her face was filthy, sweat glued her hair to the back of her neck and to her face. Her dress adhered to her body. She looked perfectly horrible; she knew it and couldn't have cared less. As her grandmother used to say: 'Even the princess can't feed the pigs in her tiara.'

He had a choice, the music box that still worked (at least it had the last time he'd wound it up), or a bunch of wildflowers. Little paper daisy things, red flowers from gum trees, a stick or two of wattle. So what if it made him sneeze?

Sam chose the flowers. At least with a bunch of flowers in his good hand she couldn't accuse him of being what he was—a thief.

She was stacking wood when he limped in.

'Anna?'

She spun about to face him and overbalanced. She was dirty, but she was the loveliest thing he'd ever seen. Sam held out the flowers. 'I didn't know it was your birthday. I guess it's one day we won't forget for a long time.'

He stood there, his bright eyes full of appreciation, a bunch of wildflowers in his hand. Anna couldn't help it. The gesture caused the sudden tidal wave of emotion. It had been building since Wednesday evening, and it exploded like a dam bursting its banks.

'Don't you like flowers?' he asked, wounded, and put the flowers down quickly. He held her tight.

'I love flowers, Sam.'

'Why are you crying if you like flowers?'

'I don't know.' For a moment, he thought he did know. And he envied her. 'It's okay. You're lucky you can cry,' he said softly. And as she bawled and clung to him, it was true. She could cry now; it was safe to. Sam was back. And he wasn't going to die.

Perhaps if she thought it often enough she'd begin to believe it.

'Papa! Come see what I found!'

Cormac appeared. His eyes widened. Leonie was leading a huge stallion into the houseyard.

'He was with Molly, Pa. He's quiet. He likes me. Can I keep him?'

Sheila appeared and almost dropped her cake bowl. 'Oh, Lordy, where'd he come from?' she cried.

'I found him back of the yards, Ma.'

'With Molly? Are you sure?' Cormac asked and inspected the weary thoroughbred which, thankfully, seemed uninjured. What a fine specimen of an animal he was.

'He's a bit of a sook, Pa. Molly kicked him and tried to bite him so he came straight to me.'

'Typical of a female,' Cormac said. 'Sink the boot in when a man's at his weakest.' He avoided Sheila's inevitable slap.

'What do you make of it?' Sheila asked when the joke had died.

''Tis a trooper's horse to be sure. Leonie, girl, fetch up a bucket of grain.'

'Oh no, you don't. You can't keep him. He has to go back to town. Right this moment.'

'Oh, Mama, I was going to call him Strider!'

'Get the grain, girl.'

Leonie ran off to collect the bucket.

'We're not keeping him. He's going back to town

and that's all there is to it.'

'In good time, wife. Stop your nagging and let a man think.'

'Think? And what if tomorrow Hannaford comes along and sees one of his horses here? He'll be arrestin' you for horse thievin'. He's after an excuse, man, and it's not you or I who'll give it to him. You hear me?'

'Yes, yes. This one'll go back to town as soon as he's been introduced to Aggie.'

'Aggie? I thought we were gettin' a service from Doolan's piebald?'

'What? When there's a thoroughbred free?'

'You're a bloody renegade, Cormac.'

''Tis why you love me,' he said with a grin. It soon faded. 'So there's a trap out there somewhere. Is the horse familiar to you?'

'Looks like Billy's to me. Daniel's isn't as tall.'

'Get that look out of your eye, Cormac Newberry. You're not about to go searching the mountains for a lost trap. Let him rot. You'll not be off searching for the likes of him.'

'Where's your humanity, woman?'

'It abandoned me on Wednesday when I visited Anna. Don't you talk to me of the law, husband, you'll be in for a fight.'

Next morning, just before dawn, Sheila watched as the stallion moved to his waiting love, Aggie. At eighteen, she was still the quickest horse Cormac had and he loved her dearly. The bay stallion siring a foal seemed a dream come true for Cormac.

Sheila nudged her wiry husband as they stood watching, arms around each's waist. 'Could be you might learn a bit if you care to watch carefully, now, husband.'

'Learn what?'

'How to please a lady.'

Cormac grunted.

Sheila teased him for the entire journey to town in the rattling buggy. The bay was bringing up the rear.

'Leonie, not a word, you hear me?'

The child pledged her silence. She'd learnt a long time ago how one whisper of Sam's name could cause his death by hanging, and she knew what death was. She was struck dumb anyway. Sam's face adorned the windows of the post office, the store and, of course, the police station where her father intended to go first. Yes, it was Sam's face but it wasn't the Sam she knew.

The poster said fifty pounds reward for information leading to his apprehension. The word's meaning eluded her but the murder did not. Fifty pounds? Pa always said people couldn't be valued: some were priceless, some worthless. A person couldn't be bought or sold, well, not normally, and it was far easier to replace an object than it was to replace a person. Fifty pounds? It seemed a fortune and it was.

If she was lucky, Pa would give her threepence and she'd run over to Ryan's and buy bags and bags of lollies. And when she saw Sam next, she would give him a sweet for a change.

Leonie tried to read the blurred print for other words she didn't understand. There were a lot of them. Her mother jerked her into the station. She hadn't heard her calling.

It was dark, gloomy, smelly, An awful place.

'Answer the sergeant, Leonie.'

'Sir?'

'Where'd you find the horse, girl?'

She glanced at her father and he nodded.

'I found him when Dog and I were rounding up the chooks, yesterday.'

'What time was this?'

Leonie shrugged. 'Not late enough for the chooks to come in. A dingo's been getting them.'

Lucas tried to smile at the child. 'You didn't see the direction the animal came from?'

'No.'

'The bridle was on?'

'Yes. So was the saddle.'

'Was the animal covered in sweat, as if he'd come a long distance?'

'I didn't look.'

'You can go.'

She looked to her father and he nodded. As she walked out, she heard him saying: 'I'll be wanting restitution for damages to my fence.'

Leonie had almost made it to the fresh air when she bumped into someone coming in. She looked up as the hand caressed her head. Daniel. Leonie beamed. He winked at her, sidestepped as if they were at a dance, and waited for a break in the ensuing argument before he could speak.

'Restitution for damages? He probably serviced every bloody mare you have, Newberry!'

'Excuse me, sir? It is Moonshine's horse. It's a sociable animal by nature, seeks company all the time. It wouldn't wander off without Billy unless something had happened.'

'That'll be all. Get off with you, you're already late by a day.'

Brannigan departed and Leonie followed him out into the bright sunshine. 'And how are you, Miss Newberry?' he asked.

'I'm good, Daniel. Am I getting taller?'

'I'll say you are,' he said as he got on his horse. 'You'll be as tall as me, soon.'

'Where are you going, Daniel?'

'I have to find Billy.'

'Pa says he's probably dead.'

'Well, you can tell your Pa I think he's right.'

Daniel and the other trooper rode off and Daniel didn't wave goodbye.

Leonie patted the bay until someone came out and took him away.

She didn't have much longer to wait for her parents. Her mother smacked her ear because she was 'Sitting like an urchin in the gutter'.

Leonie wondered what an urchin was as she was swept along towards Ryan's store. She couldn't believe her luck when her father gave her fourpence. 'Off you go, now.'

'You spoil her. The child'll want everything and not know the value of real work.'

'Sheila, stop nagging.'

Twelve

'Do you think he had a family?'

'Anna, you did what you had to. Sitting there brooding about it is no good.'

'But I—'

'We're alive, he's dead. Now be quiet.'

The tone hurt more than his words. Other questions to which she had no answers were silenced. She went back to the blue fabric in her hands. She was making another curtain. And sulking. Hurt.

'I didn't mean it to sound like that.'

Yes you did, she wanted to say. Anna remained quiet.

Lately, their only conversations came in short, curt sentences. Anna would ask how his arm was, and he'd say it hurt and it'd never get better. She'd ask if there was anything else he wanted her to do and he'd reply with a snapped denial.

Anna wondered if people who had been married a lifetime ended up like this once they'd exhausted their supply of anything worthwhile to say.

Oh, she understood he was angry. She'd be worse. She was almost as self-reliant and independent as he. Almost. But everything she tried to do was wrong. He didn't like the way she chopped the wood, because it wasn't his way. She hadn't dismembered herself yet, had she? No, but he could see it coming, or so he'd say and lope off to kick a rock. Everything he wanted to do required two hands.

Was it her fault he rode out to rob the mail coach and was shot? He should think himself lucky to be alive. What a fight those words had caused. He hadn't forgiven her at all. Now, he sat there trying to catch a semblance of a breeze. He was bare chested, rivulets of sweat coursing from his long hair down his back, down his chest. Perhaps the heat added to his anger. He was lucky. Anna had to endure a long-sleeved dress. It was not fair at all.

'Does this look like a tulip to you?' Anna asked and held up the curtain to show him the embroidered flower she was working on. It was almost finished, and she was quite proud of it.

Sam grunted. Anna exploded. She could take no more of this nonsense. 'What is wrong with you, Sam?' she yelled. Sam looked up, shocked. What was she yelling for? What'd he do this time?

'I ask you a simple question and you grunt at me!'

'You want my opinion? I don't want curtains. Why don't I want curtains? This place is supposed to look like it's falling down for a reason. No one's supposed to live here. So I don't care if I never get glass for that window and I don't want damned curtains!'

'If no one's supposed to live here, why is there a vegetable patch? Why is there so much rubbish lying about?'

'Okay. Why don't I weed it, huh? What's some abandoned shack supposed to look like? Nice and tidy? You want nice and tidy here, you won't get it.'

She was undeterred, yet her voice softened. 'You could have told me about your aversion to curtains.'

'I didn't want to hurt your feelings. Besides, it gives you something to do. At least you've *got* something to do.'

Anna threw the fabric to the floor and jumped on it. 'There! No curtains! Are you happy now? I am not a mind reader, Sam!'

The silence was thick.

'You didn't have to do that, you know,' he said calmly.

Anna grunted at him. Let's see if he likes it. He didn't notice. Sam studied the flower she'd been trying to sew. 'What'd you say it was?'

'A tulip,' she pouted.

'Ain't they yellow? That's white.'

'You're just like Michael!' she yelled. 'You're always implying I can't do anything right! Well, I can, Sam Manning. You hear me, I can!'

'I never said it wasn't a tulip.'

'You didn't have to! You insinuate I'm useless. Don't do it like that, do it like this . . . everything has to be your way!'

'What'd I say this time?'

She sent him a stinging look and headed for the door.

'Where are you going?' he asked. Anna turned. His face was blank. As blank as his brain, she thought. She didn't like him at all when he looked so utterly stupid.

'I may not be the world's best cook or cleaner or mother, and I may not be able to sew very well, but there is something I can do; something I am good at. And I intend going out there and I intend doing it whether you think it's a waste of time or not!'

The door slammed shut and Sam winced. He'd only asked where she was going.

Now she'd cut off his breeze. Sam got up and opened the door. He knew where she was going, but she'd forgotten her paints and the easel. He almost asked if she wanted them when she turned back. Sam sidestepped to let her in the door.

Anna rummaged for an enamel plate, glared at him to step aside and stomped off again.

'Ain't you gonna draw?' he asked.

222

'No!' she called without turning around.

'What you gonna do?'

'I'm going to find some gold.'

Sam leant on the porch rail and watched. She's bored, he thought. That's it. She's bored and I'm bored and we're both waiting for something, but we don't know what we're waiting for, and to fill in time we argue. Yeah, that's it. A smile lit his face.

She waded into the water. Sam waited for steam to rise. She was taking handfuls of sand from the creekbed and throwing them into the plate until it was full, and began the old routine of shake, swirl and tip. Not for the first time in his life did he wonder why people enjoyed doing this.

Sam idled over and settled himself comfortably on the lump of rock she always sat on when she wanted to think. Maybe it was the bubbling water that helped her think. Maybe he didn't know her as well as he thought. He watched until the first plate was empty and nothing was found. What'd she expect? A miracle? She started the routine over again. 'What if there's no gold here?'

'There is and I shall find it.'

'Like that?'

'Yes, like this.'

On the fifth plateful he asked, 'Want a shovel?'

Pride forced her refusal. 'I can do this on my own.'

'Be easier if you took your dress off.'

Even he could see that the wet skirts were almost drowning her. It was a good idea. Besides, it wasn't as boring if there was something nice to look at. He was surprised when she peeled the dress off.

'Sure you don't want a shovel? If there's any gold there, it's falling quicker than you can catch it like that.'

'And now you're an expert prospector, too?' Anna asked.

'I grew up near Sutter's Mill.'

'What's Sutter's Mill?'

'A goldmining town in California.'

'Oh. I suppose I'm not doing this the right way, either?'

His smile said it all. Anna was tempted to drown him, however, her anger wasn't strong enough. His grin was melting her frustrations. Still, he had a point. All she would find this way was black sand. There'd been traces of blue stone. Sapphire, she supposed.

'Would you like to use a gold pan ma'am?'

'I beg your pardon?'

'A gold pan. It'd be easier than that plate. I've got a pick and shovel somewhere, too. Maybe even a sieve.'

Anna let the enamel plate sink to the bottom of the brook. 'Why didn't you tell me?'

'You never asked. I'm not a mind reader, you know.'

She ignored that. 'You have prospecting tools and you sit there, laughing at me?'

'I suppose so. There's nothing else to do. No mail coaches to rob or pretty ladies to molest.'

'Sam Manning, must you!'

'Must I what? Look, it's not often I get to stare at a pretty lady in her underwear.'

'Sam—'

'Yes, ma'am?' he asked innocently. 'Okay. It's true. I got equipment but I don't use it. I don't see the sense in it and I never have. Do you want it or not?'

'Is this another of your jokes?' she asked cautiously, not trusting the look in his eyes.

'Do you want the stuff?' he asked slowly, emphasising each word so she'd finally understand.

'Could I?'

'All you gotta say is yes.'

'You're cranky again.'

224

'Me? Me? You got any idea how long I'd be waiting to hear you ask for anything at all? You're too proud, Anna, and that's only half your problem. What you tryin' to prove anyway?'

'You can talk of proof and pride? Do you ever listen to yourself?'

Sam mumbled and limped away.

'Don't you dare walk away from me when I'm angry!'

Sam turned back to see her trying to get out of the creek. The rocks were extremely slippery, and at her speed downright dangerous. He almost called out to be careful and next moment, all he saw were pretty white legs in the air. She came up again, wet. Very wet. Serves her right, he thought. About time the temper got cooled.

She coughed, spluttered and started cursing. He started laughing, he couldn't help it. And he had to walk away.

'Stop laughing at me!' she wailed.

He turned back. There was no more anger in her voice. It was filled with pure despair.

'I'd rather you hit me than laugh at me!'

Sam went to her even though he knew it was safer to keep walking the other way. It had to be safer. She was dripping wet. The petticoat clung to every mound of her body. He tried to swallow his thoughts, but his body wouldn't play along. His hands itched to touch. He started to ache. His mouth went dry. God, don't look at me like that, Anna. All he could see was hurt in her eyes.

'Don't move,' he said quietly, putting his finger to tongue and dabbing at her cheek. He held his finger in front of her eyes and stuck to the tip was a thin sliver of gold.

At sight of it, all was forgotten and forgiven. 'I knew there was gold in the creek!' she cried and

225

planted a hungry kiss on his face. 'Don't lose it. I have to get a bottle.' Off she ran, barefooted, towards the hut.

Sam stared at the tip of his index finger as if he'd never seen if before and then shook his head. Is this all it took to make her happy? Anna sprinted back with a small glass bottle in her hand. She ran to the creek and filled the bottle with water, holding it out to him as if he should know what to do next. Sam ceremoniously dipped his finger in and watched her eyes sparkle as the gold dropped quickly and lay unmoving on the bottom. She glanced into his face. She was smiling, victorious.

'Kiss me again,' he said.

Anna rose on tiptoe and pecked his cheek. Sam shook his head. 'Is that the best you can do?'

'Sam, I'm cold. I have to—'

'Yes, I can see you're cold.' His gaze drifted over her body. He could see straight through the wet petticoat that clung to breasts, belly, thighs. And he liked what he saw.

'I have to change,' she said quickly, taking the bottle and capping it. She went to walk away. He grabbed her hand. She didn't give him time to say anything. 'Don't, Sam. It's not right.'

'It's not wrong, either.'

'But you can't . . .'

Sam pulled her close. Very close. She felt a hard bulge against her stomach. 'I can't what?' he asked, but it wasn't a question.

Anna didn't know what to do. Hadn't this very thought touched her mind the moment she first saw him? She tried to think of a thousand reasons why this shouldn't be happening and not one surfaced. Nothing could be any defence against what she'd seen in his eyes.

Sam reached out and swept the damp hair from

226

her face. His touch lingered too long against her cheek. He put her precious bottle on the ground and he tilted her face up to his. Anna was about to protest when lips touched. The protest died. He slid the petticoat from her shoulder. His touch was light. Easy. His fingertips left goosebumps in their wake. Sam's kiss grew hungry when his hand closed over her left breast and her nipple was hard against his hand, his fingertips.

'No!'

And the spell was broken. She pushed away from him, her eyes wide, horrified. Sam stepped back, too. For a frozen moment they stared at each other and then, before he could even say her name, she'd swept up the bottle and was running for the hut. The door slammed and he was left alone. Terribly alone.

What was wrong? Was she scared of him?

The baby slept on. Anna hoped she would wake and become an excuse to escape the sudden madness Sam had created. Or had she created it? Had he seen the glow in her eyes, a glow that mirrored what she felt inside whenever he was near?

No, Anna. Get that look out of your eyes right now. Ye hear me? And Michael would push her away. Her body always was the traitor. Her body always caused trouble.

It should not be like this, she thought. It was wrong to feel such things, to want such things. It wasn't . . . proper.

Anna took off the wet, clinging petticoat. Her skin was icy, shivering. She could still taste his kiss. She could still feel his hand on her breast. Hot. Gentle. Firing her senses until no sense remained.

No, she thought. No. Only a husband is able to take pleasure from his wife's body. Only a husband.

She reached for Sheila's dress; the one which would cover her completely. The door opened. Anna froze.

227

'I can't pretend I don't want you, Anna. I can't pretend any more.'

She tried to hide her body, but she burned from his intense blue gaze. He walked to her and took the dress from her hands. Anna had no voice. Her knees were shaking. So were her hands. Sam took them between his own, crushed them gently against his chest before kissing her knuckles, nibbling her fingers.

'You know I'd never hurt you. I'd die first.' She looked up into his eyes. Lord, he meant it.

'You are so beautiful—'

She didn't think she could move. No one had ever said that before. No one. His breath was hot and tickling her ear. Sam nibbled on her neck, fingers gently touching her breasts again. It was a curious feeling. She tingled, glowed. Sam's mouth touched hers once more and this time, he found her tongue. Anna held her breath. Her heart was roaring. And his hand ventured over her belly. Between her legs. His touch was setting her alight.

'Touch me,' he whispered. 'Please.'

Anna touched Sam's chest. The hair there was soft. It was almost a lie. His skin soft and smooth. It was *all* a lie. Of course this was right. It had to be. But still she hesitated.

'Let it go, girl. You gotta let it go. Nothing's going to hurt you now. I won't let anyone hurt you again.'

'I fear what you might think of me, Sam. I'm afraid of your thoughts.'

'No,' he whispered, guiding her hand low. 'Touch me, Anna.' And slowly Anna followed his guidance, and started caressing him. Sam whispered something to her, his voice adrift. All she heard were sounds; she didn't understand what her body told her, nor did she argue. Nothing had ever felt quite like this. Sam needed her badly. She could feel it in her hand,

228

in her heart, see it in his eyes.

He lay her on the bed. He felt explosive. Her touches were unsure, but magic all the same. He looked down on her as if he'd never seen a woman quite like her before.

He hadn't.

There was no fear in her eyes now; no right, no wrong. Her body wanted him, and her eyes weren't lying this time. She returned the kiss with passion, need. Her fingers twisted in his hair and she made odd, whimpering sounds as his mouth and hands explored, slowly. He touched and kissed her in places she never knew existed and euphoria overwhelmed her when a final, fresh wave of warmth and release blossomed within. Anna stopped breathing.

'Are you all right, ma'am?' His voice sounded alarmed. Her sensations were too overpowering to allow any kind of reply.

Anna opened her eyes to see his startled face, and after a little while she smiled. Her throbbings had ceased. She was breathing heavily now.

'Take me—' she whispered. Did she think he'd cast her aside? Sam filled her to overflowing.

Anna wanted to imprison him within her forever and never let him go. He held his own weight, as hurt as he was. There was no heaviness, no pain, no animal noises. Is this how it should really be she wondered?

'Tell me to stop and I will,' he said softly.

She said nothing. She couldn't think of anything but Sam. No words were needed or enough. There was no mistake in silence and no mistake in this.

He took so long to be satisfied, and he kept worrying about hurting her. Anna only held him tighter in reply. When he had finally finished, he lay down beside her and pulled her close, saying something she couldn't hear because her heart beat too loudly.

The liquid of his seed tickled her thighs and they lay staring up at the tin roof for a long, long time.

She waited for him to tell her of his love because then it would be safe to express her own. But nothing was said. Words were not needed. After a while, Anna leaned on her elbow and looked into his eyes. 'You're not disgusted with me, are you, Sam?' He laughed away her question and pulled her close again. He loves me, she thought. Dear God this man loves me. Anna put her head on his chest and kissed his sweating skin. His heart was loud, strong. She closed her eyes.

Sam stroked her damp hair. Her breasts were hot and soft against his ribs, her entire body was soft, so soft, he too was lulled into sleep.

Lieutenant John Barton propped his head up with his hand and studied the handwriting on the envelope. There were no similarities to the writing on the six pages it contained—six pages he'd just read for the third time.

He started to cough and reached for his glass of water.

Air. He needed air. For a little while, he stared down into the traffic below, and before he looked back to the mound of files and documents all needing the commissioner's urgent attention, he sighed. It was the sigh of an impending headache.

Barton coughed again and this time he spat. Illness had sharpened his aim to perfection.

'Carmichael?'

A younger lieutenant came in.

'Is Sub-Inspector Ritchie still with us?'

'He's leaving this afternoon.'

'See to all that for me,' Barton said and gestured toward the waiting workload.

Carmichael groaned. He had enough of his own work to do. 'Going somewhere?' he asked as the lieutenant took his coat and hat from the stand near the door and tucked something into his coat pocket. It looked like a letter.

'Yes,' was all he received.

He finally found Harry Ritchie as he was heading out the back door of the building, case in hand. 'Hold up a moment, Harry. Can you delay your departure another day?'

'Why?'

'I've something here that might interest you.'

Millie Blackburn was weeding her roses when the carriage pulled up. Two policemen emerged, and one studied the house next door for some time, consulting papers before tucking them away again. The gate creaked open. Millie walked to the fence.

'No one lives there now,' she said.

The inspector turned to her. 'I see that, Mrs . . .'

'Blackburn. Millie Blackburn. If it's the Browns you're after I'm sorry to tell you they packed up and left a month ago.'

'No, we have a matter concerning Michael and Anna Hall.'

'You're two years too late. They're off chasing gold somewhere down Warwick way, I think. Perhaps Tenterfield, perhaps Stanthorpe. Knowing Michael, he'd have changed his mind a dozen times on the way, and he's probably in Victoria by now.' She smiled at both men and wondered what Mick had done this time. Killed someone in a drunken brawl, perhaps?

'So you knew them well then?'

'I knew Anna. Is something wrong? Has something happened to her?'

'Would you recognise her handwriting if you saw it?'

'Oh yes. She wrote to me twice after they first

went away. I've not heard a word for well over a year now.'

'You wouldn't have those letters, would you, Mrs Blackburn?'

'Well, yes—'

'Would it be an inconvenience if we could perhaps see them?'

Millie shrugged and invited them into her house. The inspector and lieutenant accepted her offer, but they ventured no further inside than the verandah.

'The last I heard she was expecting a baby,' Millie said and walked off to find Anna's letter. She returned a few minutes later and gave the piece of paper to the inspector. The two men compared it to something one of them held. It was kept well away from Millie's inquiring eyes.

Whatever they agreed on, Millie would never know. They thanked her, returned the letter and after a few more moments of idle converstation about the lack of rain and the incessant heat, the lieutenant thanked her again. The inspector touched his hat. They both climbed into the carriage and the driver moved on.

Millie went back to her roses and wished Anna still lived next door. Life wouldn't be as lonely if only she had Anna to talk to again.

It was dusk. Anna, sitting far enough away to avoid any flying wood chips, suddenly said: 'Something's happening, Sam.'

'Yes, I know. I'm doing something for a change.'

'No. I mean something is happening.'

Sam split the log, tossed it aside and picked up the next. 'What do you mean?'

'Someone's reading my letter.'

Sam went back to his work. If he kept quiet she'd never discover he'd lost the damned letter.

'Someone really is reading my letter. I can feel it,' she said, so sure of herself.

'You can feel it,' he mumbled and gave her one of his odd looks. Anna ignored it. 'My ears are burning, too.'

Sam tried hard not to grin. He had to turn away. He picked up another log. 'What's that mean if your ears are burning?'

'Someone's talking about me, Sam. If they do go to where I used to live, do you think Millie would remember me?'

'Millie?'

'My friend. She lived next door. A terrible gossip.'

'I think it'd be hard to forget you, Anna.'

'I often wonder how she is,' Anna mused. 'Troopers will come now.'

'Yep, just what we need. A whole army of traps.'

'Don't you see? It will soon be over, Sam.'

If he looked at her now, he'd see eagerness and innocence, a lethal combination. 'The good guys always win, right?'

'There is a chance. Even you said there was a chance.'

'I lost the letter, Anna. I don't know where it is. I think I dropped it when I got shot.'

There was the silence he expected, apart from Suzie chewing on a stick, sharpening her teeth so she could bite him again.

'Then perhaps someone found the letter and posted it,' she said quietly, still adamant her feelings were right. Sometimes her optimism was ferocious, as ferocious as Suzie when she needed to bite someone.

'Don't, Anna. Believe me, the letter's gone.'

'Why didn't you tell me?'

'Tell you what?'

'That you lost it.'

'Cos . . . I didn't. I couldn't.'

'All this time, I've been waiting for nothing. You expect me to spend the rest of my life hiding from the law? I can't, Sam. I've too much to do.'

'Making hats, I suppose.'

'Yes! What's wrong with that?'

'Opening up shops takes money, girl. Money you don't have.'

'I shall get my gold back. I will have all that's rightfully mine.'

Sam didn't want to laugh, it just happened. 'How you gonna do that?'

'You know where it is. You'll get it for me.'

If her dark eyes were the knife, he was the apple. He was being cored again. 'You assume too much, you know that?'

'It's not an assumption. I know that you know where my gold is. I know that you're simply waiting.'

'Yeah? What am I waiting for?'

'Justice to be done.'

Sam nearly choked. That word hadn't been in his vocabulary for five years.

'You're not interested in helping me at all, Sam Manning. You just want to keep me a prisoner here.'

Best to play along with her ravings. 'Whatever you say, ma'am.'

'You think if it's fine for you, it should be fine for everyone. Is that not the case? You may be able to live in isolation, perpetual boredom and utter squalor for the rest of your life, however long that may be, but I am not.'

Sam was awfully quiet. He kept splitting logs.

'Did you hear what I said?'

'I'm not deaf,' he replied at last. 'How do you know someone's readin' your letter?'

'I just do.'

'Like you knew something had happened to me the day I got ambushed, right?'

'Yes.'

'Are you some sort of gypsy with a crystal ball?'

Anna felt anger swelling. The look on his face told her she belonged in a mental asylum. It was an expression she'd seen countless times. He expected her to get angry. She wouldn't give him the pleasure. She remained quiet for a little while. There were other ways to deal with Sam Manning.

'Sam?' she asked quietly, the tone indicating she wanted something. Unless she got it, he'd suffer being nagged for a week. Sam turned to her, bored.

'Why haven't you told me to go?' she asked.

He wondered what she was up to now. Sure, at the start he'd said she'd only be staying as long as it took her to get better. He didn't want a woman about. But back then he thought she'd die. And things had changed since then, too. A lot had changed. Now what do I say, he wondered. He kept chopping wood even though his side was tearing in two. 'Maybe I can't tell you to go. Or maybe I am waiting, just like you said. Maybe I'm waiting for this justice of yours and when you've got your gold, then I'll tell you to go. Then you can go buy your shop and make your hats and be happy ever after.' *Because only then you won't need me any more, if you've ever needed anyone in your life before.*

She was quiet this time. 'That's what you want, isn't it?' Sam asked.

'Why don't you say you love me, Sam? Perhaps I wouldn't want to go if you said what's on your mind.'

'I don't think you'd like to know what's on my mind, Anna.'

'You do love me, don't you?'

He put the axe down and turned to her. Words played on his lips and in his eyes. But he couldn't say them. He turned away again, picked up a log and smashed the axe into it savagely.

Anna slowly rose to her feet. 'Someone is reading my letter. Mark my words. Justice will be done.'

He watched her walk away. Justice for who, girl, he wondered.

If he held her all night, no matter how hot the nights were, she didn't have bad dreams. And it sure was hot tonight. There was no breeze to cool sweating skins.

Sam rolled on to his back. He couldn't sleep. It was too hot, his mind was racing.

Once she said it was a like a long, dark tunnel. How life here was nothing but a long, dark tunnel. Occasionally there'd be a flicker of light at the far end, but the closer she got to it, the further away it went. Sam seemed to know the flicker of light at the other end wasn't him. It was a combination of freedom, gold and a hat shop. Nothing more, nothing less.

He'd never worried about the future as he did when she lay sleeping in his arms. He wanted her to do what she wanted and have what she wanted, but he also wanted her.

He couldn't have her and she couldn't have him and that's all there was to it, or so he told himself, and the more he said it the more he believed it. Then she'd ruin everything by asking, 'Don't you love me, Sam?' When she knew he did. He just couldn't say it. He'd never been able to. It was easier to show it.

Anna woke him before dawn. There was no sensuality in her touch. She shook him awake. He was used to her habit of springing out of bed in pitch darkness, fumbling for the light. She'd start drawing. In the morning he'd have to give an opinon on a hat she'd drawn. Lately, there were dresses to match the hats. And so, as he was shaken awake, Sam automatically told her that whatever it was, it was great, wonderful and he tried to go back to sleep.

'Sam!'

Whoever said they thought their best thoughts on awakening was lying. He sat up in bed, wide awake now, Anna leaning over him. 'Sam!' she kept calling but he didn't hear the voice. Something in her eyes chilled his spine.

'What's wrong?' he slurred.

'We have to take the baby to Sheila's; we have to get her away from here!'

'You been dreaming again, girl. It's all right. It was only a dream.' He reached out and drew her down beside him. She was quiet for a little while.

'Something's going to happen, Sam. It frightens me. I don't want you to get shot, or caught. Or hang.'

'They've tried once. Do you think I'd let it happen again? Go back to sleep. It was just a dream.'

Anna cuddled into him, his arm her pillow again. There was security in his warmth, so much of it that her dream of an old silver mine and Sam being shot faded entirely. Sam gently tangled his fingers in her hair, sighed and closed his eyes.

'Why won't you tell me about Elizabeth?'

'Huh?'

'Talk to me, Sam. You never tell me anything.' She drew circles on his chest. Tickling. Not letting him get to sleep.

'Maybe later, huh?' he mumbled, putting his hand on hers.

'And if there isn't a later? You don't want me to know. You don't trust me. After all we've been through, you still don't trust me.'

'It's not that I don't trust you. It's . . . it's the past. You start looking backwards all the time, you get in trouble. I've had enough trouble to last me forty years. It's over, Anna.'

'It will never be over. You're wanted because of her. This Elizabeth. Every time you look at me I see her face in your eyes. She's staring back at me. She's not haunting you, Sam, she's haunting me. Damn her for not letting you go.'

Christ, he thought. She'll never let me sleep now. 'Why do you want to know about Elizabeth?'

She leaned on her elbow. 'If I know, perhaps I can understand why this is happening. You're a good man, Sam. I feel it, I see it but that's all I know about you. I love you so much, and you won't talk to me.'

He wondered where to begin and his sigh was despairing.

'Luke Hannaford was one of the first friends I ever made in Australia. We were troopers together . . . Elizabeth was a friend of his wife's. A friend of Jane's. Luke and I used to be close, Anna. I know it's hard to believe, but a lot of people change with time. Get older. Sometimes get wise with it. Some folks get greedy . . . Well, before I knew what had happened, I was married, too. I gave her everything she wanted. Clothes. A nice house. I gave her everything except me. I know that now. I was never home. I'd be away for weeks, sometimes months at a time. It was hard for her but I never really knew how lonely she was.

'Elizabeth was beautiful, almost as beautiful as you. I should have known.'

He was quiet for a little while. Remembering. He was still hurting. Anna, with her head on his chest, listened to the quickening of his heart. She almost knew what he would say next.

'After I got promoted, I had to take three troopers out to a place called Lambing Flat. Trouble with the Chinese. Luke didn't come that time. His

238

daughter had some sort of fever, they thought she'd die. Well, we were supposed to be gone about a fortnight. We were back five days early. If we hadn't been back early Elizabeth would still be alive.'

Again, he was quiet. Anna was thankful for the darkness because his voice was shaking. Every time he mentioned her name, his voice shook.

'I walked in on 'em, Anna. My wife and my best friend, making love in my bed.' For a moment the silence was very thick.

'I didn't hear a word either of them had to say 'cos I knew whatever they'd say would be lies. I'd never felt anything like it. It was like something died inside me.'

Sam closed his eyes and he was back there, broad daylight, in that bedroom, looking down at the tangled bodies in the tangled sheets. Staring at Elizabeth's horrified face because she saw him first. But he turned away from the sight, the words, *Sam, you don't understand*—

At least he hadn't heard, 'It's not what you think,' because he had good eyesight. And seeing was enough.

Luke's hand on his shoulder. *We can work something out*.

Sam worked it out his own way by sending Luke through the wall, pulling the Navy Colt six-shooter, telling Luke if he wasn't out in ten seconds he was a dead man. Elizabeth screaming. Sam had never seen his wife naked in the daylight before, and nor had he heard her begging. She was clinging to the brass bedhead, screaming: 'Don't kill him! Don't kill him, Sam, I love him!'

Then Luke was trying to disarm him, a struggle for supremacy. And the gun went off. Blood sprayed the wall . . . Elizabeth's blood.

'He . . . he grabbed his clothes and ran like hell. All I could see was Elizabeth. I don't remember anything else except her face. Her eyes. It took her a long time to die.

'In court, they said I was holding her when they found us. I wouldn't let her go. I wouldn't let anyone touch her. I didn't believe she was dead. Sometimes I still don't. They said I kept whispering apologies. I don't know, Anna, maybe it did happen like they said it did. But Luke watched 'em take me away. He gave evidence in court. Said he was on his way to see me when he heard the shot. Said he tried to disarm me, I was gonna shoot him too. Said his black eye was from the struggle. He got away. Got help. He couldn't tell the truth. He was a happily married man caught making love to his best friend's wife. He had a family to consider, a career. He had a lot to lose.'

Sam said no more.

'Oh, Sam, I am so sorry.'

'He's not gonna do it again.'

All was silent except for the night sounds of the bush.

'Sam?'

'What?'

'What are we going to do?'

'I don't know yet.'

Anna studied his face in the half-light of the dawn. 'Perhaps we could find somewhere else to go, somewhere no one would know us or find us or . . .'

'Fifty pounds is a lot of money. People have died for a lot less. I'm still wanted, Anna. There's always a shadow around my neck.'

'A shadow?'

'Yeah. The shadow of a rope.'

'But you could grow a beard and we could go somewhere no one would know us—'

'Anna, I been told it's my eyes that people remember most. And I can't take you and Suzie along with me.'

'Why not? I love you, Sam. So does the baby. She knows you as her father.'

'Anna, no. No. The law'd see you as an accomplice. If I ever got caught you'd hang too. That's how it is.'

'It's not right! You are innocent!'

Innocent? How he wished he could live in her dream world.

'Anna, all we gotta do is wait a little longer. If we can wait long enough, Luke is gonna make the first mistake.'

'Perhaps he's waiting for you to do the same.'

'Maybe. Guilt won't destroy him. If he's scared enough, a mistake just might. And when people are scared, they get a little impatient. That's what I'm hoping for. I'm hoping he thinks you're dead, and I'm also hoping he knows you're not. That sort of pressure's enough to break anybody.'

'I don't understand you, Sam.'

'Maybe you will get your gold back, and go buy that hat shop you want. Trust me, that's all you have to do.'

'And what about you, Sam? What will you do?'

'I don't really know. Be a farmer, I guess.' He touched her face very gently and held her tight. The words he wouldn't say aloud were but a whisper in his kiss, his touch.

'Sam?'

'Mmm—'

'Who is Ginger-Lee?'

Thirteen

If it hadn't been for the axle, Maddy would have been home on 23 December. She didn't know what was worse, too long at Aunt Rachel's or travelling on the packed coach. Or, for that matter, the many ten-mile inns offering cold porridge, sour milk and beds full of tiny crawling things. It took a day to mend the axle, and that one day seemed to take forever.

She knew what would be waiting for her at home. A mess. Her father wouldn't have cleaned the kitchen, or changed his sheets, or washed himself or his clothes. Maddy didn't want to even think about the cells. Still, it would be good to get home again, no matter what state it was in. It would be good to see Daniel again, too.

Maddy was far too embarrassed to ask for a stop. Her mother wouldn't have hesitated, but Jane would now be choosing what to wear to Lady McTaggart's Christmas luncheon. With eyes watering from the strain, Maddy studied the other people's faces. Most of the seven passengers were sleeping until the driver exclaimed, 'Steady up there!'

The driver was first down.

Maddy was almost trampled in the rush to disembark, and head west or north, south, east.

She ran towards a huge boulder off the road a way, out of sight of everyone else. A little while later, her heart froze. She heard the driver exclaim again, 'Everyone in? Good-o. Hey up there!'

Maddy tried to scream but all she could say was,

'Don't leave me!' in a tiny horrified squeak.

When she was finally able to run back to the roadway, all she could see was the coach's dust turning to mud in Mitchell's Crossing. She waited, praying that someone would actually notice she wasn't on board.

No one did. No one at all. All they would notice for half an hour was the sudden comfort. There would seem to be much more room and in half an hour, someone would ask, 'Where's that girl? She didn't get off at Warwick, did she?' They would see then that she wasn't there. And the driver would be made aware of his oversight and he would, rather cranky now, turn around and go back to Mitchell's Crossing.

But Maddy Hannaford wouldn't be there.

Of all people to lose, it had to be the sergeant's daughter.

Sam was taking aim at a fat scrub turkey and just as his finger began to squeeze he heard the low, animal-like moaning that immediately chilled his spine. He lost interest in shooting Christmas dinner because the turkey heard the noise, too.

The moan became a wail. Something like an Irish banshee, but not quite.

What the hell's that?

He soon tracked the noise to its source—a girl sitting squarely in the middle of the narrow, rocky road.

Sam walked his horse down to where she sat, crying. At least that's what he thought she was doing.

'Hey! You okay?' he called loud enough to cover the noise. A red, puffed, blotched face looked up, and instantly recognised him. Sam had never seen anyone move as fast. 'Slow down, I'm not gonna hurt you.' She slowed down by falling over.

It must have been his year for strays.

Terror flooded her eyes as he dismounted. 'The stage left you behind, huh?' he asked.

She nodded. Face to face with Sam Manning and Maddy was speechless with terror. What if all the lies were true? What if . . . Sam reached down and pulled her to her feet.

'Stop it, come on, stop the noise.'

After a few heavings and bubblings, she did. Almost.

'You live in town?' he asked. Maddy nodded and couldn't look into his face. 'Okay, you listening?' Maddy did look up this time and wished she hadn't. Sobs began to surface again, big, huge ones. 'There's no coach for another week and it's thirty miles to town. Now I can leave you here to wait if you want, or you can come with me. It's up to you.'

Her chin trembled as she choked on another howl. 'But it's Christmas tomorrow, I have to get home.'

'Maybe the coach'll come back, maybe it won't. You can wait here if you want. Your choice.'

'Would you leave me out here on my own?' she asked.

'That's up to you, like I said.' And for the smallest of moments, Sam wondered where he'd seen her before. Familiarity was a faint itch. Unreachable. 'Trouble is, I can't get you to town now. It's too damned late. You know who I am?'

Maddy nodded.

'If I help you, girl, you better promise to keep your mouth shut. No one knows, right?'

'I promise.' Her voice was a whisper, her legs were turning to jelly. All her daydreams were dissolving.

Sam hesitated for a moment. 'I promith.' The lisp, too, was haunting. It's nothing, he thought. She's just a stranded girl. 'Turn around.'

Maddy obeyed. Sam took a scarf from his pocket and wrapped it around her eyes. Blindfolded, confused, she was helped onto the horse after some ordeal. Once on, she blindly clung to his waist. If she hadn't been so disturbed, she might have enjoyed it. But this was no dream. This was reality.

Hadn't she imagined something like this ages ago? Maddy clung tighter as the horse moved off. She was dizzy. It was always the way when she couldn't see where she was going.

'What's your name?' he asked.

'Maddy.'

Maddy? Something registered. His voice was cautious and curious.

'Maddy who?'

He felt her entire body stiffen. He repeated his question. Impatient now.

'Maddy Hannaford, sir.'

His heart leapt in his chest. Finally, Sam said quite calmly, 'It's been a long time, Maddy Hannaford.' The truth of course. From a thin, sickly kid with plaits pinned on her head to this full-blown young woman.

A gift from the gods.

Anna thought she was hallucinating when Sam dismounted and helped his passenger to the ground. She opened her mouth and was silenced with a gesture of his hand. Sam untied the blindfold.

Maddy squinted into the sunset. She didn't know where she was and she turned in a circle before she finally saw Anna standing on the porch with the baby in her arms. She didn't know Sam had married again. No one had told her about this.

'Get yourself inside, girl,' Sam ordered.

Maddy took a few tentative steps towards the woman and glanced back at Sam. He was unsaddling the horse, setting it free.

'Go on,' he said, gently reinforcing the first order.

'I don't think she'll eat you.'

The woman had caution in her eyes. The baby studied her eagerly. As Maddy drew closer, the child reached out to touch. 'The coach left me behind,' was all she could think of to say.

'What's your name?'

'Maddy.'

'Come inside.'

Anna let Maddy go in first and she put the baby down. Susan crawled to Maddy, grasped a handful of skirt, heaved herself to her feet and gave the newcomer a huge grin. Maddy thought she was wonderful. She'd always loved babies. 'She is a sweet baby.'

'Sit down, Maddy. It's important we keep the door closed or the baby crawls off outside. Would you like some tea?'

'Yes, please,' Maddy said softly and sat down. Susan tried to crawl into her lap. 'May I hold her?' Maddy asked.

'If you want. She might bite, be careful.'

'That's all right, Mrs Manning. I've been bitten by worse than a baby.' Maddy picked up the infant.

'I'm not Mrs Manning. My name is Anna Hall.'

Maddy glanced at the woman. Can't be, Maddy thought. She's dead. Maddy had a wonderful mind for names and faces, those she cared to remember, of course. The baby tried very hard to chew on her nose and poke at her eyes. 'You can't be Anna Hall. She's dead.'

She'd spoken without thinking again. She suddenly wished she had remained quiet. She was bombarded with questions. How did she know Anna Hall was dead and, more importantly, who was she? Maddy had no choice but tell the truth. And when the woman heard her name, she snatched the baby away as if she thought Maddy would hurt it. Maddy felt tears fill her eyes. She didn't know what was happening. Nor did the baby.

'Get out of this house!'

'I've nowhere to go—'

'Get out of my sight!'

'What have I done?' Maddy pleaded as she cringed by the door. The entire room was blurred from stinging tears. She was so confused she could hardly speak.

Anna's moment of temporary rage ended. There had been so much sudden anger towards the girl—the girl who was lost, left behind. The girl who obviously didn't understand a thing. Anna turned away from the tears, the sobs. 'Go and sit down. I'm sorry.'

Maddy gave the woman a very wide berth. She sat down, and the woman took the baby and fled.

Sam knew it was only a matter of time now. He'd prepared himself for the inevitable yet he still cringed when he saw the approaching thundercloud—Anna. 'I almost had a turkey.'

'Instead, you brought that girl home.'

'I couldn't leave her out there. It's Christmas.'

'This is not a joke, Sam. She's the sergeant's daughter.'

'I know she's the sergeant's daughter. I still couldn't leave her out there.'

Anna ground her teeth in her attempt to remain calm. 'If she doesn't arrive home, he'll think she's been kidnapped and we know who he will blame, don't we, Sam!'

Sam smiled and tore the skin from the rabbit. It made a horrible noise, one she couldn't bear and he knew it. Anna looked away.

'Do you have any idea at all what you've done now?'

'Uh-huh,' he said.

'She is *his* daughter.'

Sam's smile broadened. It almost drowned his entire face.

'Do you honestly expect me to be civil to her?'

'Yep. You can't blame that girl for someone else's actions. I expect you to trust me, Anna. She's our ticket to freedom.'

'A ticket to more trouble, Sam Manning.'

'You think you can see past tomorrow but you can't.'

'And you can?' Anna asked, not really a question; it was more like a shaking enraged whisper, a little hiss before the eruption.

'Luke doesn't value much at all except her. Trust me.'

'Trust you! You'll only be satisfied when we're all dead!'

'Of old age, I hope.'

She stifled her anger and walked off in a huff.

Sam wondered how much Maddy remembered. Most of all he wondered how much Maddy knew. She'd have to be fifteen or sixteen by now.

Anna tried her best to be as nice as possible, and the girl seemed to sense it. She offered to help in any way she could. In fact, Maddy was so persistent that Anna relented with a genuine smile. Sam was right. The poor girl hadn't chosen her parents, nor had she chosen this situation. Being left behind in the middle of rugged bushland would be enough to daunt anyone—Anna knew how she would feel. But she was still faced with one appalling fact—this girl was the sergeant's daughter who had a thousand questions she dared not ask. Anna could see them all bubbling in her pale eyes. She had her father's eyes.

'It would be nice to live here where no one would bother you.'

'It's not from choice, Maddy.'

Maddy studied Anna cautiously. 'You really are the lady from Bitter Creek, aren't you?'

'You're not surprised?'

'Not really,' Maddy whispered and went back to peeling the potato in her hand.

'Sam found us and brought us here. I was almost dead.'

Maddy didn't voice what she was thinking. The answer to one question would only prompt another forty questions and, somehow, Maddy already knew the answers. The truth was not what she was wanting to hear.

Daniel had been right all along. Maddy's heart had also spoken the silent truth. 'Sam didn't kill anyone, did he?'

'Sam isn't a murderer, Maddy.'

Maddy reached for the second potato and pretended not to watch the woman holding her baby. She couldn't remember ever being hugged or told how good she was, and there was this tiny child, trying hard to walk now and being encouraged for it. So many smiles. Maddy was both happy and sad. Even when she'd tried her best at school there was no reaction from Mother or Papa, except perhaps a sad expression in her father's eyes when he studied her report. Was it her fault she wasn't a genius? Or a boy? Mother kept telling her not to worry, it wasn't important for a girl to do well at anything until she became a wife. And then her mother would regard her rather sadly. Maddy was not terribly attractive. Even Daniel told her she tried too hard. How she loved Daniel, yet he treated her like a sister.

'I suppose you'll be expected home tonight?' Anna asked, breaking the train of thought. Maddy was glad of the interruption.

'I think so.'

'You think so?'

'It depends upon my father receiving my letter, Mrs Hall.' Maddy washed the potato until it shone, then she took up another. Everything the girl did was accomplished with slow, deliberate perfection. 'If Papa isn't waiting, Daniel will be. I hope.'

'Daniel?'

'Daniel Brannigan, ma'am. Daniel is a good man. He knows Sam isn't responsible for Bitter Creek. He knows Sam is just a nuisance.'

'Is he?' a deep voice said from the doorway. Maddy almost fractured her neck from her sudden turn. She dropped the potatoes and had to chase them across the floor. The more she tried to regain a semblance of composure the worse she became.

Sam didn't notice a thing except a clumsy girl chasing potatoes around the floor. Only Anna had half an inkling of what Maddy was feeling. She'd been through it herself. But where Sam was concerned shyness was simply a word, not a state of being.

'Nuisance, huh?' he laughed and put the rabbits down. He retreated. As soon as he left, Maddy calmed. Her face was still bright crimson. 'Perhaps we'll have that tea now,' Anna said.

Over one cup of tea, Anna discovered a lot about Maddy Hannaford. She liked to cook and clean and sew. She had a special beau but was too shy to admit who he was. Anna suspected this was Daniel. She also suspected the admiration wasn't reciprocated. And Maddy was adept at turning conversation, too.

'Mr Manning can't use his left arm. Is that where he was shot?' she asked.

'You know about this?'

'Oh yes. Papa and Daniel both wrote and told me. It seems that James, one of the new troopers, was killed. Sam is in trouble again. Where Papa says Sam shot James, Daniel tells me he saw it happen, and it was not Sam's bullet at all . . . but I suspect Sam knows and he can hide away for a while longer. He's always being blamed for things he didn't do.'

Anna told her to find Sam and tell him what she knew. Maddy didn't question. Outside in the encroaching darkness, she began calling for 'Mr Manning'.

Sam stood behind her for quite some time before she realised he was there. She squealed in fright again and Sam wondered why she was so nervous. She never used to be. 'Mrs Hall said I had to come and tell you straight away.'

'Tell me what?'

'About the trooper.'

'And?'

'Papa says you shot him.'

'Shot who?'

'The trooper. Daniel says he saw it happen. Do you know Daniel?' Maddy asked. 'He seems to know you.'

'Daniel? Yeah, I know him. Is he dead?'

'Daniel's fine, Mr Manning. At least, I hope he is.'

'Not Daniel! The trooper!'

Tears filled her eyes, and her fingers went to her mouth because he'd yelled. Instantly apologetic, Sam touched her arm. 'Just tell me what you know, Maddy. And don't start crying again. I'm sorry for yelling.'

'In his letter, Papa said you shot the trooper while you were escaping. Everyone saw you do it. But Daniel told me in his letter that he saw it, too, and it wasn't your bullet which killed James.'

There was silence for a little while.

'This James got caught in crossfire didn't he?'

'That's what Daniel told me. What Daniel said makes sense. If you were riding away down the creek,

251

how could you shoot someone in the back if he was facing you?'

Sam looked down into her eyes. The girl had a good brain. He thought it was a shame she looked like Luke instead of Jane. 'So Daniel's on my side. That's good to know. Whose side are you on, Maddy?'

'My own heart never lies to me, Mr Manning.' Maddy gazed up into his bright blue eyes, and swore she was drowning. What a lovely feeling it was.

Then he smiled at her and thanked her for her honesty. 'Seems to me like you should always listen to your heart.' He touched her face, winked at her and walked away. Maddy wanted to run after him and say how sorry she was that all this had happened, but she couldn't move. He had touched her face!

Sam went back to where he'd been pegging out his rabbit skins. Maddy, composed now, forced herself to follow him.

'When can you take me home, Mr Manning?'

'I don't think I can now, Maddy.'

'But you said . . .'

'I know what I said.'

'You promised!'

'No, I didn't promise. You thought I did. Look, I'm sorry, I really am, but you're gonna have to stay here for a while.'

'But I can't stay here! I have to be home for Christmas. I have to tell Papa . . .'

Her words failed very quickly. Sam's suspicion arose. 'Tell him what?'

More tears formed now but Sam was unmoved this time. For all he knew this could have been another trap. But no, he hadn't been followed. Not even Luke would plant his own daughter like that. Or would he? The past came back to haunt him for a moment and it stung. 'Tell him what, Maddy? I want to know.'

'That Mother's not coming back,' she sobbed.

'That she doesn't want me, that she sent me home to Papa. But he doesn't want me either because if he did, he wouldn't have sent me away in the first place.'

Oh God, Sam thought. This is all I need. The poor kid was howling and he couldn't blame her. 'Maybe it's not as bad as you think,' he tried.

'It's worse,' Maddy sobbed and walked away.

Sam's idea of a trade-off slowly crumbled. His stomach knotted because now Luke was losing it all, too. Full circle. Everything Sam loved had been either stolen or swept from him. Now it was Luke's turn.

And Maddy was caught in the middle.

She had to be coaxed to the table to eat. Once seated, Sam thought he understood Luke's need to steal— maybe he couldn't afford to feed his daughter. The joke was so bad Sam had to smile in spite of himself. 'I want to go home,' she said, sniffling. Sam looked at Anna and wondered when she would start, too, but she stayed quiet. Watchful. That was worse than talking. She was boiling inside. Sam knew it. He could feel it. Anna could see no reason for this situation.

'I want to go home,' Maddy repeated in case he hadn't heard. She emphasised 'home'.

'I need you here, Maddy,' Sam said softly.

Anna's eyes flickered to Sam, caught his gaze for a long moment and released when she heard the girl say: 'I don't think Papa would appreciate it if I helped you hold up mail coaches every Wednesday, Mr Manning.'

Sam let it ride. 'I didn't kill them miners, girl,' he said.

'Those miners,' Anna corrected.

'I know that, Mr Manning, and so does the whole town.'

'But I know who did kill them.'

'Sam, don't you dare!'

Sam glanced at Anna.

'It's all right, Mrs Hall. I can tell Papa and Daniel who is responsible. They'll believe me.'

'You won't have to, girl. I'll tell your father myself.'

'When?' she asked cautiously, knowing certainly that the moment her father saw Sam he would shoot him.

'When he comes looking for you in a couple of days.'

Silence fell. Maddy glanced at Anna. The woman continued pushing her food around her plate. She would look at no one now.

'Your old man'll shoot me the minute he sees me, girl, but if you're with me, he won't.'

Anna saw it all unfolding in her mind's eye. How could the sergeant shoot if Sam was holding his daughter as a shield? Gun at her head, too, no doubt. But he wouldn't, surely. She glanced at Sam, saw something in his eyes she had never seen before. Oh, my God, he would, Anna thought. He can't be that desperate, surely?

'Mr Manning, Papa hates you so much he'd shoot you no matter who was with you. But if you took me home, I could tell Inspector Ritchie who was responsible and I promise I won't say how I found out. Or I could tell Daniel. Daniel keeps secrets better than anyone else I know.'

'Tell her, Anna.'

Anna glanced up. She was feeling ill. Very ill. 'Tell her what?'

'What happened to you. Who did it.'

'You must be mad,' she said quietly, trying not to look at Maddy. She felt the sudden grip on her forearm. Anna looked up into Sam's bright eyes and was frightened of what she saw there.

'Tell her. She might believe it from you. Show, her, Anna.'

The cold, callous threat brought on tears.

'I can't. I can't! For God's sake, she's only a child!'

'I know what you can't tell me, Mrs Hall,' Maddy said quietly. 'It was my father, wasn't it?' She was staring at her food, her hands were shaking. Her eyes were glazed. Vacant. 'It was my father and those men he pays. Those horrible men.' Maddy looked at Sam, then at Anna. Her eyes were filling with tears now and their faces blurred. 'I heard Daniel talking to Papa. I listened at the door. Daniel never saw the mother or her baby with all the dead bodies at Bitter Creek. He loves babies, you see. He would have told Papa about the baby first.'

Anna stared at her plate. She wondered if her heart would ever beat again.

'I saw the cut on Papa's face. I had to wash the blood out of his clothes. "Don't show your mother, Maddy," he said to me. "You know how she is with blood." So you see, I've known, just like Daniel, but I didn't want to believe it either. Papa thinks I don't know very much. He thinks I'm not very bright. But he's my father and I love him. I can't help it.'

'Oh, Jesus,' Sam whispered.

'But I don't want to know anything else. I don't want to know what happened.' Maddy pushed away from the table and ran out into the darkness. She was howling.

'Go after her, Sam, please?'

'I can't, Anna.' He was despairing. There were tears in his eyes, tears he didn't want anyone to see. Tears he tried to hide.

Anna grabbed his hand. 'Please, Sam?'

Lucas waited patiently on the verandah of the station

in the cool, drowsy breeze. His watch said six forty-five. An hour ago, or so it felt, it was six-forty. The cook at the pub was keeping a plate warm for Maddy. He even planned to let her enjoy a glass of red wine as well. He'd missed her quiet unassuming presence about the place. Most of all, he missed her quiet goodnights, good mornings and her never-ending, 'Is there anything I can do, Papa?'

The place had been like a tomb for the weeks she'd been away.

Six-fifty now. Still no sign of the coach.

'Brannigan?'

Daniel duly appeared, fighting to roll a cigarette. He'd recently taken up smoking and still hadn't acquired the art. His fingers were thumbs.

'Are you sure she said today?'

'Maybe the wheel fell off again.'

Hannaford grunted.

'Or maybe Manning's decided to branch out into kidnapping as well as murder. That'd be interesting.'

Luke threw him a cold glance. 'Have you been drinking again?'

'No,' Daniel said. He didn't bother with *sir* lately. It seemed a waste of breath. He was a little relieved though, when the coach appeared. The relief was short-lived. His quip of a moment before, born of exasperation and what little humour he had left inside proved . . . well, he hoped it wasn't true. Maddy wasn't on board.

'But how in God's name could you leave my daughter behind?'

Daniel waited for someone to have the guts to answer.

'We went back, Sergeant, but she wasn't there. All of us searched for an hour or more. There wasn't a sign. I'm sorry.'

'You're sorry? Is that all you can say?'

Daniel finally lit his cigarette. You're not sorry yet, friend, he thought. You'd better start looking for a new job. I can guarantee you won't find one in this town now.

'Manning has my daughter,' the sergeant said.

'I'll take a search party out for her in the morning. She'll survive one night in the bush. She's not stupid,' Daniel assured gently.

'Manning has my daughter! We may never find her.'

'You don't know that for certain.'

The sergeant turned to him and his eyes were glazed with what, Daniel wondered. Was it fear? If Maddy hadn't been missing, Daniel would have laughed at the look on the man's face.

'Do you want me to inform Inspector Ritchie, Sergeant?'

'No. Don't bother him now. What he doesn't know can't hurt. As he said, he won't be back on duty for a week yet. He has friends to entertain.'

Daniel turned away from the hunted look in the man's eyes. 'I'll organise the party to leave at dawn, sir. Do you want to be involved?'

'I won't be here. I'm leaving you in charge.'

'Where are you going?'

There was no reply.

'Maddy?'

Her heart beat so fast it hurt in her ears. She used to like playing hide and seek, she used to enjoy the thrill of the chase and being chased, the butterflies in her stomach, then getting caught. But this was not a game. She wanted to be lost and never found.

'I don't want to hurt you, Maddy! You know I wouldn't do that!' he called.

It was a lie. Of course he wanted to hurt her. Everyone wanted to hurt her. Everyone. Aunt Rachel,

Mother, Papa, Daniel. Everyone. 'Leave me alone!' she yelled, only then realising she'd led him to her hiding place and it was too late and too dark to find somewhere else.

Footsteps now.

'How the hell did you get in there?' came the question. She was no wilting flower and she was crammed into a tiny niche between two rocks a little too close to his stash for comfort. 'Come on out, Maddy. Running away isn't gonna help anyone. Certainly not you if a bigfoot gets you.'

Maddy refused to budge. 'Bigfoot?' she asked.

'Yeah. A big hairy man that eats girls.'

'I am not a child you can scare with fairytales.'

Sam sat down and sighed. 'Maddy, I never said you wouldn't get home. It's just a matter of when. I need your help. I need you to co-operate. I know what you're feeling.' Sam reached for her hand. Maddy huddled into a smaller knot.

'No, how could you know? I want to be on my own. Forever.'

'That's not a good idea. You'll go as crazy as me if you stay on your own too long.'

'I love my father—'

'I used to, too, you know. Come on out. You never used to be scared of me.'

'I was six years old then.'

'Maddy, Anna is the only witness to a very serious crime. If you don't help us, she'll die and so will the baby. They're supposed to be dead, you know that. Now, I'm not worrying about myself but she's got a life to live. She's a rich woman. More than that, she deserves to have what she worked for. It was all stolen. Every last bit of it.'

'I don't care,' Maddy sobbed. 'I'm going to stay right here for the rest of my life.'

'Know something, Maddy? You weren't stupid

when you were six years old. How come you're so stupid now?'

'I'm not stupid!' she yelled.

'What'd you say to me before? Something about your heart never lies to you? What's it saying now?'

There was silence for a little while. Sam saw the hand appear. He took it and she squeezed out of her hiding place.

'There's something important I want you to do for Anna.'

Swollen eyes tried to focus on his face.

'I want you to write to your father. I'll tell you what to say. Will you do that for me?'

Maddy nodded and Sam pulled her close for a little while. 'We better get back inside. Anna's worried about you.'

An hour later, Sam put the letter into his pocket and rode off into the night, alone, armed.

'Papa won't come alone,' Maddy whispered into the darkness.

'Sam knows he won't,' Anna replied with a voice as numb as she felt.

'If Papa comes at all. I don't think he loves me enough, Mrs Hall.' The voice was shaking, despairing. Confused. Anna didn't know what to say, perhaps nothing was really needed. Anna rolled over and took hold of the girl's hand. After a while, Maddy said quietly, 'Did he hurt you badly?'

'Maddy, don't—'

'I saw the scar under your breast when you undressed. It was a knife, wasn't it?'

'Maddy, what do you want me to say? This is not helping. Please try to sleep. Please.'

'No matter what he's done or what he is, he's my father and I still love him.'

'I can understand.'

'That is why you hated me when you found out my name.'

'I'm so sorry for that.'

'It's all right, Mrs Hall. It's not the first time that's happened to me. People don't like me because my father's a trooper. Everyone fears him. But I still love him. Why?'

The quiet of the night was very loud. Outside, a multitude of crickets played their symphony. Anna remained silent.

'Do you believe Mr Manning is doing this for you and your baby?'

'Yes.'

'He wouldn't deliberately hurt me, would he?'

'No, of course not. The last thing Sam wants to do is hurt anyone. The least of all, you. Try to sleep.'

And a moment later, Maddy's arm was around her and she had cuddled very close. She was like a small child, starving for love, reaching out for it wherever it might lie.

Anna wondered how and when this would end as she held the sergeant's daughter tight.

Daniel was awake on the hour every hour until two o'clock when he finally gave up the idea of trying to sleep and opened his window wide. He sat by the billowing curtain and stared out at the darkness. It's Christmas, he thought.

On the chest by the bed was his present for Maddy—a neatly wrapped box of lace hankies. He'd bought them after her last letter in which she'd said: *I'm sure you shall find your present very useful.*

Her luggage had arrived intact. The present already wrapped and labelled with his name had been thrown at him. The long, thin box lay on his dresser, unopened. It was probably an engraved pen. Maddy was always very practical.

Yes, it would be useful. Useful for writing reports and signing papers when he was left in charge of the station. Even though Inspector Ritchie was back in town, he was still off duty. The trouble had begun after Mrs Ritchie had made the discovery of the missing bath tub.

Now Maddy had disappeared.

Oh, what a lovely Christmas this was going to be.

Daniel reached for his tobacco and took some between his fingers. His concentration was diverted by the sound of a horse on Burns Street. Daniel looked out of the window.

A grey.

Manning.

Manning! Daniel dropped the tobacco and swooped on his pants. He was still limping into them as he tried to run barefooted into the street. But then he'd lost sight of the rider. Dogs barked at the unexpected presence in the early morning darkness.

Daniel rounded the corner in time to see Manning get off his horse and slip something under the station door.

Daniel started to run. *No!* he wanted to scream. *Come back, we need to talk!* But the bushranger had already disappeared into the waiting blackness.

Silence fell again, as thick and as complete as before. If it hadn't been for the rivulets of sweat tickling his back and icing in the breeze, Daniel would have sworn it was all a dream.

He returned to his house for the keys and opened the station proper. Lit the light. Tore the letter open. The letter addressed to 'Papa'. Yes, it was Maddy's writing. But they weren't Maddy's words.

'Spencer's Brook on the 26th if you want to see me again?' he whispered to himself as he read. For a moment he wished it was all a dream because he found himself half-naked at three in the morning on

Christmas day knocking on Inspector Ritchie's door.

'Daniel? Is that you?' Mrs Ritchie asked, bleary-eyed, rather stunned.

'It's about Maddy Hannaford, ma'am. I need to talk to the inspector.'

'Come in, boy, no one's about to bite you. It's Christmas.'

The inspector appeared, half-asleep and cranky. Daniel wondered what his problem was, at least he could sleep. Before he was castigated for being out of uniform, Daniel thrust Maddy's letter under Ritchie's nose. 'It was delivered by Manning himself, sir, not an hour ago. It seems he has Maddy.'

'And you didn't try to apprehend him?'

'I'd like to remain breathing, Inspector.'

Getting cheeky in his old age. He would not have dared say such a thing a week ago. Now he didn't care at all.

'I'd like to talk to you, sir. About Bitter Creek.'

Ritchie sighed and turned to his wife. 'Make us some tea, Florrie.'

Daniel was urged to sit, and he did, not sure where to begin. 'Sir, how many times has Ryan's supply wagon made the trip to Bitter Creek diggings and returned with up to a thousand ounces of exchanged gold?'

'What are you getting at?'

'The accusation that Manning is the perpetrator of the Bitter Creek massacre, sir. It's not right. I know it's not. If he wanted gold, he'd have taken it long ago. Granted, he led me to the diggings but how else could he report it? More to the point, sir, I counted fourteen bodies and there was no woman or child amongst them. There are sixteen graves at Bitter Creek, sir.'

'And?' the inspector asked patiently. Daniel wondered why his eyes were sparkling.

'Two of those graves are empty. That woman and her baby are not dead. Sam Manning has them, too.'

'Can you prove this?'

'Not at this time, no, sir. I can't. You've read Porter and Gradys' reports of Smith-Johnson's death, sir?'

There was a nod in reply. Mrs Ritchie brought the tea out and she lingered until she was told nicely to go back to bed.

'Were you shown my report?'

'No.'

'It wasn't Manning's bullet that killed James. It was Porter's. I saw it happen. I could do nothing to prevent it. Manning did return fire but he was wounded and his bullets went wide of any man.' Daniel picked up the cup of tea and his hand shook.

'Is there anything else you'd like to tell me?'

'Yes, sir. There's something else I've kept to myself in the hope some kind of justice would be done. It seems to have been futile. When Manning was shot and wounded, a letter dropped from his coat. I recovered it. I told no one about it. I read it, sir, even though it was addressed to—'

'The Commissioner and written by a supposed dead woman.'

'You know?'

Ritchie smiled. 'Where have I been, Daniel?'

'At Headquarters, sir, preparing for the Duke of Edinburgh's visit.' Daniel understood the light in the inspector's eyes. He felt like an idiot.

'I know your handwriting, lad. Drink your tea.'

Daniel's hand still shook but not as badly.

'Where did Hannaford say he was going when he rode out this evening?'

'He didn't tell me. He simply left me in charge.'

'When he returns you'll show him this note, Daniel. You know nothing you understand? If, and I stress, if he disappears again, I want you to follow him.'

'Yes, sir.'

Daniel took a tentative sip of the over-sweet tea and from peripheral vision he caught the movement as a shadow appeared in the doorway. A man coughed, loosely.

'Brannigan, this is Lieutenant Barton from the Commissioner's office. He drew this matter to my attention in the first place.'

Daniel was on his feet. Hot tea spilled on his bare chest.

'You forwarded the letter, Constable?'

'Yes, sir.'

'I want Manning alive, son,' the pyjama-clad lieutenant mumbled.

Sam chewed on some grass to alleviate the boredom as he gazed down at the old miner's hut a stone's throw from the deserted silver mine at Spencer's Brook. The grass was breakfast of a kind.

He had planned on going down to see what else he could find in Luke's stash, knowing of course that Anna had probably been right all along. Her gold would be there. All the gold from Bitter Creek would be there. Including Tom's. Sam supposed it was rightfully his, now.

Luke was there, too.

Maddy hadn't stepped off the stagecoach and he'd panicked. He was probably in there now, taking inventory, seeing how much Sam had stolen. From one thief to another. A vicious circle.

As dawn broke over the hills, Sam felt that yes, here seemed a place as good as any to die. No matter how hard he tried, he couldn't see past tomorrow.

He wasn't necessarily scared of dying—hell no, he'd started dying the moment he'd held Elizabeth's limp, heavy body all those years ago. He'd started to die long before he was dragged into the courtroom. Luke had got what he wanted back then. Sam knew what he wanted now and it wasn't going to happen.

Luke came out of the miner's hut with a heavy satchel over his shoulder. He was looking older lately. Older, more worried. Sam watched him get on his horse and ride away.

Whatever he was carrying was not heavy enough to be a sack of gold. That much he knew. Money?

Sam waited until he was certain Luke had gone. He made his way carefully to the hut. The last thing he needed to do was fall into one of the open shafts—some of them were a thousand feet deep.

Something had been burnt in the fireplace. It wasn't recent, the ashes were cold. Sam guessed the papers had been a stack of mining rights. It was futile to determine what had been reduced to ash, nothing useful or recognisable remained.

Doubts rose. Maybe this wouldn't work. Maybe it was lunatic. Crazy. Maybe Anna was right. Maybe I am insane, he thought.

He pulled up the floorboards anyway and climbed down into the deep, dark, stinking abyss.

Match struck boot. The sulphur smelled fragrant compared to this tomb of riches. He was nearly as familiar with the layout of Luke's stash as he was with his own. It had been quite a while since he'd ventured down here, though, and a lot more had been added in his absence.

Sam opened a heavy metal chest. Inside lay what everyone had died for. Gold. And some of it was Anna's. Some of it was his. But most of it belonged to a lot of dead men who couldn't take it with them anyway.

Fourteen

As Daniel watched he knew why he was a constable and Ritchie was a sub-inspector. There were no such things as hunches or guesses—it was simply a case of twenty years more experience with human nature, such as it was. Twenty years of learning which Daniel was trying to digest during a few weeks of hell.

He lay on his belly trying to blend in with the bush and the truth rolled over him in clear, concise waves. He felt no elation that his intuitive feelings were correct. He felt nothing really. He simply wondered what lunacy prompted his decision to leave farming for this: a uniform that didn't fit, a few shillings in pocket each month and living amid the antagonism that being a trooper seemed to generate.

You're mad, Daniel, Rose had once told him. *You're mad. It's the worst criminal who wears a uniform.*

He hadn't believed her then, but he always was a gullible lad. For some idiotic reason, Daniel had always believed there was an ounce of good in everyone. Ha.

Ritchie and Barton had been right in their predictions. Hannaford would most likely enlist his mates once more for the confrontation at Spencer's Brook. And of course when the sergeant and his small troop duly arrived at the appointed place and on time, why, there'd be nothing but slaughter to meet their eyes. The sergeant's daughter, by some miracle of God, would be left unharmed. That's what they said.

It had sounded unlikely to Daniel but it made awful sense now because he was watching Hannaford with

266

his renegade friends. If only he knew where in the Girraween wilds Manning lived, he could be forewarned.

Perhaps Sam Manning already knew what to expect.

A tired Sam returned to an empty house. 'Anna?' he called, without the inflection of urgency in his voice, urgency he certainly felt. 'Anna?'

No reply. It was unlike her not to be waiting with a smile of welcome; not that she had a lot to smile about lately. Who did?

He unsaddled the horse and went inside. The place looked cleaner than usual. Apart from that nothing had changed. Suzie's cot was still there. Empty. The kid's clothes were in the chest where they usually were, so Anna hadn't left home. She hadn't fled with Maddy. Where would they go, anyway? Sam shook his foolish thought aside.

Something was simmering in a pot. Whatever it was smelled good. He looked. Rabbit. 'Must be hungrier than I thought,' he whispered. He replaced the lid and sighed. Some Christmas dinner.

They'd probably taken a walk. Anna was always getting bored and taking walks, often making him go, too, when all he wanted to do was sleep.

Sam checked under the bed. Sure enough, the easel was gone. So she's drawing hats again, with dresses to match. Typical of Anna. We could all be dead tomorrow and she's drawing hats.

Sam uncapped his whisky bottle, took three wholesome gulps and felt the liquid burn a trail to his toes. He walked off in search of them.

He was tired and hungry but eating alone and sleeping alone now seemed as alien to him as having permanent company would have felt three months ago. But it had to end. Everything had to end. Soon, she'd be free. She'd be gone.

He didn't know how he would survive without her.

'It's wonderful!'

'You're not just saying that, Maddy?'

'No, it's truly beautiful. My mother would wear that to a garden party. She would love it.'

'And you?'

Maddy shifted the baby to her other knee. 'Perhaps if these rosebuds here were small feathers? Could you not have removable ornaments?'

'Would it be hard to make?' Anna asked.

'I don't think so. The design is simple enough.'

Sam approached and listened to the chatter. A small part of him felt happy, the rest was torn. She was working on her dream again. It didn't have much longer to wait.

Susan saw him first. 'Dad-dad-dad,' she gurgled, and held her arms out towards him. When she did that he felt special, warm and very happy.

'Hey, Suzie,' he said, taking her from Maddy. It was good to hold the baby. He liked her a lot. No, he loved her. She grabbed his nose.

'Sam, where have you been all day?' Anna asked.

'Away,' he said, eyes twinkling. 'More hats, huh? They look good. What do you think of Anna's idea, Maddy?'

'While there are ladies and sunshine, Mr Manning, there will always be a need for hats.' And while there's people, Sam thought, there'll always be a need for grave diggers, too.

'I'm starving,' he said. 'What's cooking inside?'

'Christmas dinner. It won't be ready for a while yet.'

'Perhaps I can get you a snack, Mr Manning?' Maddy offered.

This is service, Sam thought. 'That'd be good. Thanks.'

He watched Maddy walk away and when the girl was out of earshot, Anna asked, 'Where did you go?'

'For a ride.'

Anna resumed her drawing. 'You delivered the ransom note.'

'It's not a ransom note.'

'It may as well be. What if you'd been caught? Captured? Perhaps shot again? What if you'd been killed, Sam?'

Sometimes he had to wonder at some of the things she said. 'I'm here, ain't I?'

'That's not the point. I don't know where I am or even where the nearest signs of civilisation are. I know nothing because you won't tell me.'

'You never asked me before, and maybe I have a reason not to tell you where you are.'

'Is it the same reason which made you bring poor Maddy in blindfolded? What if Susan took ill? I wouldn't know how to get to Sheila's, let alone to a town.'

'Just follow the creek south for ten miles. You can see the house from the creek. It's a sandstone—'

'Stop it, Sam!'

They stared at each other.

'Why couldn't you have left things well enough alone? Why involve that innocent girl in this?'

'It has to be resolved.'

'I don't want it resolved! I want things to be as they were. Just you and me and Susan, and that silly horse of yours.'

'Maybe I don't.' Shock froze any more words before they emerged. Anna couldn't believe what she'd heard. 'Maybe I don't want you here any more.'

'You don't mean that.'

'Just keep drawing your hats, Anna.'

'I thought you loved me!'

'It makes no difference if I do or I don't. I'm a dead man. You don't belong with me. No one does.'

'How can you say that? I love you. I've never loved anyone the way I love you.'

'No, you don't, Anna.'

'You know I do.'

'No. No, I cannot listen! Why do you have to make it so hard? I was fine before you came along. I was fine—'

The baby had a curious expression on her face.

'You're saying you've never loved me? You've never felt anything for me?'

'What I feel's got nothing to do with it, Anna. If it works out tomorrow you'll have your gold. You'll have your freedom. You can go off and chase your dream. I just hope it's enough for you.'

'All I want is you, Sam. Please don't push me away. Not now.'

Maddy could always sense when she wasn't wanted. After so many years of practice, making herself scarce at the right time came naturally. Which is why she'd offered to get Mr Manning something to eat. All he had to do now was come in, sit down and tuck in. Maddy had made some cakes that morning. But he was taking so long. Perhaps they'd had no time alone lately?

Who would believe she'd spent Christmas day, 1867, with a bushranger? What proof would there be except memories? How could anyone prove a memory?

Christmas. No gifts. No turkey.

Maddy went to the door and looked down towards the creek. Well, she knew what was causing the delay now. Mr Manning was kissing Mrs Hall, and the baby was tucked under his right arm.

Maddy sighed and leaned against the door. She studied her feet and wondered if Daniel was worrying about her. They would all know by now, of course. Her luggage would have arrived without her. Perhaps her father had found the presents she'd already wrapped? Would Daniel have opened his or would he be waiting until he saw her again?

There would be no threepences in the Christmas pudding this year because she hadn't been home to bake one. Do you miss me, Papa? The thought faded when she saw Sam coming. He looked happy now. He smiled at her. 'Anna tells me you're a good cook.'

'I like cooking.'

'I don't,' Sam said and squeezed past her.

Christmas dinner was quiet. No one spoke except Maddy and the baby. Anna was sad. Maddy supposed she would be, too, in her position. Tomorrow, Anna would have her freedom again. Not Sam, though. Freedom he could never have.

'I was nearly killed by a threepence last Christmas,' Maddy said.

Two faces peered at her.

'It's true. I choked on one in the Christmas pudding. Daniel hit me on the back and saved my life.' A smile touched Anna's face. All this talk of Daniel. Daniel this, Daniel that.

'You like this Brannigan, don't you?' Sam asked.

'I must be talking too much again, I'm sorry.'

'Does he like you?' Sam persisted.

'I don't know.'

'He's a fool if he don't.'

'Doesn't,' Anna corrected.

'Is she supposed to be walking?' Maddy asked and indicated the baby, who was taking three tentative steps towards Sam. When all eyes turned to her, she looked up, grinned and collapsed on her behind. She sat on the bare floor, chewed on her fist, dribbled and grinned at Sam. She held her arms up, as if knowing he would oblige.

Sam looked down at her, sitting there in the middle of the room. 'You walk to me and I'll consider it, Suzie. Come on. Show me some of that determination you got from your mother.' He held his arms out to her. Enticing her.

Anna watched as her daughter rose unsteadily. She had such a huge smile on her little face. She took a few shaky, unsure steps. Anna glanced at Sam, who seemed to be helping her. He was tense, waiting to catch her next fall. But the baby stumbled on until she reached him, and Sam lifted her and was on his feet, throwing her high into the air as he always did.

She screamed with happiness.

Anna wished she could capture the look on Sam's face and hold it in her heart for the rest of her life. Tears flooded her eyes.

'Mrs Hall, why are you crying?'

'My baby's walking,' Anna said softly and reached for Sam's bottle of whisky. He didn't object.

It was Christmas.

Hannaford kicked the bedcovers off and stared at the fading flowers on the wallpaper. Moonlight rendered them colourless smudges, akin to how he was feeling.

Where were the subtle lies for comfort now? What was left to cling to that would help him believe Maddy would survive, unharmed? How far would Manning take his revenge? This unending torment?

Nothing but silence and emptiness remained like the unopened gifts on a dusty dining-room table. No one to nag him about a tree to decorate. No wife to complain about pine needles dropping on her floor, no daughter to clean up the mess.

One more month; four more weeks and they would all have been in Sydney. Jane would have had anything she wanted. A finishing school for Maddy. Now there was no more Jane. He'd known she wasn't coming back the morning she'd said goodbye. He had expected it long before this, of course. This was her revenge. Manning was getting his share as well. Lucas closed his eyes. He saw Elizabeth as if it were only yesterday.

Elizabeth. Such a lonely beauty. How could one woman's death destroy two other lives? Like the ghost of his wife Sam always appeared, returning to haunt, to taunt, to torment.

A lot of time might have passed but memories didn't fade.

Now Sam had Maddy.

Lucas whispered his daughter's name and as if in reply, the three o'clock breeze billowed the dusty curtains and echoes of a drunk's shout drifted in: *Merry Christmas*.

Archibald was at it again.

Daniel had no sooner opened the station when Eli Wallis stormed in, fuming. Someone had pinched his prized gander. A wayward goose began a fateful day.

Daniel stepped into Eli's backyard and was instantly bitten by a brown dog. All that remained of the gander was a head, some feathers and two feet. The guts were discovered in Noggy Burns' vegetable patch but, of course, Noggy hadn't known anything about a missing goose. He said something about the smell of roast goose drifting across the street from the Cunningham's kitchen . . .

Eli threatened to fix them all and kicked the dog,

273

which was, for Daniel at least, the only enjoyable part of the morning.

'Be ready to ride at ten, boy,' came the order as Daniel tried to find a bandage.

Two hours to Spencer's Brook. Arriving on time for once, Daniel thought. But there was an hour more to wait, so he took off his boot and inspected the bleeding dog bite on his right calf. He wrapped his leg as best he could and not for the first time did he remind himself to stay behind Hannaford today. At all costs.

They left before dawn, with Anna riding Aggie, the Newberrys' old galloper. Maddy clung tightly to Sam for the first few miles across the mountains. The women were obviously relieved when two miles west of Spencer's Brook, he eased off his horse and helped Maddy to the ground.

Sam could have sworn the grey sighed with relief. He watered her in the shallow creek and looked back. The girls had been on horseback for two and a half hours and there they were, sitting on a log. The baby was trying to crawl away—Anna had a tight grip on her pants.

'Make the most of it. We won't be here long,' Sam said and walked downstream.

'Has he gone?' Maddy asked.

'Yes. Be quick about it. I have to go, too.'

Maddy exited for the nearest tree and listened for the telltale rustle of a goanna, or snake. Already today she'd seen two of each. Daniel often said that if you saw a black snake it was a sign of impending rain. Perhaps it's going to flood, Maddy thought. Instead of reptilian rustles in the grass, she heard voices. Strange voices. Was there no privacy anywhere? Without too much noise, she ran off as quietly as she could to where she'd last seen Sam. He was bent over at the edge of the creek, using cupped hands to drink. 'Mr Manning, I heard men's voices. That way.'

Sam straightened and his gaze followed her pointing hand. Spencer's trail.

Sam's intense blue eyes fired. 'Show me,' he said, grabbing her arm and hurrying her along the steep, grassy slope. At the top he pushed her down. Maddy could see no sign of movement below but that was where she'd heard the voices. The men had been walking along that trail down there. 'How many?' Sam asked.

'Two, perhaps three.'

They both heard the movement and turned. Sam went for his knife and seeing who it was, he slipped it away quickly. If he'd had a gun, he might have fired. It was Anna, baby in arms. She was nervous, wide eyed, pale. 'It's them, Sam. It's those men. I remember their faces.'

He grabbed Maddy again and pulled her down the hill. 'Keep that kid quiet,' he said to Anna and withdrew his Spencer repeater and two of his Navy Colt pistols from the grey's saddle. He stuck one pistol into his belt and threw the rifle to Maddy. 'You know how to use this?'

'Yes, sir. Papa taught me when I was —'

'Great. Stay here and stay quiet. You see anything you shoot to kill. Just make sure it ain't Anna or me.'

He turned to Anna. 'Keep the baby quiet.'

'For God's sakes be careful, Sam.'

'Careful's my second name,' he said and headed off into the bush. As he did he was checking the load in his pistol. He knew where they were heading. He'd half expected this. It only proved how right he'd been.

Sam lay in the grass and waited. Wouldn't be long now.

When Luke's two 'friends' finally came into view, he noted they were on foot, they were armed and they were making their leisurely way along the donkey trail that led to the old silver mine. And one of them had bright red hair. He could almost hear their laughter. Probably had orders to kill everyone except Maddy. It'd look good on Luke's report. Sam could see the written words on the paper: On arrival at Spencer's Brook we discovered bodies of—

Maddy's banshee scream scared him back to the present.

'You bastard, get away from him!'

Sam spun to see the figure standing not ten feet away, and he heard the sudden crack from the repeater. The boy fell instantly.

Maddy was galloping up the hill towards him, the rifle across her chest like a soldier in battle retreat. She was screaming. Sam jumped to his feet, grabbed for the weapon before she shot him in her terror and he tackled her to the ground.

'Where's Anna?'

'I . . . she was . . . I don't know.' Before Maddy could think to answer, Anna flashed by on Aggie. One arm was tight around her baby as down the slope she cantered, across the trail and into the waiting cover of the scrub below.

Sam didn't have time to curse at her. He barely had time to think. Was she drawing them out into the open? One appeared; too far away for the rifle to be deadly accurate. Sam had no choice. The man fell after two shots. 'Bushwhacking bastard,' Sam mumbled.

Maddy screamed again. A third raider was almost on top of her and this time it was reflex action on Sam's part. The redhead's stomach exploded and Maddy was hit by his full weight. Her screams split Sam's eardrums. 'Get him off me! Get him off me!'

It took a couple of minutes to calm the girl down and when the noise died, the only sounds were a baby's cries, far off. Distant.

When she saw him coming, Anna cringed. She held the baby a little tighter as Sam slid from his horse. He was shaking with rage. Poor Maddy, covered in blood, was sobbing, dazed. She tumbled to the ground and lay there, heaving.

'You're trying to kill yourself,' he said quite calmly. 'You're trying to kill yourself and you want to take Suzie with you.'

'For heaven's sakes—'

'Don't you for heaven's sakes me! I have never seen anything so stupid in all my life!' His voice was shaking with rage.

'I took them by surprise! I drew them away from you both and it worked!'

'I told you to stay put!'

'You told me to keep Susan quiet!'

'Stop fighting and tell me what's happening!' Maddy wailed.

Sam glanced back at Maddy and tore the old horse's reins from its tether. He thrust them at Anna. 'Get on this horse and follow me. Do as I say for once. Think you can manage that?'

His anger was intimidating. She had never seen him this angry and she never wanted to again. Anna obeyed.

Sam heaved Maddy into place behind him. 'I owe you two, girl.'

'You owe me?' she sobbed.

'You saved my life. Twice. Not bad for one day.'

'That's all right, Mr Manning. I don't mind.'

'Just don't tell your father.'

Maddy rested her dirty, bloodied face against Sam's back. It wouldn't really matter what she told her father, or Daniel, or Inspector Ritchie because soon,

Sam would be dead. They all would be, most likely. Papa wouldn't come alone, that much she knew.

'Watch your feet. Some of these shafts go all the way to hell.'

On foot now, Maddy inched her way up the barren slope towards the abandoned mine. She had heard about Spencer's Brook silver mine but had never seen it or the smelter the Chinese had built years ago. It now stood in a red-brick ruin, guarded by armies of jumper ants. Sam led the way through the warren of uncovered, dangerous shafts. Some were big enough to lose a horse down.

There was no one here of course, it was too early. The fewer questions Maddy asked the fewer lies she'd be told. She felt it was better to know little and endure. In a few hours, it would all be over and she would be home again.

The shelter—she wouldn't have called it a house— was built of wood and bricks most likely stolen from the chimney stack of the abandoned smelter. And once it had a roof. Now it resembled a skeleton— the whole place an old, tired graveyard. Even the trees were dying. It was quiet. Spooky. It would have been completely dead were it not for the ants. 'Don't stand still too long,' Sam warned.

'Who lived here?' she asked.

'A man called Spencer, I suppose.'

Maddy fell quiet. She wondered if she'd been talking too much again. She had one question which couldn't be contained for long.

'What will happen now, Mr Manning?'

'Your old man'll ride in, and expect everyone to be dead. Except for you. I'd bet my life on it.'

'The greatest gamble of all,' Anna said quietly.

'Don't you start. What you did was the stupidest thing I've ever saw.'

'Seen,' she corrected. 'Besides, I've seen you shoot before.'

Ignoring her, Sam tied the horses and unpacked the two sacks containing Anna's things. The girls followed him inside.

'I said I was sorry, what else do I have to do?'

'You can sit down and feed Suzie.' Sam took the bottle of milk from one of the sacks and found Susan's cup.

'Sam, please. I can't bear it when you look at me like that.'

Maddy didn't know what to do. She sat quietly by the fireplace and studied her hands. 'Please don't fight,' she whispered.

Sam sat down beside Anna and handed her the cup.

'You would have done exactly the same thing,' Anna said quietly as she held the cup of milk for Susan to drink.

'You could have been killed.'

'I'd rather die now than live the rest of my life without you.'

'Don't say things like that.'

Nothing at all was said for quite some time.

'Is my gold here?' Anna asked, voice shaking.

'Right under your feet.'

And even Maddy looked down at the rotting floorboards.

'There's a shaft directly below us.'

'How much gold was stolen from you, Mrs Hall?' Maddy asked.

'We had forty-three ounces, Maddy.'

Her eyes widened. 'You're rich! What will you do with it all?'

'She's going to have a hat shop. That's what she's going to do.'

Anna said absolutely nothing. Is that all he thought

she cared about? Gold? Didn't he know her by now?

'I'll show you where it is, Maddy. Come here, girl.' He heaved up the floorboards and when the black, putrid shaft was exposed, he grabbed Maddy's hand and led her down. He helped her off the final slippery rung.

'It's like a tomb,' she whispered.

Sam took her hand and the shaft was illuminated by the strike of a match. The flame flickered and almost died. Maddy could barely breathe. Even a hand over mouth and nose didn't help. The smell was unbearable.

Then she saw the treasures Sam displayed for her. Something hard and heavy was pressed into her hand. 'Here.'

'It's a nugget of gold,' she said.

'It's from Bitter Creek. I know it's gonna be hard, girl, but I need you to tell Daniel about this. He'll know what to do. I want you to show him. When this is over, you bring him down here and show him. Promise me, Maddy.'

'Yes, sir.'

Sam's hand closed over hers. 'The nugget in your hand belonged to an Irishman called O'Leary. I was there the day he found it. I got drunk with him. Feel it? Look at it, Maddy. It even looks like Ireland.' Sam watched her eyes fill with tears as she studied it and nodded in agreement. She repeated, 'Ireland,' as a whisper.

'I don't know what it's worth these days but this chest here's half full of gold. It's more than enough to make a man kill.'

Papa. Papa promised the world and most promises were broken.

'Maddy, I never wanted this either but I'm not gonna hang for something I didn't do. Forty-three ounces of this is Anna's. I don't know how much belonged to my father but it's mine now and I want Anna to have it. Tell Daniel, girl. I'm trusting you, Maddy. I want you to trust me.' Maddy dropped the nugget back into the chest and Sam touched her face. 'Do you trust me?'

Forgive me, Papa, she thought. 'Yes,' she whispered. 'I trust you.'

'It might get rough out there today.'

'I know. You've told me what to expect.'

'Believe that I am not going to hurt you, Maddy.'

'Yes, Mr Manning.'

'Tell Daniel. He'll have a list of the dead. They'll have to find the widows, the families. Things like that. This gold belongs to those families, Maddy.'

She started to cry and the noise was deafening. Sam held her, and gradually the sobbing ceased. His shirt was wet. 'Do something for me when all this is over, girl.'

'If I can,' she sniffled.

'Tell Anna I love her and I'll never forget her.'

Maddy pulled away and fumbled in the dark for the ladder. She began to climb it. 'You should say that yourself, Mr Manning, before it's too late. You may never have the chance again.'

As they waited, he watched Anna holding her sleeping baby and he remembered her face, hidden under her old hat that first day; how she'd looked up and a mixture of fright and interest had flashed into her eyes. She'd caught him off guard. She'd caught him with her eyes and held him fast. He'd loved her then, and he loved her now.

But he couldn't have her then, and he couldn't have her now. He'd turned away on too much in his life. Running away was habit, and bad habits were hard to break. So he'd leave her with a few months of memories and what had been hers all along, more than enough riches to buy a dream he hoped she'd realise, sooner than later. And he'd be left with nothing.

'Annabelle's Millinery,' Sam said, loud enough for her to hear. Anna glanced up at him, hated the despair she saw in his eyes and turned away from it.

'I hate waiting,' Maddy said quietly.

'Not much longer, now,' Sam said. He wanted to hold the baby. He wanted to hold Anna. Hold them both. He stood up slowly and stretched his back. As he did so often, he looked outside carefully, as if he knew from which direction they would come. He walked back to Anna and stood over her for a little while. She looked up into his face. He crouched in front of her and put his hand over hers. 'I love you,' he said very softly. 'No matter what happens, I want you to remember that I love you, Anna. You're probably the best thing that's ever happened to me. No, you're the only thing that's ever happened to me. Anything good, anyway.'

Tears filled Anna's eyes, and the baby in her arms woke. Sam touched the fine, soft hair. She went back to sleep.

'Mr Manning?'

He turned to Maddy, who had been watching.

'I can go outside if you'd like?'

Sam looked into Anna's eyes. She nodded.

With no expectations there can be no disappointments.

The sergeant's expectations mirrored the disbelief in his eyes. Surprised there's no bodies all over the place, are you, Sarge? Daniel wanted to ask. He remained quiet and wished he wasn't so bloody alone.

'There's shafts everywhere, boy. Watch your step.'

Been here before have you? he wanted to ask again. Keep it friendly, there'll be no suspicion, he thought.

However, being swallowed whole by a shaft seemed more welcoming than this. Daniel wondered if he'd get a bullet in the back. By mistake of course.

Quartz glittered in the blinding sun. It stung his eyes.

Shoot on sight.

Yes, sir.

Daniel's stomach rolled over and played dead. He was limping now from that dog bite. His whole leg was paining. Where are you, Inspector? Lieutenant? Porter . . . they weren't in the vicinity. Barton's ceaseless coughing wasn't heard.

'Here, you go first.'

Holy Jesus. It was an order, too. Gone the resolution to stay behind at all costs. Daniel cringed from the forceful yell that seemed to decalcify his entire spine. He'd rather it be a bullet so he'd be spared this.

'Where's my daughter, Manning?'

The call echoed.

'Doesn't look like anyone's here,' Daniel weakly offered, trying to fight the instinctive urge to jump on his horse and gallop off.

Fear rose. Fear for Maddy because it was too quiet. Too still.

'I know you're in there, Manning!'

Daniel squinted as two figures appeared in the doorway of the old shack some thirty feet away.

'Shoot him,' the sergeant mumbled.

Daniel swallowed his heart. 'I can't. I'll hit Maddy. Jesus. She's covered in blood. Jesus—'

There was a short silence. What looked to be an affectionate embrace was marred by the pistol at Maddy's head. 'Now what do we do?' Daniel asked, his voice no more than a whisper. His scalp was crawling. He wished his superior wouldn't hide behind him like that.

'Get rid of the armoury, Luke! All of it! Down the hole, then we talk! You hear me?'

'Do as he says,' Hannaford said calmly and Daniel seemed frozen solid.

'Daniel!' Sam called.

Daniel looked to the bushranger. He knows my name?

'Yeah, you! Throw it down the hole!'

Daniel glanced at the sergeant for confirmation. It came in a fierce nod. Daniel gathered the two rifles, the pistols. Manning called to him again.

'Daniel!'

'What?'

'You interested in some stolen goods?'

'Let Miss Hannaford go and then we'll talk!'

'Nice try, kid,' was all Sam said, amused.

Daniel threw the guns down the shaft. He listened for three seconds before the final, far-off crash was heard. He stepped away from the hole before it reached out to take him, too.

'I got somebody here I want you to take back to town, Daniel, and you better take her back alive!'

'Let my daughter go, Sam! Let her go, I'll give you five minutes!'

Sam? First names again? Five minutes? Sam thought that was highly amusing. Luke never had much sense of time or loyalty. 'Sure, Luke! Like you gave me five minutes when Elizabeth died? Remember that, Luke?' Sam tightened his grip on Maddy, more to ease her shakings and stop her slipping than to give the impression he'd shoot her at any given moment. The poor girl was scared half to death and Sam didn't blame her in the least. He could feel her powerful heartbeat against his arm. She was crying, 'Don't, don't,' just as he'd asked her to.

'Is Anna Hall this person you speak of?' Daniel

called, and as he did she appeared. She was holding the baby which was supposed to be dead as well. Daniel turned to the sergeant, but all he saw was a white face with widened, horrified eyes. It was pure terror there. Daniel could almost feel it.

'Why did you do it, Papa?' Maddy screamed.

Luke moved so quickly even Sam was taken by surprise. Daniel was pushed aside and he fell at the shaft's gaping, hungry edge. Sam saw the glint of metal.

A hidden gun. He should have known.

He pushed Maddy away as two bullets sped past. Sam screamed at the girls to get inside. Daniel was screaming too, caught on the crumbling edge of the bottomless hole.

Hannaford tried to run. He heard his daughter's screams as the first bullet hit him high in the back and pierced a lung. The second shattered his spine. He fell face first into a slag heap of rough, cutting quartz. Traces of silver winked at him. He couldn't move. He could barely breathe. Maddy was still screaming but strangely, she wasn't screaming for him. He heard the footsteps. He felt Manning's boot crush the hand which still held the small pistol.

'You're not gonna hang me this time, are you, Luke? Your daughter knows everything. And she knows where all the gold is, too. The gold you stole. She knows 'cos I showed her.'

Sam moved Luke on to his back. The fifty calibre bullet from the Spencer had torn a gaping hole in the man's chest. Sam felt nothing at all, because he didn't want to feel. He didn't want to see the eyes, either, even if they were begging him for a quick end. Elizabeth died slowly too.

Elizabeth.

Now they did have a reason to hang him.

Sam took the gun from the ground near Luke's

hand. He wasn't much of a threat now. Blood foamed at his mouth. He was dying. 'Get it over with—' Luke managed to say.

Sam stared down at him for a long time. He heard none of the girls' screams for he was lost in the past.

'Why?' he asked and for a second he thought Luke was going to tell him. Then he saw the smile amid the blood and he knew nothing had changed.

Sam shook his head. 'No, I'm not gonna kill you.'

'Sam! For God's sakes, quickly!'

Sam turned, saw the girls. Anna was on her stomach, one arm around the baby, the other hand clinging to Daniel's wrist. Maddy, too, was clinging with all her might to his other wrist. Sam moved, and before he realised he was running he was on the edges of the shaft. It was crumbling quickly from the added weight. Both girls were still screaming for help. Sam grabbed for Daniel's shirt and heaved but the cloth tore. 'Help me, Maddy!' He pushed Anna away in case she dropped the baby down the shaft, and he grabbed for the arm Anna had. Maddy's nails were drawing blood around the young trooper's wrist.

'Now! Pull!'

Terror added to each's strength.

Daniel came up from the edges of the dark shaft, gasping, almost crying from terror. Sam dragged him further away from the gaping abyss and rolled him over. The poor kid's face was white. Maddy collapsed and started to howl. Sam rose to his feet and offered his hand to Daniel. A shot cracked from nowhere.

Or so it seemed.

Sam felt the sudden fire and it thrust him forwards. He landed heavily, his feet whipped out from under him by the impact. He couldn't move. He couldn't breathe. Brilliant colours appeared in his mind. Wheels. Geometric shapes. I'm gonna die, he thought.

From the edges he heard Anna screaming something that felt like his name as well as another voice's deep-throated curse, 'Porter, you bloody idiot! I wanted him alive!'

Is that all they have to say? Sam thought.

And then there was nothing.

Maddy was frozen, detached. She felt nothing. She was numb.

Her father.

Daniel.

Sam.

Inspector Ritchie.

'Papa!' she screamed and suddenly found her legs were able to move. Inspector Ritchie was leaning over her father. Maddy stared down at him. He was trying to talk and each time he tried to take a breath, more blood flowed from his mouth. Maddy knew what he was trying to say, even if he couldn't talk. He was watching her. Then someone touched her.

'Maddy, come away. Please.' It was Daniel, tugging weakly on her arm. Maddy pushed him away and dropped to her knees close to her father. He tried to hold her hand and say her name but Inspector Ritchie was in the way, talking about murders and robberies. Possession of stolen goods. Asking questions that would never be answered. 'Papa, no! Don't leave me on my own!'

'Would you get this girl away, Brannigan!'

'Papa?' she whispered and felt Daniel's hands pulling her away.

'No, Maddy. He's dead.'

'No!'

'Come on, Maddy. Please,' Daniel begged.

Maddy looked into Daniel's eyes. 'What am I going to do now?' she asked. Daniel held her tight.

'Mrs Hall?'

Anna looked up but her vision was a blur. 'You're too late,' Anna whispered.

'Come now, my dear. It's over. Come on, with me. We've a lot to discuss. A lot of questions remain unanswered.' Anna wiped her eyes on her sleeve. This stranger in a fancy uniform was holding her baby.

'Come, now. Let him go.'

She looked down at Sam, limp and heavy in her arms. His blood was warm and wet against her skin. The gingham dress he'd given her was bloodied. She held his face tighter to her breast.

'Anna, my dear, let him go.'

The stranger reached out.

'Don't touch me! You're too late!' she screamed and clung tighter to Sam, as if holding him close would rekindle the life that was there only a moment ago.

Fifteen

'Sam?'

Daniel turned away. He couldn't bear to watch any more of this.

'Do you think he can hear me?' Anna asked, turning her head towards him, looking at him with eyes full of hopelessness. She wasn't the same lady he'd seen at Bitter Creek. That one was young and pretty. This one looked older, and so weary.

Lost.

'I don't know if he can hear you, Mrs Hall. Why don't you go with Mrs Ritchie? She'll see you have a bath, have something to eat. You should do as the doctor says. You need to sleep.'

'I can't leave him.'

'Please? You'd better come out now. You shouldn't even be in here.'

'Come on, dear. You've had a perfectly horrible time—'

Anna looked at the inspector's wife. She had kind eyes, wise eyes. Anna looked back at Sam, white-faced, naked to the waist, propped high on pillows on the bunk of the narrow cell. The doctor had removed the bullet from his back, and had said he would probably survive long enough for them to hang him. He would be awake soon, the doctor had said, but that was hours ago. Anna watched his chest rise and fall. How she longed to take his hand but she couldn't, not while so many were about, watching.

'Daniel? Will you promise me you'll stay here all night? Will you promise to come and get me the moment he wakes?'

Daniel nodded. 'Go with Mrs Ritchie.'

'Can I not stay? I could sleep here, no one need know—'

Mrs Ritchie went into the cell, took Anna by the hand and led her away. There was no resistance— she was too weak now for fighting or for tears.

'He saved Daniel's life, Mrs Ritchie. He wasn't going to kill him. Why did this happen? Why did that trooper shoot Sam? He's an innocent man. You can't let them hang him.'

'Come, my dear. The doctor has left a medicine to help you sleep.'

Outside, the afternoon sun was blinding. The street seemed full of curious people.

'Susan? Where's my baby?'

'She's fine. Zelda's been taking good care of her. You needn't worry about your child.'

'And Maddy?'

'Sleeping.'

'Poor Maddy,' Anna said as she walked with Mrs Ritchie, taking the steps of an exhausted soul, often looking back at the police station where her heart lay in what it feared the most—a jail cell. 'Sam needs a hospital.'

'It's more than forty miles to Warwick. The journey would certainly kill him.'

'He's not a bad man, Mrs Ritchie,' Anna said softly, but Mrs Ritchie wasn't listening.

'Sh, now. We're almost home. Zelda!' Mrs Ritchie called as they reached the gate and a plump middle-aged woman appeared at the front door. She was wiping her hands on her apron. 'Prepare us another bath if you please.'

Daniel locked the station door and slowly, wearily, removed most of his uniform. The heat was stifling. There wasn't a sound coming from the cell where his wounded prisoner lay.

All he could remember was the fear—fear of that damned gun going off, Maddy dropping dead. Then the terror while he clawed at the edges of that abyss. Maddy's horrified face, her nails like claws on his wrist. Then Manning was there, the strong hands gripping his arm. He saw daylight once again. The bushranger's grin, the compassion in the eyes and then Sam was falling. Shot. Bleeding. Dying. Or so it seemed.

Daniel sighed. He was finally alone now. How often had he imagined this? In charge of the station . . .

The sarge was dead. Lying in a coffin over at Harry's. And Daniel felt nothing. All he wanted to do was sleep.

Manning was in the largest cell, the one with two cots. Daniel took the key and went in, drew the cell door to a close and lay down opposite his prisoner.

Everything could wait until tomorrow.

He closed his eyes and opened them again when he heard the hoarse whisper: 'You're not gonna let 'em hang me, are you, Daniel?'

Anna woke to the morning sun filtering through rose-coloured curtains. She lay in a comfortable bed on a soft pillow. There was a large mahogany wardrobe on the far wall, a dressing table with mirror to match. A porcelain jug and washbowl. And on the floor near the door was the canvas bag containing all her worldly things.

From somewhere in this huge house, she could hear Susan laughing. Anna rose from the bed. Her back ached, her legs ached. She was not used to comfort. She drew the curtains aside and looked out of the window. By the shadows she could tell it was seven o'clock, then she saw the clock on the wall. Five minutes past.

Anna looked down at the nightdress she wore. It was far too large. She smelt of powder. Powder? It had been so long since she had smelled such luxury.

The door to the bedroom opened a little way and a face peered in. It was Zelda. 'Oh, you're awake. How did you sleep?'

'Well, I think.'

'May I come in?'

'Of course.'

Zelda came in and went to the wardrobe. From it she took four dresses and placed them on the bed. Anna asked, 'Have you heard how Sam Manning is this morning?'

'Don't know, none of my business. I keep this house running, not the whole town. These are Caroline Ritchie's dresses. Mrs Ritchie says you can wear them while you stay. Miss Caroline's away at school in Sydney.'

'I have my own clothes,' Anna said and emptied her canvas bag on to the bed.

'If you prefer. Inspector Ritchie is in the dining room. He'd like to see you as soon as you can manage it.'

'Tell him I'll be there very soon. How is Susan?'

'Sitting up eating everything she finds,' Zelda said and left quietly.

Anna dressed in the pale green dress Sam had given her, and she washed her face, rolled her hair and pinned it on her head. She didn't like what she saw in the mirror. Another luxury she hadn't realised she'd missed. How she had aged in so short a time. Her skin was not pale any more but almost bronze. Her hands were rough, her nails broken.

As she found her way to the dining room, she thought of Sam. Had he slept well? She refused to think that he might have died and this was what Inspector Ritchie needed to talk to her about. She pushed open the dining room door. Susan was in a baby's chair. She was eating a biscuit. The inspector looked up when Anna came in.

'Good morning,' she said softly.

He stood quickly. Anna noticed Daniel's presence in the room. He stood, arms folded, head bent, in front of the bookcase. Her heart leapt in her chest so quickly and painfully she had to sit or fall.

'Sam?'

'He's gone,' Daniel said without looking at her. 'He was supposed to be almost dead. How was I to know he'd escape?'

Anna's eyes widened. 'Escape?'

Daniel had a strange look on his face; a look the inspector couldn't see. 'We'll find him,' he said and gazed directly into her eyes.

'Anna, dear, I'd like you to tell me all that you know,' Inspector Ritchie said quietly.

'Again?'

'It's very important. Zelda! Make us some tea if you will!'

'Do you think Anna will tell them about us?' Cormac asked.

'No,' Sam said, wincing as Sheila made him lift his arms higher so she could strap his ribs. 'She knows you're the only friends I've got. She won't.'

'You could have said goodbye to the lass. She loves you, Sam, and you love her. I see it in your eyes.'

'I couldn't say a thing, Sheila. And I'm only staying here until I'm strong enough to go north. I might get work at Gympie.'

'On the goldfields? You?'

'Maybe. Find some gold, buy a farm. I don't know.'

'You're not a farmer, Sam.'

'I can learn,' Sam said, wincing.

'I still think he was seen,' Cormac said. 'What

excuse do you think Daniel will give?'

'He'll say he fell asleep; I guess it's as good an excuse as any.'

'Enough talk you two. Out with you, Cormac. You, Sam, can sleep.' Sheila pushed Sam down on the spare bed in Leonie's room. Dog nuzzled Sam's hand. 'Leonie, get this dog out of the house!'

'You're not going to die, are you, Sam?' Leonie asked, tears in her eyes.

'Not me, sweetheart. Takes more than a bullet to kill me.'

'I kept a sweet for you. Would you like it?'

He nodded and watched the girl open one of her drawers. She took out a small paper bag and gave it to him.

'It's your favourite, Sam. It's a peppermint.'

'Leonie!'

'I have to go now.'

Sam nodded, coughed, and pain tore through his entire body.

'Will you see Mrs Anna again, Sam?'

'I don't know, Leonie. I hope so.'

She took the dog outside and Sam closed his eyes and tried to sleep. He kept seeing Anna's face, and he kept hearing her voice, feeling the touch of her hand, the warmth of her body, almost feeling her quiet agonies all over again.

Oh, Anna, where are you?

'I want to come with you, Daniel.'

'It's police business, ma'am.'

'It's my property you're going out to recover. Sam asked Maddy to show you where it is. I know where it is, too, Daniel. Please?'

'Porter?'

Porter peered cautiously out from the cells.

'You'll ride the bay. Mrs Hall will accompany me

294

in the wagon.' Daniel turned to Anna. 'We'll be leaving in half an hour and we may have to camp out.'

'I understand, Daniel. Thank you.' Anna turned towards the door and hesitated. 'Have you seen Maddy today?' she asked.

'No, ma'am.'

'I'm sure she'd appreciate a visit.'

Daniel rubbed his face. 'Yes, ma'am.'

'She thinks the world of you, Daniel. You're all she has left, now.'

'Yes, I know. Half an hour, Mrs Hall.' Daniel watched her walk out. 'Ma'am?' She turned back. 'Thanks for taking care of Maddy.'

'She needs you, Daniel.'

The lad looked embarrassed and he tried hard not to smile.

Daniel walked quietly into Mrs Macauley's spare room. The flame of auburn hair spread across the white pillowcase. Maddy was still asleep, more peaceful today than yesterday. He wished she would wake. He had the Christmas gift in his hand. It was two days late, but she wouldn't mind.

Daniel touched her hand. 'Maddy?'

She opened her eyes. She wasn't pretty until she opened her eyes. She winced at the sunlight the curtains refused to shut out. How much medicine had that drunken doctor given her anyway? She could barely focus on his face. 'Daniel?'

'I thought I'd give you this now because I have to go back to Spencer's Brook.' Daniel put the small gift into her hand, leant over and kissed her forehead. He didn't wish her a merry Christmas because the words would sound foolish.

'Are you coming back?' she asked.

'I'll be back,' he said softly, and with a touch to

her face he left without another word.

Maddy sat up in the bed, and with shaky fingers opened the small present. She knew what it was. He always gave her lace handkerchiefs. There was a note on the plain piece of paper on top of the lace.

With love, Daniel.

The journey in the wagon was rough but the fresh air on Anna's face was a wonderful feeling. Daniel was very quiet, very thoughtful. Anna thought he was a very handsome lad indeed now that she had time to study him closely. His hazel eyes were flecked with green and his eyes smiled each time he looked at Susan, asleep in her arms.

'Daniel?'

'Yes, ma'am?'

'What price to tell me where Sam Manning is?'

He looked to see how far ahead Porter was. 'Porter and I'll be camping at Spencer's Brook overnight. I'll take you to Cormac and Sheila Newberry. You can spend the night there. You know them anyway, don't you?'

'Sam's with the Newberrys?' Anna asked quickly.

Daniel said nothing but his eyes smiled at her this time.

'Is he going to live?'

'It'd take more than a bullet to kill him. Or so he told me. And as soon as he can travel I never want to see either of you again.'

'Dad-dad-dad,' the baby babbled.

'Soon,' Anna said quietly. 'Soon.'

'Mama? Quick!'

Sheila came out of the house. Visitors, of all times. 'Leonie, take Sam's clothes from the washline, girl. Quickly. And close the door to your bedroom.'

For once, Leonie didn't protest.

As the wagon drew nearer, Sheila could see the two on it. Daniel. Daniel and . . .

Anna!

Thank God she'd come. There was a trooper with them, though. He was younger than Daniel if it were possible. And the baby, oh how she'd grown!

'Mrs Newberry, could you do me a favour, please, and find a bed for this lady for one night?'

Anna smiled politely at Sheila as if she'd never seen her before. Sheila smiled politely in return. 'What a charmin' baby.' Susan gave Sheila a huge, dribbling grin and held her arms out. Anna glanced at Andrew Porter. He wasn't even watching. Daniel helped Anna to the ground and she thanked him with a word, a touch to his hand, a sparkle of deep gratitude in her dark eyes. 'Under the floorboards, Daniel. There's quite a lot there. It might take you and Constable Porter a long, long time to recover it all.'

'A long, long time for sure. We'll see you tomorrow then. It might be very late,' Daniel said and noted Porter's boredom.

'Thank you for being so understanding.'

Daniel climbed back into the wagon and drove it away.

Anna grabbed blindly for Sheila's hand and she squeezed it very tightly. 'I don't know how to thank you, Sheila.'

'Just keep watching and smiling until they go.'

'Why can't they hurry?'

'Patience, lass. Sam's not about to run off. He's a little better and he's very cranky and sick of himself already. You're welcome to him. When he's better, of course,' Sheila added quickly.

The wagon was almost out of sight when Anna turned, lifted her skirts and sprinted to the house, calling Sam's name like a madwoman. He was asleep when he heard her voice. A soft hand touched his face. 'Sam?' He opened his eyes. All was hazy for a little while.

'Anna?'

'Oh, Sam, I never thought I'd see you again.'

He reached for her. Yes, it was Anna. She was crying. He tried to wipe the tears away. 'Don't cry—'

'We're not being parted again, Sam. We're not. I'll buy us a farm somewhere far away. Somewhere no one knows of us.'

'How's Suzie?' he asked.

'She's well and happy. She's here with me. She's with Sheila.'

From the next room came the sounds of a baby's laughter and it was music. Sam's pain faded.

'I told Inspector Ritchie about Elizabeth's death. He said he'd look into it.'

'Won't make any difference. I'm still wanted for murder. Nothing's changed, Anna. Nothing.'

If nothing had changed why was he holding her hand so tightly?

'Sam, all my gold would mean nothing if you weren't with me. There'll be no Annabelle's Millinery. That's a dream that can wait. What do you say?'

'No hat shop?'

'Not if it means I have to live without you.'

How long had he waited to hear those words? Sam pulled her close and stroked her hair. 'I hear there's some good cattle country a couple of hundred miles west of here —'

'I don't care where it is. Daniel said . . .'

'Soon as I'm able to travel, he don't want to see us again. Right?'

'Right.'

Sam held her for a long time. 'We'll have to change our names. Suzie's too.' Anna drew back and studied his face intently. 'You must promise me one thing,

Sam.' Sam didn't like the word, must. He looked at her very cautiously.

'You must promise me you'll try to be an honest man from now on.'

Pain touched his face and that sparkle returned to his bright blue eyes. It was the look Anna could never trust at all.

'Promise me, Sam, please?'

But he was looking past her, now, to the doorway where Suzie stood, swaying on little bowed legs. 'Dad-dad-dad,' she dribbled and took six quick, stumbling steps towards the bed.